CONCISE REVISION COURSE
CSEC®
Integrated Science

T0312363

Anne Tindale, Peter DeFreitas & Shaun deSouza

Collins

William Collins' dream of knowledge for all began with the publication of his first book in 1819. A self-educated mill worker, he not only enriched millions of lives, but also founded a flourishing publishing house. Today, staying true to this spirit, Collins books are packed with inspiration, innovation and practical expertise. They place you at the centre of a world of possibility and give you exactly what you need to explore it.

Collins. Freedom to teach.

Published by Collins
An imprint of HarperCollins*Publishers*
The News Building
1 London Bridge Street
London
SE1 9GF

HarperCollins*Publishers*
Macken House, 39/40
Mayor Street Upper,
Dublin 1, D01 C9W8,
Ireland

Browse the complete Collins Caribbean catalogue at
www.collins.co.uk/caribbeanschools

Authors: Anne Tindale and Peter DeFreitas
Reviewer: Shaun deSouza
Publisher: Dr Elaine Higgleton
Commissioning editor: Tom Hardy
Product developer: Natasha Paul
Copy editor: Aidan Gill
Proofreader: Mitch Fitton
Illustrator: Ann Paganuzzi
Production controller: Sarah Burke
Typesetter: Ken Vail Graphic Design Ltd.
Cover designers: Kevin Robbins and Gordon MacGilp
Cover photo: Yurchanka Siarhei/Shutterstock
Printed and bound by Ashford Colour Press Ltd.

MIX
Paper | Supporting responsible forestry
FSC™ C007454

This book contains FSC™ certified paper and other controlled sources to ensure responsible forest management.

For more information visit: www.harpercollins.co.uk/green

About the reviewer

Shaun deSouza has 20 years' experience teaching science subjects at CSEC® and CAPE® levels, producing excellent results. Shaun has been an assistant examiner for CSEC® Human and Social Biology and CAPE® Environmental Science for several years. She currently lectures at the Montego Bay Community College, Jamaica.

Acknowledgments

The publishers would like to thank the following for permission to use their photos in this book:
p8 chris kolaczan/Shutterstock; p11 Alfred Pasieka/Science Photo Library; p16l zcw/Shutterstock; p16c dourleak/Shutterstock; p16r isak55/Shutterstock; p26l Addyvanich/Shutterstock; p26c Southern Illinois University/Science Photo Library; p26r Image Point Fr/Shutterstock; p34l John Bill/Shutterstock; p34r hareluya/Shutterstock; p35l1 Anat Chant/Shutterstock; p35l2 Vitalii Hulai/Shutterstock; p35l3 Eric Isselee/Shutterstock; p35l4 Robert_s/Shutterstock; p35r1 Tatiana Belova/Shutterstock; p35r2 Feathercollector/Shutterstock; p35r3 Roland Birke/Getty Images; p35r4 FLPA/Alamy Stock Photo; p39 Phanie/Alamy Stock Photo; p40 Shutterstork/Shutterstock; p52 plenoy m/Shutterstock; p61 Luis Carlos Jimenez del rio/Shutterstock; p73 Wikrom Kitsamritchai/Shutterstock; p85 ARZTSAMUI/Shutterstock;

p86 Vlue/Shutterstock; p95 jaiman taip/Shutterstock; p99l gualtiero boffi/Shutterstock; p99r gualtiero boffi/Shutterstock; p100 Bellovittorio/Shutterstock; p133l Brandon Seidel/Shutterstock; p133r Pi-Lens/Shutterstock; p150 Fabien Monteil/Shutterstock; p152 Andre Nitsievsky/Shutterstock; p155 Ecelop/Shutterstock; p170tl NPeter/Shutterstock; p170tr Nicolas Primola/Shutterstock; p170br Alex Mit/Shutterstock; p170bl Yuriy Mazur/Shutterstock; p172 D1min/Shutterstock; p177l Sasa Kadrijevic/Shutterstock; p177r NASA/JPL-Caltech; p194l Photovolcanica.com/Shutterstock; p194r Yvonne Baur/Shutterstock; p195 Route55/Shutterstock; p204t Pumidol/Shutterstock; p204b Mike Shooter/Shutterstock; p206t Hennadii H/Shutterstock; p206b Buncha Lim/Shutterstock.

Maps on p187 and p194 © Collins Bartholomew Ltd 2019

Contents

The pathway to success

About this book

This book has been written primarily as a **revision course** for students studying for the CSEC® Integrated Science examination. The facts are presented **concisely** using a variety of formats which makes them **easy to understand** and **learn**. Key words are highlighted in **bold** type and important **definitions** which should be learned are written in *italics* and highlighted in colour. A**nnotated diagrams** and **tables** have been used wherever possible and **worked examples** have been given where appropriate. **Questions** to help test knowledge and understanding, and to provide practice for the actual examination, are included throughout the book.

The following sections provide **valuable information** on the format of the CSEC® examination, how to revise successfully, successful examination technique and key terms used on examination papers.

The CSEC® Integrated Science syllabus and this book

The **CSEC® Integrated Science syllabus** is available online at **http://cxc-store.com**. You are strongly advised to read through the syllabus carefully since it provides detailed information on the specific objectives of each topic of the course and the format of the CSEC® examination. Each chapter in **this book** covers a particular topic in the syllabus.

- **Chapters 1 to 8** cover topics in Section A, **The Organism and its Environment**
- **Chapters 9 to 14** cover topics in Section B, **The Home and Workplace**
- **Chapters 15 to 19** cover topics in Section C, **Earth's Place in the Universe**

At the end of each chapter, or section within a chapter, you will find a selection of **revision questions**. These questions test your **knowledge** and **understanding** of the topic covered in the chapter or section. At the end Chapters 8, 14 and 19 you will find a selection of **exam-style questions**, which also test how you **apply** the knowledge you have gained and help prepare you to answer the different styles of questions that you will encounter in your CSEC® examination. You will find the answers to all these questions online at **www.collins.co.uk/caribbeanschools**.

The format of the CSEC® Integrated Science examination

The examination consists of **two papers** and your performance is evaluated using the following **three** profiles:

- **Knowledge and comprehension**
- **Use of knowledge**
- **Experimental skills**

Paper 01 (1 ¼ hours)

Paper 01 consists of **60 multiple choice questions**. Each question is worth **1 mark**. Four **choices** of answer are provided for each question of which one is correct.

- Make sure you read each question **thoroughly**; some questions may ask which answer is **incorrect**.
- Some questions may give two or more correct answers and ask which answer is the **best** or **most suitable**; you must consider each answer very carefully before making your choice.
- If you do not know the answer, try to work it out by **eliminating** the incorrect answers. Never leave a question unanswered.
- Make sure you use a **B** or a **2B** pencil when answering multiple choice items.

Paper 02 (2½ hours)

Paper 02 is divided into **Sections A** and **B**, and consists of **six compulsory questions**. Each question is divided into several parts and the answers are to be written in particular **spaces** provided in the answer booklet. These spaces indicate the length of answer required and answers should be restricted to them. Take time to **read the entire paper** before beginning to answer any of the questions.

- **Section A** consists of **four** compulsory **structured questions** whose parts require short answers, usually a word, a sentence or a short paragraph.

  Question 1 will be a **practical/investigative type question** which is worth **25 marks**. You will usually be provided with some form of **data** that you will be expected to analyse and answer questions about. The data might be in the form of a table or a graph. If you are given a table, you may be asked to draw a **graph** using the data and may then be questioned about the graph. Make sure you know how to draw graphs (see pages 4–5). This question might also test your planning and designing skills.

  Questions 2, 3 and 4 are each worth **15 marks**. They may begin with some kind of **stimulus material**, such as a diagram or a table, which you will be asked questions about.

- **Section B** consists of **two** compulsory **essay type questions**, each worth **15 marks**. These questions require a greater element of **essay** writing in their answers than those in Section A.

The marks allocated for the different parts of each question are clearly given. A total of **100 marks** is available for Paper 02 and the time allowed is **150 minutes**. You should allow about 35 minutes for Question 1 and about 20 minutes for each of the other questions. This will allow you time to read the paper fully before you begin and time to check over your answers when you have finished.

Successful revision

The following should provide a guide for **successful revision**.

- **Begin your revision early**. You should start your revision at least two months before the examination and should plan a **revision timetable** to cover this period. Plan to revise in the evenings when you do not have much homework, at weekends, during the Easter vacation and during study leave.

- When you have a **full day** available for revision, consider the day as three sessions of about three to four hours each, **morning, afternoon** and **evening**. Study during two of these sessions only, do something non-academic and relaxing during the third.

- **Read through the topic** you plan to learn to make sure you **understand** it before starting to learn it; understanding is a lot safer than thoughtless learning.

- Try to understand and learn **one topic** in each revision session, more if topics are short and fewer if topics are long.

- **Revise every topic** in the syllabus. Do not pick and choose topics since **all questions** on your exam paper are **compulsory**.

- **Learn the topics in order**. When you have learned **all** topics **once**, go back to the first topic and begin again. Try to cover each topic **several times**.

- **Revise in a quiet location** without any form of distraction.

- **Sit up to revise**, preferably at a table. Do not sit in a comfy chair or lie on a bed where you can easily fall asleep.

- Obtain copies of **past CSEC® Integrated Science examination papers** and use them to practise answering exam-style questions, starting with the most recent papers. These can be purchased online from the CXC® Store.

- You can use a variety of different **methods** to **learn** your work. Chose which ones work best for you.

  - **Read the topic several times**, then close the book and try to write down the **main points**. Do not try to memorise your work word for word since work learned by heart is not usually understood, and questions test **understanding** as well as the ability to repeat facts.

- **Underline** or **highlight** key points, and important definitions, examples and concepts.
- **Summarise** the **main points** of each topic on **flash cards** and use these to help you study.
- **Draw simple diagrams** with **annotations**, **spider diagrams** and **flow charts** to summarise topics in visual ways which are easy to learn.
- **Practise labelling diagrams** that you have been given. You may be asked to do this in your exam.
- **Use memory aids** such as:
  - **acronyms**, e.g. **Roy G Biv** for the seven colours of the visible spectrum of light; red, orange, yellow, green, blue, indigo, violet.
  - **mnemonics**, e.g. 'all zoos in Thailand contain snakes' for the order of reactivity of the metals; aluminium, zinc, iron, tin, copper, silver.
  - **associations between words**, e.g. tricuspid - **right** (therefore the bicuspid valve must be on the left side of the heart), arteries - **away** (therefore veins must take blood towards the heart).
- **Test yourself** using the questions throughout this book and others from past CSEC® examination papers.

Successful examination technique

- **Read the instructions** at the start of each paper very carefully and do **precisely** what they require.
- **Read through the entire paper** before you begin to answer any of the questions.
- **Read each question at least twice** before beginning your answer to ensure you clearly **understand** what it asks.
- **Underline the important words** in each question to help you answer precisely what the question is asking.
- **Reread** the question when you are **part way through** your answer to check that you are answering what it asks.
- **Give precise** and **factual answers.** You will not get marks for information which is 'padded out' or irrelevant. The number of marks awarded for each answer indicates how long and detailed it should be.
- **Restrict** your answers to the **lines** or **spaces** provided in your answer booklet. **Do not** write in the **margins** because your scripts will be scanned and marked online and any work in the margins will be lost in the scanning process.
- **Use correct scientific terminology** throughout your answers.
- Give any **numerical answer** the appropriate **unit** using the proper abbreviation/symbol e.g. cm³, g, °C.
- If a question asks you to give a **specific number of points**, use **bullet points** to make each separate point clear.
- If you are asked to give **similarities** and **differences**, you must make it clear which points you are proposing as similarities and which points as differences. The same applies if you are asked to give **advantages** and **disadvantages**.
- **Watch the time** as you work. Know the time available for each question and stick to it.
- **Check over your answers** when you have completed all the questions.
- **Remain in the examination room** until the **end** of the examination and recheck your answers again if you have time to ensure you have done your very best. Never leave the examination room early.

Some key terms used on examination papers

Account for: provide reasons for the information given.

Annotate: add brief notes to labels of drawings to describe the structure and/or function of the structure labelled.

Calculate: give a numerical solution which includes all relevant working.

Compare: give similarities and differences.

Construct: draw a graph, histogram, bar chart, pie chart or table using data provided or obtained.

Deduce: use data or information provided or obtained to arrive at a logical conclusion.

Define: state concisely the meaning of a word or term.

Describe: provide a detailed account which includes all relevant information.

Determine: find a solution using the information provided, usually by performing a calculation to find the value of a physical quantity.

Design: plan and present with appropriate practical detail.

Develop: expand or elaborate on an idea or argument by giving supporting reasons.

Discuss: provide a balanced argument which considers points both for and against.

Distinguish between or **among:** give differences.

Explain: give a clear, detailed account which makes given information easy to understand and provides reasons for the information.

Give an account of: give a written description which includes all the relevant details.

Identify: name or point out specific components or features.

Illustrate: make the answer clearer by including examples or diagrams.

Label: add names to identify structures or parts indicated by pointers.

Name: give only the name.

Outline: write an account which includes the main points only.

Predict: use information provided to arrive at a likely conclusion or suggest a possible outcome.

Relate: show connections between different sets of information or data.

State or **list:** give brief, precise facts without detail or explanation.

Suggest: put forward an idea or explanation deduced from information given or from previous knowledge.

Note that **other terms**, which are used less frequently, can be found in the **CSEC® Integrated Science syllabus.**

Drawing graphs

Graphs are used to display numerical data. When drawing a graph:

- Use a **sharp HB pencil**, preferably a mechanical pencil with a 0.5 mm lead.
- Plot the **manipulated variable** on the **x-axis** (horizontal axis) and the **responding variable** on the **y-axis** (vertical axis):
  - The **manipulated variable** is the factor that is **changed** by the person carrying out the investigation. It will be given in the **left column** of the table of data.

- ♦ The **responding variable** is the factor that is **measured** by the person carrying out the investigation. It will be given in the **right column** of the table of data.
- Choose appropriate **scales** which are easy to work with, and which use more than half of the graph grid in both the x and y directions. Avoid using scales having multiples of 3, 7 or 9 which make plotting difficult.
- **Label** each axis with its correct **quantity** and **unit**, if any. To do this, use the **column headings** in the table of data.
- When drawing a **line graph**:
  - ♦ Plot each **data point** accurately using a **small dot** surrounded by a circle, i.e. ⊙ , to locate it. Alternatively, a small cross (X) may be used.
  - ♦ When drawing a **typical line graph**, join successive data points by drawing a straight line between them.
  - ♦ When drawing a **best-fit line graph**, draw the best straight line or smoothest curve between the data points so that the total deviation of the points from the line at each side is minimum. The line does not necessarily need to pass through any of the data points.
- When drawing a **histogram** or **bar chart**, the height of each bar indicates the value of the responding variable:
  - ♦ Draw **vertical bars** of equal width and draw an accurately positioned **horizontal line** to show the top of each bar.
  - ♦ When drawing a **histogram** ensure that the bars **touch** each other.
  - ♦ When drawing a **bar chart** ensure that **spaces** of equal width are left between the y-axis and the first bar, and between each of the other bars.
- Give the graph an appropriate **title** which must include reference to the responding variable and the manipulated variable.

School-Based Assessment (SBA)

School-Based Assessment (SBA) is an integral part of your CSEC® examination. It assesses you in the **Experimental Skills** and **Analysis and Interpretation** involved in laboratory and field work, and is worth **20%** of your final examination mark.

- The assessments are carried out at your school by **your teacher** during Terms 1 to 5 of your two-year programme.
- The assessments are carried out during **normal practical classes** and not under examination conditions. You have every opportunity to gain a high score in each assessment if you make a **consistent effort** throughout your two-year programme.
- Assessments are made of the following **five skills**:
  - ♦ Manipulation and Measurement (MM)
  - ♦ Observation, Recording and Reporting (ORR)
  - ♦ Planning and Design (PD)
  - ♦ Drawing (D)
  - ♦ Analysis and Interpretation (AI)

As part of your SBA, you will also carry out an **Investigative Project** during the second year of your two-year programme. This project assesses your **Planning and Design,** and **Analysis and Interpretation** skills.

You will be required to keep a **laboratory notebook** in which you record all of your practical work and this may then be moderated externally by a CXC® moderator.

Section A – The organism and its environment

1 Matter and cells

Everything around us is made of **matter**. All matter has both volume and mass. All living organisms are made of **cells**. Cells are so small that they can only be seen with a microscope and not with the naked eye.

The states of matter

Matter is anything that occupies space and has mass.

All matter is made of **particles**. On Earth, matter can exist in **three** common **states**:

- The **solid** state.
- The **liquid** state.
- The **gaseous** state.

Three different **types** of particles make up these three common states: **atoms**, **molecules** and **ions**.

Table 1.1 *Comparing the three states of matter*

Property	Solid	Liquid	Gas
Shape	Fixed.	Takes the shape of the part of the container it is in. The surface is always horizontal.	Takes the shape of the entire container it is in.
Volume	Fixed.	Fixed.	Variable – it expands to fill the container it is in.
Arrangement of particles	Packed closely together, usually in a regular way:	Have small spaces between and are randomly arranged:	Have large spaces between and are randomly arranged:
Forces of attraction between the particles	Strong.	Weaker than those between the particles in a solid.	Very weak.
Energy possessed by the particles	Possess very small amounts of kinetic energy.	Possess more kinetic energy than the particles in a solid.	Possess large amounts of kinetic energy.
Movement of the particles	Vibrate about their mean position.	Move slowly past each other.	Move around freely and rapidly.

Changing state

Matter can exist in any of the three states depending on its **temperature**. It can be changed from one state to another at particular temperatures by **adding** or **removing heat** because adding or removing heat causes a change in the **energy** and **arrangement** of the particles.

- When a **solid** is **heated**, its particles gain energy and it changes state to a **liquid** at a particular temperature, known as its **melting point**. If the liquid is heated further, its particles gain more energy and it changes state to a **gas** at a particular temperature known as its **boiling point**. The temperature of the substance **remains constant** at both the melting and boiling points until it has changed state completely because all the heat energy supplied during these periods is used to weaken the forces of attraction between the particles.

- When a **gas** is **cooled**, its particles lose energy and it changes state to a **liquid** at its **boiling point**. If the liquid is cooled further, its particles lose more energy and it changes state to a **solid** at its **freezing point**.

*The **melting point** is the constant temperature at which a solid changes state into a liquid.*

*The **boiling point** is the constant temperature at which a liquid changes state into a gas.*

*The **freezing point** is the constant temperature at which a liquid changes state into a solid.*

Note that the melting and freezing points of a specific **pure** substance will have the same value, e.g. pure ice will always melt at 0 °C and pure water will always freeze at 0 °C, while pure lead will melt and freeze at 327.5 °C.

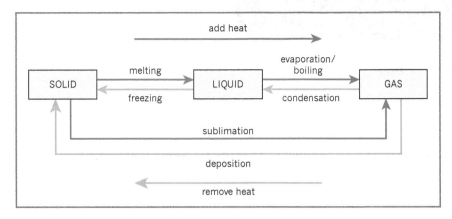

Figure 1.1 *Changing state*

Evaporation is the process by which a liquid changes to a vapour or gas at temperatures below its boiling point. Evaporation differs from boiling in two ways:

- Evaporation can take place at **any temperature**, whereas boiling takes place at a specific temperature.

- Evaporation takes place at the **surface** of the liquid only, whereas boiling takes place throughout the liquid.

Substances that **sublimate** (or **sublime**) change directly from a solid to a gas. The reverse process, in which a gas changes directly to a solid, is called **deposition**. Examples of substances that sublimate and undergo deposition include carbon dioxide (dry ice), iodine and naphthalene (moth balls). The formation of snow in clouds is an example of deposition. Here water vapour turns directly into ice crystals of snow, without going through the water phase.

Plasma

Plasma is another state of matter that is rare on Earth, but which makes up stars including the Sun. Plasma is thought to be the most common state of matter in the universe. A plasma is an **ionised gas** consisting of negatively charged **electrons** and positively charged **ions** which possess very large amounts of kinetic energy. A plasma is usually formed when a gas is heated strongly enough that the atoms in it lose electrons, i.e. they **ionise**.

Like gases, plasmas do not have fixed shapes or volumes. **Unlike gases**, plasmas conduct an electric current and are attracted to magnetic fields. Plasmas are found in neon signs, fluorescent light bulbs, lightning and auroras.

Figure 1.2 *An aurora in northern Canada*

Cells

The **cell** is the basic structural and functional unit of all living organisms. Some organisms are **unicellular**, being composed of a single cell; others are **multicellular**, being composed of many cells.

Plant and animal cells

All plant and animal cells contain structures called **organelles** which are specialised to carry out one or more vital functions. Examples of organelles include the nucleus, mitochondria, ribosomes, chloroplasts and vacuoles. Organelles are found within the **cytoplasm** of the cells and most are surrounded by one or two **membranes**.

The following structures are found in **all** plant and animal cells:

- a **cell membrane** or **plasma membrane**
- **cytoplasm**
- a **nucleus**
- **mitochondria** (singular mitochondrion)
- **ribosomes**.

In addition to the above, **plant cells** also possess:

- a **cell wall**
- **chloroplasts**
- a large **vacuole**.

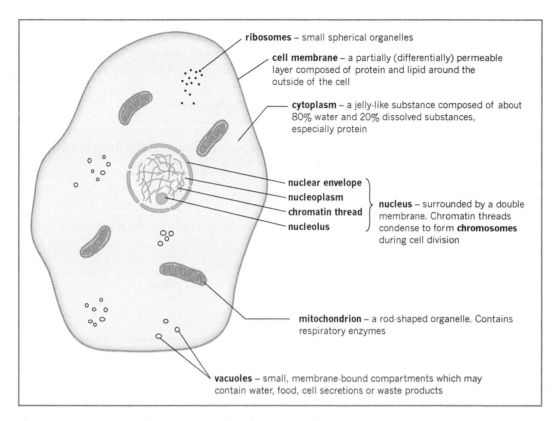

Figure 1.3 *Structure of an unspecialised animal cell*

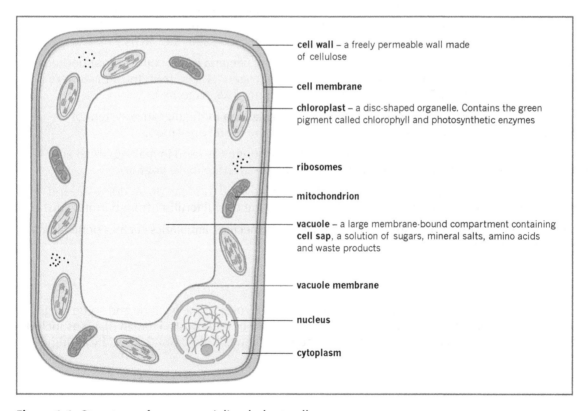

Figure 1.4 *Structure of an unspecialised plant cell*

Note that **plant cells** have **regular shapes**, usually round, square or rectangular, because they are surrounded by a rigid cell wall, whereas **animal cells** can have a **variety of shapes** because they are not surrounded by a cell wall.

Table 1.2 *A summary of the functions of the different cell structures*

Cell structure	Function
Cell membrane	Controls what substances enter and leave the cell.
Cytoplasm	Supports the organelles. The site of many chemical reactions.
Nucleus	Essential for cell division. **Chromosomes** in the nucleus contain genetic information in the form of DNA which controls the characteristics and functioning of the cell.
Mitochondrion	Where **respiration** occurs to release energy for the cell.
Ribosome	Where proteins are synthesised (produced).
Vacuole	Stores food, cell secretions and cell waste. Supports plant cells when turgid (firm).
Cell wall	Supports and protects the cell and gives it shape.
Chloroplast	Where **photosynthesis** occurs to produce food for the plant.

Microbes

Microbes or **microorganisms** are extremely small organisms that include **viruses**, **bacteria** and some **fungi**. They play an **important role** in maintaining life on Earth; however, some can also be extremely **harmful**.

Positive effects of microbes

- Microbes **recycle nutrients** in nature. **Saprophytic bacteria** and **fungi** decompose dead organic matter (plant and animal remains) and release **chemical elements**, e.g. carbon, oxygen and nitrogen, back into the environment in a form that can be reused by plants (see pages 183–185).
- Microbes **fix nitrogen** from the atmosphere. **Nitrogen-fixing bacteria** in the soil and root nodules of leguminous plants, e.g. peas and beans, convert or 'fix' nitrogen (N_2) gas from the atmosphere into a form that plants can use to manufacture **protein** (see Figure 16.5, page 185).
- Microbes enable herbivores to **digest their food**. Certain **bacteria** in the digestive system of herbivores, e.g. cows and rabbits, digest the cellulose in the herbivores' food.
- Microbes are used in **food production**. **Yeast**, a unicellular fungus, is used in making bread and alcoholic beverages. Certain **bacteria**, e.g. *Lactobacillus*, are used to make yoghurt.
- Microbes are used in **sewage treatment**. Certain **bacteria** are used to break down domestic and industrial organic waste in sewage treatment plants, forming useful **fertiliser** from harmful waste.
- Microbes, mainly **bacteria** and **yeast**, are used to produce **vaccines**, **antibiotics** such as penicillin, and other **drugs**, including insulin.

Negative effects of microbes

- Some microbes can cause **disease** in plants or animals. All **viruses**, some **bacteria** and some **fungi** are **pathogens**, meaning they are parasites that cause **disease** in their hosts. Human diseases include AIDS (caused by a virus), cholera (caused by a bacterium) and athlete's foot (caused by a fungus).

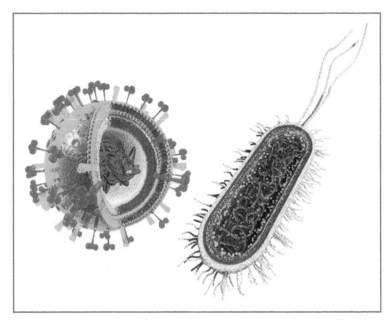

Figure 1.5 *The influenza virus (left), and the E. coli bacterium that can cause diarrhoea (right)*

- Some microbes **damage food crops**, reducing yields. Certain **viruses**, **bacteria** and **fungi** grow parasitically on crops, e.g. fungi cause rice blast and potato blight, which destroy rice and potato plants.
- Some microbes cause **food to spoil. Saprophytic bacteria** and **fungi** decompose food, causing it to **spoil**, e.g. fungi, especially moulds, grow on bread, fleshy fruits and vegetables (see page 40).

Diffusion, osmosis and active transport

Substances can move into and out of cells, and from cell to cell by **three** different processes:

- **diffusion**
- **osmosis**
- **active transport.**

Diffusion

Diffusion is the net movement of particles from an area of higher concentration to an area of lower concentration until the particles are evenly distributed.

The particles (molecules or ions) are said to move **down a concentration gradient** because they move from a region of higher concentration to one of lower concentration. Particles in gases, liquids and solutions are capable of diffusing. Diffusion is the way cells obtain many of their requirements and get rid of their waste products which, if not removed, would poison them.

The importance of diffusion in living organisms

- **Oxygen** for use in aerobic respiration moves into cells by diffusion, and **carbon dioxide** produced in aerobic respiration moves out of cells by diffusion.
- Some of the **glucose** and **amino acids** produced in digestion are absorbed through the cells in the walls of the small intestine and capillaries, and into the blood by diffusion.
- **Carbon dioxide** for use in photosynthesis moves into leaves and plant cells by diffusion, and **oxygen** produced in photosynthesis moves out of plant cells and leaves by diffusion.

Osmosis

Osmosis is a special form of diffusion.

*Osmosis is the movement of **water molecules** through a partially (differentially) permeable membrane from a solution containing a lot of water molecules, e.g. a dilute solution (or water), to a solution containing fewer water molecules, e.g. a concentrated solution.*

In any cell, the **cell membrane** is partially (differentially) permeable. There is always **cytoplasm**, a solution of protein and other substances in water, on the inside of the membrane, and usually a solution on the outside. **Water molecules**, therefore, move into and out of cells by **osmosis**.

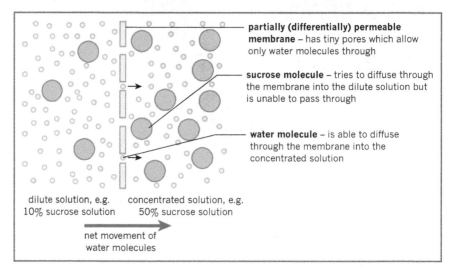

partially (differentially) permeable membrane – has tiny pores which allow only water molecules through

sucrose molecule – tries to diffuse through the membrane into the dilute solution but is unable to pass through

water molecule – is able to diffuse through the membrane into the concentrated solution

dilute solution, e.g. 10% sucrose solution

concentrated solution, e.g. 50% sucrose solution

net movement of water molecules

Figure 1.6 *Explanation of osmosis*

The importance of osmosis in living organisms

- **Water** moves into animal cells from blood plasma and body fluids by osmosis. This keeps cells **hydrated.**
- **Water** is absorbed from the intestines into the blood by osmosis. This ensures the body obtains the water it needs from consumed food and drink.
- **Water** is reabsorbed from the filtrate in the kidney tubules into the blood by osmosis. This prevents living organisms from losing too much water.
- **Water** is absorbed from the soil by the root hairs of plants and moves through the cells of roots and leaves by osmosis. This ensures that leaves get a constant supply of water for **photosynthesis.**
- **Water** moves into plant cells by osmosis. This keeps them **turgid** (firm), so that non-woody stems stand upright and leaves are kept firm.

Active transport

Active transport is the movement of particles through cell membranes against a concentration gradient using energy released in respiration.

During active transport, **energy** released in respiration is used to move the particles (molecules or ions) through cell membranes from areas of **lower** concentration to areas of **higher** concentration. Active transport allows cells to build up high concentrations of important substances, e.g. glucose, amino acids and ions.

The importance of active transport in living organisms

- Some of the **glucose** and **amino acids** produced in digestion are absorbed from the small intestine into the blood by active transport.
- **Useful substances** are reabsorbed from the filtrate in the kidney tubules into the blood by active transport.
- **Mineral ions** move from the soil into plant roots by active transport.

Revision questions

1 Water can exist as solid ice, liquid water and gaseous steam. State the differences among these three states in terms of their shape, the arrangement of their particles, the movement of their particles and the forces of attraction between their particles.

2 By referring to particles, explain what happens when:

a a liquid is heated until it becomes a gas

b a liquid is cooled until it becomes a solid.

3 What is a plasma?

4 **a** Draw a simple labelled diagram to show the structure of an unspecialised animal cell.

b Identify TWO structures found in plant cells but not in animal cells.

5 State the function of EACH of the following cell structures:

a the nucleus   **b** a mitochondrion   **c** the cell membrane

d a chloroplast   **e** ribosomes

6 **a** What are microbes?

b Give THREE examples of microbes.

c Suggest THREE ways in which microbes are important in maintaining life on Earth and TWO ways in which they have harmful effects.

7 Define EACH of the following terms:

a diffusion   **b** osmosis   **c** active transport

8 Give TWO reasons to support the fact that diffusion is important to living organisms.

9 Cite THREE reasons why osmosis is important to living organisms.

2 Reproduction and growth

All living organisms must **produce offspring** in order for their species to survive. There are two types of reproduction: **asexual reproduction** and **sexual reproduction.** Offspring produced during reproduction must then **grow** and **develop** before they in turn can reproduce.

Reproduction is the process by which living organisms generate new individuals of the same kind as themselves.

Asexual and sexual reproduction compared

Asexual reproduction occurs in unicellular organisms, e.g. *Amoeba* and bacteria, in fungi, in some plants and in a few animals. **Sexual reproduction** occurs in most plants and animals.

Table 2.1 *Asexual and sexual reproduction compared*

Asexual reproduction	Sexual reproduction
Involves only **one** parent.	Involves **two** parents, one male and one female.
Does not involve the production of gametes (sex cells).	Involves the production of male and female **gametes** in male and female reproductive organs.
Offspring are produced by a type of **cell division** known as **mitosis** occurring in the parent.	Offspring are produced by the **fusion** of a **male gamete** and a **female gamete** during **fertilisation** to form a single cell called a **zygote**. The zygote then divides repeatedly to form an **embryo** and ultimately an **adult**.
All offspring produced asexually from one parent are **genetically identical** to each other and to their parent, i.e. they do not show variation.	Offspring receive genes from both parents, therefore they possess characteristics of both parents, i.e. they show **variation**.
The process is **rapid**, so **large numbers** of offspring can be produced **quickly**.	The process is **slow** because it involves gamete production, finding a mate, mating, fertilisation and embryo development, so **small numbers** of offspring are produced **slowly**.

Asexual reproduction

Cell division and asexual reproduction

During cell division known as **mitosis**, each chromosome in the nucleus of the parent cell **duplicates** itself. The nucleus then divides, with the chromosomes split equally between the two newly formed nuclei. The cytoplasm then divides to form two **genetically identical** cells, known as daughter cells.

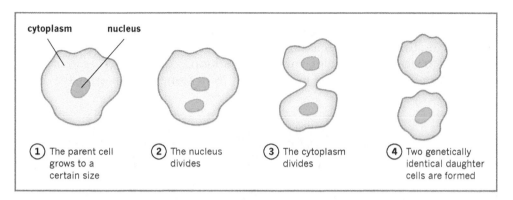

Figure 2.1 *Simple cell division*

Table 2.2 *Advantages and disadvantages of asexual reproduction*

Advantages	Disadvantages
• All offspring will be **well adapted** and have a high chance of survival if the parent is well adapted to its environment, because they are all **identical**. • **Beneficial** or **desirable characteristics** are retained within populations because all offspring are **identical**. • Population sizes can increase **rapidly** because the process is **rapid** since it does not involve gamete production, finding a mate, mating, fertilisation and embryo development.	• **All** offspring will be adversely affected if environmental conditions change for the worse, because they are all **identical**. • Species cannot change and adapt to changing environments, meaning they **cannot evolve**, because all offspring are identical. • It can lead to overcrowding and **competition** because offspring usually remain **close** to the parent.

Methods of asexual reproduction

There are several different methods of **asexual reproduction**, and all offspring produced asexually from one parent are collectively called a **clone**. Asexual reproduction in **plants** is known as **vegetative reproduction** and humans can make use of this process to **artificially propagate (produce)** plants.

• **Budding.** This occurs in some unicellular organisms, e.g. yeast and bacteria, and some simple animals, e.g. coral polyps, jellyfish and hydra. In these animals, the new individuals develop from **buds** produced by cells dividing repeatedly by mitosis in specialised areas of the animal's body.

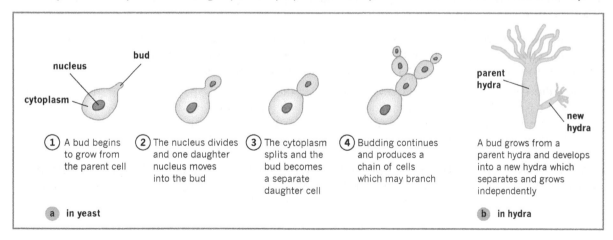

Figure 2.2 *Budding in yeast, a unicellular fungus, and in hydra, a simple multicellular animal*

- **Storage organs.** Some plants use **underground storage organs** to reproduce, including corms, e.g. eddo, rhizomes, e.g. ginger, bulbs, e.g. onion, and tubers, e.g. sweet potato and yam. These contain **stored food** and allow plants to survive during unfavourable conditions, e.g. the dry season or winter. When conditions improve, several new plants can grow from a single organ using the stored food.

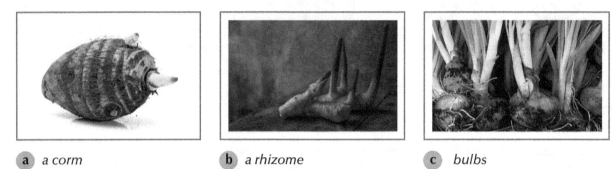

a *a corm*　　　　**b** *a rhizome*　　　　**c** *bulbs*

Figure 2.3 *Asexual reproduction using storage organs*

- **Runners.** Some plants produce **runners**, e.g. savannah grass and spider plant. These are **horizontal stems** that grow from the base of the parent plant and have buds at their tips that develop into new plants.

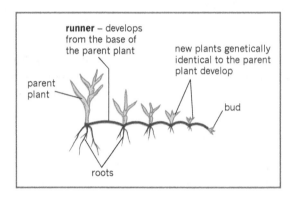

Figure 2.4 *Asexual reproduction using runners*

- **Cuttings.** Farmers and gardeners can artificially propagate plants such as sugar cane and hibiscus by taking **cuttings**. These are parts of plants, usually stems, which develop roots and shoots to become new plants if given suitable conditions.
- **Grafting.** Farmers and gardeners can **graft** a shoot, known as the **scion**, from a plant showing a desirable characteristic, such as bearing large fruits, onto the stem of an established root system, known as the **rootstock**. Citrus and mango trees are usually grafted.
- **Tissue culture** is used to artificially propagate plants such as orchids, potatoes and tomatoes. Small pieces of tissue called **explants** are taken from a parent plant and grown in a nutrient-rich culture medium, under sterile conditions, to form cell masses known as **calluses**. Each callus is then stimulated with appropriate plant hormones to grow into a new plant.

If **cuttings**, the **scion** and **rootstock**, or **explants** are taken from plants with **desirable characteristics**, e.g. a high yield, high quality, resistance to disease or fast growth rate, then all plants produced will have the same desirable characteristics. This is useful to farmers when producing **crops**.

Cloning in animals

To **clone** an animal, a nucleus is removed from an **ovum** of a female donor. A **cell**, still containing its nucleus, is taken from the animal to be cloned and is fused with the ovum. This **new ovum** is placed into a **surrogate mother** where it is stimulated to develop into an embryo. The surrogate then gives birth to a new individual that is **genetically identical** to the animal from which the **original cell** came. A very low percentage of cloned embryos survive to birth, and those that do often have health problems.

Sexual reproduction in flowering plants

Flowering plants produce **flowers** for **sexual reproduction**. A flower consists of an expanded stem tip, the **receptacle**, which usually bears four whorls (rings) of flower parts: **sepals**, **petals**, **stamens** and one or more **carpels** in the centre.

Most flowers contain both female and male reproductive parts. The female parts are the **carpels**. These produce one or more **ovules**, which contain the female gametes. The male parts are the **stamens**. These produce **pollen grains**, which contain the male gametes.

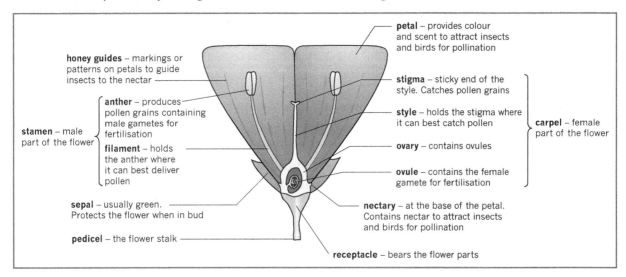

Figure 2.5 *A longitudinal section of a generalised flower showing the function of the parts*

Pollination

Pollination is the transfer of pollen grains from the anthers to the stigmas of flowers.

There are two types of pollination:

- **Self-pollination** occurs when a pollen grain is transferred from an anther to a stigma of the **same flower** or to a stigma of another flower on the **same plant**.
- **Cross-pollination** occurs when a pollen grain is transferred from an anther of a flower on one plant to a stigma of a flower on a **different plant** of the **same species**.

Cross-pollination has certain **advantages** over self-pollination:

- It leads to **greater variation** within the offspring, which increases their chances of survival in changing environments.
- Some offspring may have **superior characteristics** to both parents, e.g. greater resistance to disease.
- The seeds produced tend to be more **viable**, meaning they are capable of surviving longer before germination and are more likely to germinate.

Agents of pollination carry the pollen grains between flowers. These include the **wind**, **insects** and some **birds**, e.g. hummingbirds. Flowers are usually **adapted** to be pollinated either by wind or by insects.

Table 2.3 *Comparing flowers adapted for wind pollination and insect pollination*

	Wind pollinated	Insect pollinated
Flower	Usually small and inconspicuous.	Usually large and conspicuous.
Petals	Usually small, green and have no scent, nectar or honey guides.	Usually relatively large, brightly coloured and scented, and have nectaries and honey guides to attract insects.
Pollen grains	Small, smooth, light and produced in large quantities.	Relatively large, sticky or spiky and produced in smaller quantities.
Stamens	Anthers are large and loosely attached to long, thin filaments and they hang outside the flower.	Anthers are firmly attached to short, stiff filaments, usually inside the flower.
Stigmas	Long, branched and feathery and hang outside the flower.	Flat or lobed and sticky and usually situated inside the flower.
Examples	Grasses, maize, sugar cane.	Pride of Barbados, flamboyant, allamanda.

Fertilisation

After pollination has occurred, the male gamete has to reach the female gamete for **fertilisation** to occur.

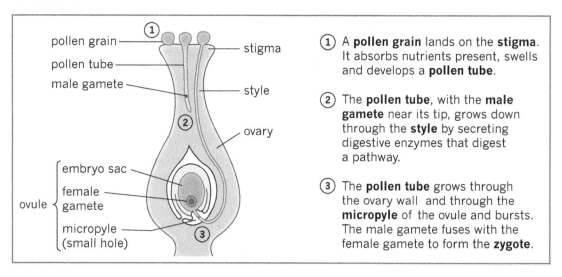

Figure 2.6 *Section through a carpel outlining the mechanism of fertilisation*

Events following fertilisation

After fertilisation:

- Each **ovule** develops into a **seed**. The **zygote** divides by **mitosis** forming the **embryo** which is composed of three parts: the **plumule** or embryonic shoot, the **radicle** or embryonic root, and one or two **cotyledons** that usually store food. The embryo is surrounded by the seed coat or **testa** (see Figure 2.16, page 29). Water is withdrawn from the seed and it becomes **dormant**.

- The **ovary wall** develops into the **fruit** which may be **succulent** (**fleshy**), e.g. mango and tomato, or **dry**, e.g. pride of Barbados and pigeon pea. A fruit contains one or more **seeds**. Fruits **protect** the seeds and they help to **disperse** (spread) the seeds they contain.

Revision questions

1 **a** Distinguish between sexual and asexual reproduction.

   b Give TWO advantages and TWO disadvantages of asexual reproduction.

2 Describe TWO different natural ways in which living organisms can reproduce asexually and TWO different artificial ways humans can propagate plants asexually.

3 What is the importance of flowers to plants?

4 Give the function of EACH of the following parts of a flower:

   a the petals   **b** the sepals   **c** the anther

   d the stigma   **e** the ovule

5 **a** What occurs during pollination?

   b Distinguish between self-pollination and cross-pollination.

6 Outline the events that occur in the carpel of a flower following pollination that lead to the development of the seed and the fruit.

Sexual reproduction in humans

The female reproductive system

The female gametes are called **ova** and they are produced in two **ovaries** which form part of the female reproductive system. Usually one **mature ovum** is released from one of the ovaries each month between **puberty** and **menopause**.

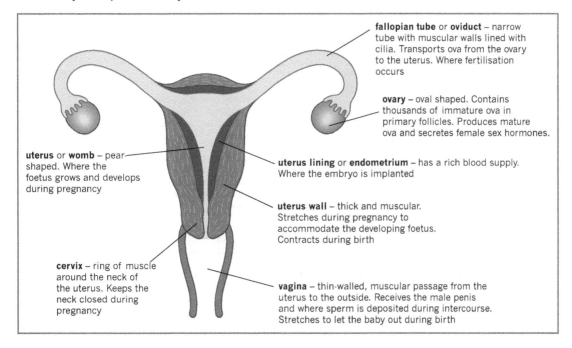

fallopian tube or **oviduct** – narrow tube with muscular walls lined with cilia. Transports ova from the ovary to the uterus. Where fertilisation occurs

ovary – oval shaped. Contains thousands of immature ova in primary follicles. Produces mature ova and secretes female sex hormones.

uterus or **womb** – pear-shaped. Where the foetus grows and develops during pregnancy

uterus lining or **endometrium** – has a rich blood supply. Where the embryo is implanted

uterus wall – thick and muscular. Stretches during pregnancy to accommodate the developing foetus. Contracts during birth

cervix – ring of muscle around the neck of the uterus. Keeps the neck closed during pregnancy

vagina – thin-walled, muscular passage from the uterus to the outside. Receives the male penis and where sperm is deposited during intercourse. Stretches to let the baby out during birth

Figure 2.7 *Structure and function of the parts of the female reproductive system*

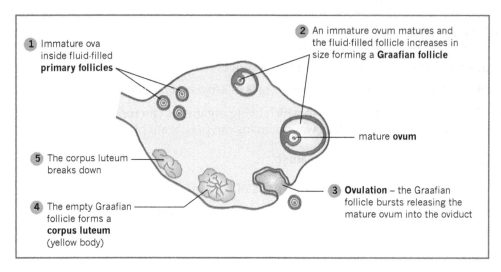

Figure 2.8 *Production of an ovum in an ovary*

The male reproductive system

The male gametes are called **sperm** or **spermatozoa** and they are produced continuously from **puberty** in the **testes**, which form part of the male reproductive system.

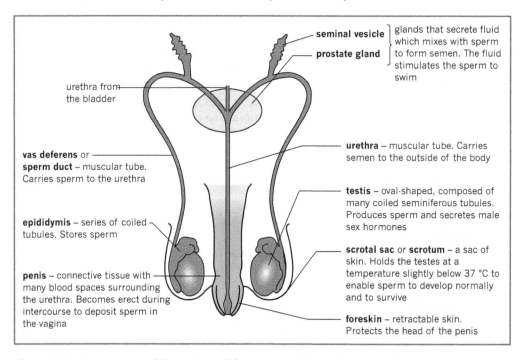

Figure 2.9 *Structure and function of the parts of the male reproductive system*

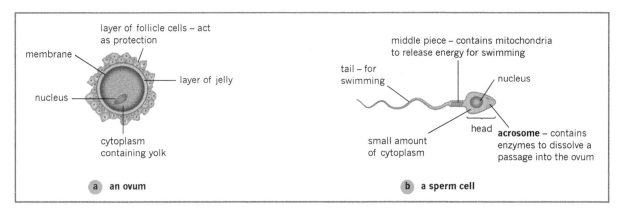

Figure 2.10 *Structure of an ovum and a sperm cell*

The menstrual cycle

This is a cycle of about 28 days which begins when a female reaches **puberty**. The cycle comprises two main events:

- **Ovulation**, which is the release of an **ovum** from an ovary.
- **Menstruation**, which is the loss of the **uterus lining** from the body. This starts to occur about 14 days after ovulation if fertilisation has not occurred.

The **start** of each cycle is taken from the start of menstruation and it is controlled by several hormones, including **oestrogen** and **progesterone**. These hormones synchronise the production of an ovum in an ovary with the uterus lining being made ready to receive it if fertilised:

- **Oestrogen** is produced by the **Graafian follicle** mainly during the second week of the cycle. It stimulates the uterus lining to thicken and its blood supply to increase after menstruation.

- **Progesterone** is produced by the **corpus luteum** during the third week of the cycle. It causes the uterus lining to increase slightly in thickness and remain thick. If fertilisation does not occur, the corpus luteum degenerates during the fourth week and reduces secretion of progesterone. The decrease in progesterone causes the uterus lining to begin to break down.

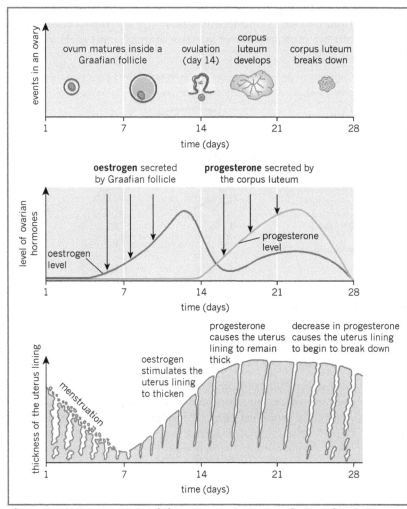

Figure 2.11 *A summary of the events occurring during the menstrual cycle*

Menopause

Menopause occurs in females when they are about 45 to 50 years old. During menopause, the secretion of oestrogen and progesterone decreases, the production of mature ova and menstruation stop, and a female can no longer become pregnant.

Bringing sperm and ova together

When a male becomes sexually excited, blood spaces in the penis fill with blood. The penis becomes **erect** and is placed into the female vagina. **Semen**, composed of sperm and secretions from the seminal vesicles and prostate gland, is **ejaculated** into the top of the vagina by muscular contractions of the tubules of the epididymis and sperm ducts. The **sperm** swim through the cervix and uterus and into the fallopian tubes.

Fertilisation

If an **ovum** is present in one of the fallopian tubes, one **sperm** enters leaving its tail outside. A **fertilisation membrane** immediately develops around the ovum to prevent other sperm from entering and the nuclei of the ovum and successful sperm fuse to form a **zygote**.

Implantation

The zygote divides repeatedly to form a ball of cells called the **embryo**, which moves down the fallopian tube and sinks into the uterus lining, a process called **implantation**. Food and oxygen diffuse from the mother's blood into the embryo, and carbon dioxide and waste diffuse back into the mother's blood.

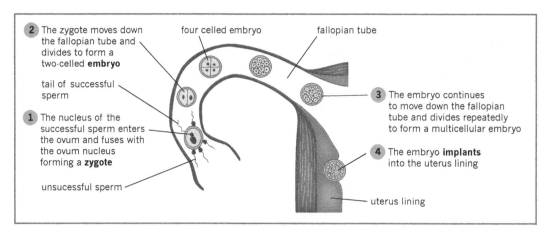

Figure 2.12 *Fertilisation and implantation*

Pregnancy and development

The cells of the embryo continue to divide and some develop into the **placenta**, which is a disc of tissue with finger-like projections called **villi** projecting into the uterus lining. The embryo is joined to the placenta by the **umbilical cord**, which has an **umbilical artery** and **umbilical vein** running through it. These connect the capillaries in the embryo with capillaries that run throughout the placenta. The placenta allows the exchange of materials between the mother's blood and the embryo's blood (see Figure 2.13).

The developing embryo is surrounded by a thin, tough membrane called the **amnion**, which forms a sac containing **amniotic fluid**.

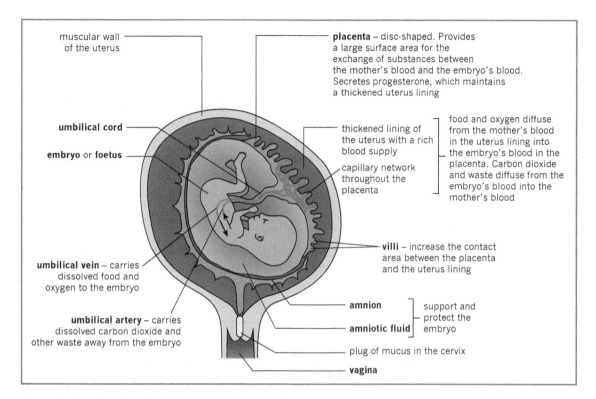

Figure 2.13 *The developing human embryo/foetus in the uterus*

Table 2.4 *Development of the human embryo/foetus*

Time after fertilisation	Characteristics
7 to 10 days	A hollow ball of cells that is implanted in the uterus lining.
4 weeks	The brain, eyes and ears are developing along with the nervous, digestive and respiratory systems. Limb buds are forming and the heart is beginning to beat.
8 weeks	The embryo has a distinctly human appearance. All the vital organs have formed and limbs with fingers and toes are developed.
10 weeks	The embryo is now known as a **foetus**. External genitals are beginning to appear, fingernails and toenails form, and the kidneys start to function.
11 to 38 weeks	The foetus continues to grow and the organs continue to develop and mature.
38 weeks	Birth occurs.

Note that the **gestation period (pregnancy)** is considered to last for 40 weeks or 280 days since it is calculated from the first day of the last menstrual cycle and not from the time of fertilisation.

Birth

The foetus turns so it lies head down. Secretion of progesterone by the placenta is reduced and this stimulates the **pituitary gland** to secrete the hormone **oxytocin**. Oxytocin stimulates muscles in the uterus wall to start contracting, i.e. **labour** begins. The amnion bursts and the contractions strengthen and cause the **cervix** to gradually **dilate**. When fully dilated, strong contractions push the baby, head first, through the cervix and vagina. The baby starts to breathe and the umbilical cord is clamped and cut. The placenta is then expelled as the **afterbirth** by further contractions of the uterus wall.

Prenatal and postnatal care

Prenatal or antenatal care

Prenatal care, or care before birth, is essential to ensure the foetus **grows** and **develops normally** and **healthily**, and that the mother **remains healthy** throughout her pregnancy. During pregnancy the mother must:

- Attend regular **prenatal checkups** with her doctor or clinic to monitor her health and the development of her baby.
- Have two **ultrasound scans** if possible, one at about 6 to 8 weeks and the other at about 18 to 20 weeks. These scans use high-frequency sound waves to create an **image** of the baby to monitor its growth and development, and to detect any abnormalities.
- Eat a **balanced diet** which contains adequate quantities of protein, carbohydrates, vitamins and minerals, especially calcium and iron, to ensure the foetus obtains all the nutrients it needs to grow and develop.
- Not use **drugs** of any kind, especially alcohol, cigarettes and illegal drugs, which will harm the developing foetus, and she must protect herself against harmful **X-rays** and **infectious diseases**.
- **Exercise** regularly to maintain fitness.
- Prepare her body for the birth by attending **prenatal classes** which teach correct exercises and breathing rhythms as well as how to care for her baby after the birth.

Postnatal care

Postnatal care, or care after birth, is essential to ensure the baby **grows** and **develops healthily**, and that the mother remains both physically and emotionally **healthy**.

- The **newborn baby** should be **breastfed** if possible for a minimum of 6 months because:
  - Breast milk contains all the **nutrients** the baby needs in the correct proportions.
  - Breast milk contains **antibodies** that protect the baby against bacterial and viral diseases.
  - Breast milk is **sterile** so reduces the risk of infection, is at the correct **temperature** and is **available** whenever needed.
  - Breastfeeding lowers the baby's risk of developing **asthma**, **allergies** and other **non-communicable diseases** as it grows older.
  - Breastfeeding creates a strong **emotional bond** between mother and baby.
- The **newborn baby** should be kept **warm** and **clean**, have plenty of **interaction** with both parents and its surroundings, and be taken for regular **check-ups** with the doctor. As the baby grows it should be **vaccinated** to **immunise** it against infectious diseases, **weaned** onto semi-solid and solid food, **cared for** physically and emotionally, and given continual **teaching**.
- The **mother** should continue to eat a **balanced diet**, not use **drugs** of any kind, **exercise** regularly and be given both physical and emotional **support**.

Birth control (contraception)

Various **methods** are available to prevent pregnancy from occurring. They are designed to **prevent fertilisation** or to **prevent implantation**, and they can be natural, barrier, hormonal or surgical. Two methods, **abstinence** and the **condom**, also protect against the spread of sexually transmitted infections (STIs) such as HIV/AIDS. When choosing a method, its reliability, availability, side effects and whether both partners are comfortable using it must be considered.

Table 2.5 *Methods of birth control*

Method	How the method works	Advantages	Disadvantages
Abstinence	• Refraining from sexual intercourse.	• Completely effective. • Protects against sexually transmitted infections.	• Relies on self-control from both partners.
Withdrawal	• Penis is withdrawn before ejaculation.	• No artificial device needs to be used or pills taken, so it is **natural** and therefore is acceptable to all religious groups.	• Very unreliable since some semen is released before ejaculation. • Relies on self-control.
Rhythm method	• Intercourse is restricted to times when ova should be absent from the oviducts.	• No artificial device needs to be used or pills taken, so it is **natural** and therefore is acceptable to all religious groups.	• Unreliable since the time of ovulation can vary. • Restricts the time when intercourse can occur. • Unsuitable for women with an irregular menstrual cycle.
Spermicides	• Creams, jellies or foams inserted into the vagina before intercourse. • Kill sperm.	• Easy to use. • Readily available.	• Not reliable if used alone, should be used with a condom or diaphragm. • May cause irritation or an allergic reaction.
Condom	• A latex rubber or polyurethane sheath placed over the erect penis or into the female vagina before intercourse. • Acts as a **barrier** to prevent sperm entering the female body.	• Very reliable if used correctly. • Easy to use. • Readily available. • Protects against sexually transmitted infections.	• May reduce sensitivity so interferes with enjoyment. • Condoms can tear allowing sperm to enter the vagina. • Latex may cause an allergic reaction.
Diaphragm	• A dome-shaped latex rubber disc inserted over the cervix before intercourse. Should be used with a spermicide. • Acts as a **barrier** to prevent sperm entering the uterus.	• Fairly reliable if used correctly. • Not felt, therefore, does not interfere with enjoyment. • Easy to use once the female is taught.	• Must be left in place for 6 hours after intercourse, but no longer than 24 hours. • Latex may cause an allergic reaction. • May slip out of place if not fitted properly.

Method	How the method works	Advantages	Disadvantages
Intra-uterine device (IUD or coil)	• A T-shaped plastic device, usually containing copper or progesterone, inserted into the uterus by a doctor. • Prevents sperm reaching the ova or prevents implantation.	• Very reliable. • Once fitted, no further action is required except an annual check-up. • No need to think further about contraception. • Few, if any, side effects.	• Must be inserted by a medical practitioner. • May cause menstruation to be heavier, longer or more painful.
Contraceptive pill	• A **hormone** pill, taken daily, which contains oestrogen and progesterone, or progesterone only. • Prevents ovulation. • Makes cervical mucus thicker and more difficult for sperm to swim through.	• Almost totally reliable if taken daily. • Menstruation is lighter, shorter and less painful.	• Ceases to be effective if one pill is missed. • May cause side effects in some women, especially those who smoke.
Surgical sterilisation (**vasectomy** in males, **tubal ligation** in females)	• The sperm ducts or oviducts are **surgically** cut and tied off. • Prevents sperm leaving the male body or ova passing down the oviducts.	• Totally reliable. • No need to think further about contraception. • No artificial device needs to be used or pills taken.	• Usually irreversible.

Note that one **disadvantage** of all methods except abstinence and condoms is that they do not protect against sexually transmitted infections.

a *condoms*

b *diaphragm*

c *an intra-uterine device (IUD)*

Figure 2.14 *Different methods of birth control*

Sexually transmitted infections (STIs)

Infections passed on during **sexual intercourse** are called sexually transmitted infections or STIs. When **controlling** any of these diseases, the aim is to **prevent further development** and **spread** of the disease so that its incidence in the population is gradually reduced. **Treating** a disease is always one method to control it.

Methods of **preventing** and **controlling** STIs vary; however, some methods can be used to prevent and control **all** STIs. These include:

- Set up **education programmes**.
- **Abstain** from sexual intercourse or keep to **one**, uninfected sexual partner.
- Use **condoms** during sexual intercourse.
- **Trace** and **treat** all sexual contacts of infected persons.

Table 2.6 *Causes, symptoms, prevention and control of sexually transmitted infections*

Infection	Cause	Symptoms	Specific methods of prevention and control
Gonorrhoea	**Bacterium** – *Neisseria gonorrhoeae*	- Discharge from the vagina or penis. - Pain or burning sensation when urinating.	- Treat with antibiotics. - No vaccine exists.
Syphilis	**Bacterium** – *Treponema pallidum*	- Painless, round sores on the genitals lasting 3 to 6 weeks. - A red, non-itchy rash that spreads over the body. - Swollen glands in the neck, groin and armpits. - In the longer term, brain damage and stillbirths.	- Treat with antibiotics. - No vaccine exists.
AIDS – acquired immune deficiency syndrome	**Virus** – human immunodeficiency virus (HIV)	- **Primary infection:** Flu-like symptoms lasting 1 to 2 weeks may develop 2 to 6 weeks after infection. - **Asymptomatic stage:** No symptoms are usually experienced for 10 years or more, but the virus is damaging the immune system. - **Symptomatic stage:** Common symptoms include weight loss, prolonged fever, severe tiredness, night sweats, chronic diarrhoea, swollen glands and skin rashes. Severe damage to the body's immune system also leaves the person vulnerable to **opportunistic infections**, e.g. pneumonia, tuberculosis and lymphoma (see page 59).	- Treat with antiretroviral drugs to slow reproduction of the virus, drugs to enhance the immune system and drugs to treat opportunistic infections. - Don't use intravenous drugs or share cutting instruments. - Use sterile needles for all injections. - Test all human products to be given intravenously for HIV. - No cure or vaccine exists.

Infection	Cause	Symptoms	Specific methods of prevention and control
Genital herpes	**Virus** – HSV or herpes simplex virus	• Recurrent painful blisters on the genitals and surrounding areas.	• Treat with antiviral drugs to reduce symptoms. • No cure or vaccine exists.
Hepatitis B	**Virus** – HBV or hepatitis B virus	• Flu-like symptoms, nausea, vomiting, diarrhoea, dark coloured urine and jaundice (yellowing of the skin) lasting up to six months. • Can lead to serious liver damage if left untreated, e.g. cirrhosis or liver cancer.	• Treat with antiviral drugs to slow reproduction of the virus. • Don't use intravenous drugs or share cutting instruments. • Use sterile needles for all injections. • Test all human products to be given intravenously for HBV. • Vaccinate all children, adolescents and at-risk individuals.
Candida or **thrush**	A yeast-like **fungus** – *Candida albicans*	• In females: white vaginal discharge, itching or soreness of the vagina and surrounding area, vaginal burning during intercourse or urination. • In males: irritation or burning at the head of the penis. • Much more common in females than males.	• Treat with antifungal tablets. • Wear loose-fitting cotton underwear. • Don't sit around in wet clothing. • Avoid hot tubs, hot baths and douching.

Growth patterns in living organisms

Growth is a permanent increase in size of an organism.

Growth can be measured by measuring changes in various growth **parameters**, e.g. height, length, mass or number of organisms in a population over time. If the parameter is then plotted against time, a **growth curve** is obtained that is similar for most organisms and populations, and is described as being **sigmoid** or **S-shaped**.

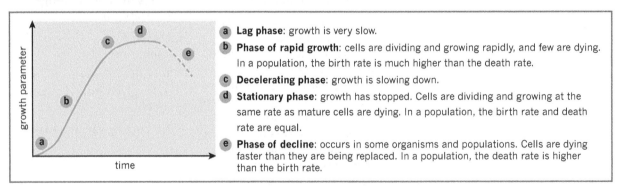

a **Lag phase**: growth is very slow.

b **Phase of rapid growth**: cells are dividing and growing rapidly, and few are dying. In a population, the birth rate is much higher than the death rate.

c **Decelerating phase**: growth is slowing down.

d **Stationary phase**: growth has stopped. Cells are dividing and growing at the same rate as mature cells are dying. In a population, the birth rate and death rate are equal.

e **Phase of decline**: occurs in some organisms and populations. Cells are dying faster than they are being replaced. In a population, the death rate is higher than the birth rate.

Figure 2.15 *A sigmoid growth curve*

Germination and growth in annual plants

Germination is the process by which the embryonic plant in a seed grows into a seedling.

A **seed** contains the **embryo** of the plant, which consists of the **radicle** and **plumule** joined to one or two **cotyledons**. In a seed such as a bean or pea seed, the two cotyledons contain **stored food** that is used by the radicle and plumule (embryonic plant) during germination.

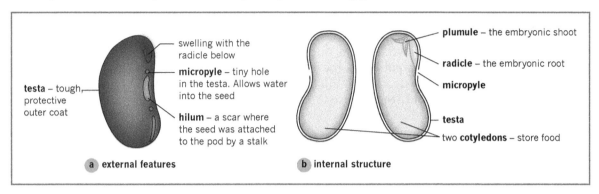

Figure 2.16 *Structure of a bean seed*

Seeds require **three conditions** to germinate:

* **Water** to activate the enzymes so that chemical reactions can occur.
* **Oxygen** for aerobic respiration to produce energy.
* A **suitable temperature**, usually between about 5 °C and 40 °C, to activate enzymes.

Water is absorbed through the **micropyle** causing the seed to swell and activating enzymes. The enzymes break down stored insoluble food in the cotyledons into soluble food that the radicle and plumule use for **respiration** and **growth**. As the **radicle** grows, it emerges from the testa and grows downwards. The **plumule** then emerges and grows upwards.

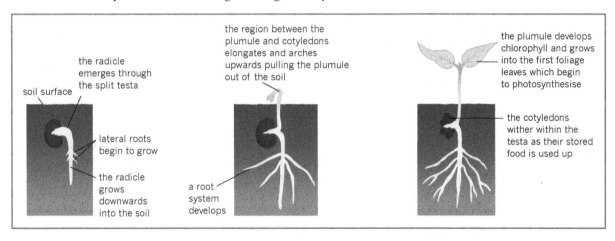

Figure 2.17 *Germination*

Annual plants complete their life cycle in **one year**, e.g. balsam and marigolds. Their seeds germinate at the beginning of the growing season, usually the summer months or rainy season. After germination, growth continues through the growing season as the plants make their own food by photosynthesis, produce flowers and reproduce. Once seeds have been produced and dispersed, the plants **die** and their seeds remain **dormant** (inactive) until the next growing season when they germinate. Many **crops** are annuals, e.g. beans, peas, maize (corn) and other grains.

Growth of humans

Humans have two phases when growth is **rapid**, one whilst in the **womb** and during **infancy** up to about 2 years, and the other during **puberty** somewhere between 11 and 16 years. Between infancy and puberty, growth is slower, but steady, and once **adulthood** is reached, growth stops. Most people then become slightly shorter in **old age** because the discs in their vertebral column (see page 63) compress slightly.

Human population growth

The world **human population** is currently in the **phase of rapid growth**. It is growing at about 1.1% per year and has grown from 1 billion in 1804 to 7 billion in 2011. It is expected to reach just over 9 billion by 2040.

The effects of human population growth

Predictions are that if this **rapid growth** of the human population continues it will:

- Cause **shortages** of food, water, other natural resources, and land for housing, crops and livestock.
- Increase **pollution** and the **destruction** of the environment.
- Increase **overcrowding** and the spread of **disease.**
- Increase **unemployment** and **poverty**.
- Decrease **living standards** and the **quality** of life.

Education and using **birth control** can help to **reduce population growth**, which should increase the availability of food, water and other natural resources, reduce pollution, the destruction of the environment, overcrowding, the spread of disease, unemployment and poverty, and increase living standards and the overall quality of life.

Effects of teenage pregnancy

Teenage pregnancy is contributing significantly to human population growth; it is estimated that about 16 million girls under 18 years of age give birth every year. Teenage pregnancy is also associated with **risks** to both the teenage mother and her baby including:

- Increased **health risks** for mother and baby, usually due to inadequate prenatal care and the teenager's body not being fully mature.
- Babies being born **prematurely** and often with **low birth weights**, leading to a number of **health** issues.
- Children born to teenage mothers growing up with increased **social**, **emotional** and **health problems.**
- Teenage mothers suffering **social consequences** such as not finishing their education, being single parents, and abusing alcohol and other drugs.

Revision questions

7 By means of a labelled and annotated diagram, indicate the function of EACH of the different parts of the female reproductive system.

8 Construct a table to give the function(s) of EACH of the following parts of the male reproductive system: the testes, the epididymis, the sperm ducts, the prostate gland and the penis.

9 **a** What happens during ovulation and menstruation?

b Explain the role of oestrogen and progesterone in the menstrual cycle.

c Outline what happens during menopause.

10 Explain how ova and sperm are brought together for fertilisation to occur.

11 What part does the placenta play in the development of a human embryo?

12 Outline what happens during birth.

13 **a** Jacia is 3 months pregnant. Outline some of the steps she should take to ensure the health of her developing baby during her pregnancy.

b After Jacia gives birth, she is strongly advised to breastfeed her baby for a minimum of 6 months. Give FOUR reasons to support this advice.

14 Construct a table that explains how EACH of the following methods of birth control prevents pregnancy, and includes ONE advantage and ONE disadvantage of EACH method: the contraceptive pill, surgical sterilisation, the rhythm method and the condom.

15 Outline some of the symptoms experienced by a person who is suffering from AIDS and give FOUR ways of controlling its spread.

16 What is meant by EACH of the following terms?

a growth   **b** germination

17 Describe the events that occur when a seed germinates until its first foliage leaves form above the ground.

18 Discuss the need for the human population to be controlled.

3 Food and nutrition

All living organisms need **food** to provide them with energy and to enable them to grow and produce important chemicals for cellular processes. Plants make their own food and are known as **autotrophs**. Animals take in ready-made food and are known as **heterotrophs**.

Photosynthesis in green plants

Photosynthesis is the process by which green plants convert carbon dioxide and water into glucose by using energy from sunlight absorbed by chlorophyll in chloroplasts. Oxygen is produced as a by-product.

Photosynthesis takes place mainly in the **leaves** of plants. During photosynthesis the green pigment, **chlorophyll**, in the leaves absorbs **energy** from **sunlight** and uses it to bring about the reaction between **carbon dioxide** and **water**. The reaction produces **glucose** and **oxygen** and is known as a **photochemical reaction** because it is initiated by the absorption of **light energy**. This light energy is converted into **chemical energy** that is stored within the glucose molecules.

Photosynthesis can be summarised by the following **equation**:

$$\text{carbon dioxide} \ + \ \text{water} \ \xrightarrow[\text{by chlorophyll}]{\text{energy from sunlight absorbed}} \ \text{glucose} \ + \ \text{oxygen}$$

$$\text{or} \qquad 6CO_2 \ + \ 6H_2O \ \xrightarrow[\text{by chlorophyll}]{\text{energy from sunlight absorbed}} \ C_6H_{12}O_6 \ + \ 6O_2$$

The plants then use some of the glucose they produce in **respiration**, during which the stored **energy** is released and used by the plants. The remaining glucose is converted into other organic compounds such as **proteins** which the plants use for growth, and **starch** which the plants store. The presence of **starch** in a leaf is proof that the leaf has been photosynthesising.

Photosynthesis requires the following **substrates**:

- **Carbon dioxide**, which diffuses into the leaves from the air through the **stomata** (see page 69).
- **Water**, which is absorbed from the soil by the roots.

In addition to the above substrates, photosynthesis requires the following **conditions**:

- **Energy from sunlight**, which is absorbed by the chlorophyll in chloroplasts of leaf cells.
- **Chlorophyll**, the green pigment that is present in chloroplasts.
- **Enzymes**, which are present in chloroplasts.
- A **suitable temperature** between about 5 °C and 40 °C so that enzymes can function.

Crop production

Farmers and gardeners use a variety of methods to produce **crops** to provide food for humans.

Table 3.1 *Methods used in the production of crops*

Method	Description
Strip planting	Different crops are grown in alternating **strips** or **bands** across a field or following the contours of sloping land. This reduces soil erosion.
Contouring or contour ploughing	Sloped land is ploughed and crops are planted along the natural **contours** of the land, rather than up and down the slope. This conserves rainwater by reducing runoff and it reduces soil erosion.
Terracing	**Flat areas** are cut out of the sides of hills or mountains to form terraces in which crops are planted. These terraces reduce rainwater runoff and soil erosion.
Crop rotation	Different crops are grown in **succession** on a piece of land; one of these is usually a legume such as peas or beans to replenish nitrates in the soil. Crop rotation maintains soil fertility, reduces soil erosion and helps control diseases and pests.
Greenhouse farming	Crops are grown in **greenhouses** that have walls and roofs made from a transparent material such as glass. This allows the climate in the greenhouse, particularly temperature, to be carefully controlled so that many different kinds of crops can be grown in places where the climate would not normally be suitable.
Hydroponics	Crops are grown in a **mineral-rich solution** without soil. The solution is pumped around the plant roots, which may be suspended in the solution or supported in an inert growing medium such as gravel or perlite. Hydroponics eliminates damage due to soil-borne diseases and pests, and high yields can be produced in limited space.
Tissue culture	See page 16. **Explants** are taken from plants with desirable characteristics and are grown in a sterile, nutrient-rich culture medium. Large numbers of plants with desirable characteristics can be produced in a fairly short time.
Container gardening	Food crops and herbs are grown in large **containers**, e.g. half-barrels and tubs, containing soil instead of planting them in the ground. This is used especially when outdoor space is limited.
Rooftop farming	Food crops are grown on **flat rooftops** using a variety of growing techniques including hydroponics and container gardens. This utilises otherwise unused space and provides a means of feeding growing urban populations with fresh produce.
Indoor farming	Food crops and herbs are grown entirely **indoors** where environmental conditions can be carefully controlled. Techniques such as hydroponics are used together with artificial lighting such as LED lights.
Organic farming	No synthetic inputs are used. Farms use only **natural** pesticides, herbicides and fertilisers, crops and livestock are rotated, organic matter is recycled back into the soil, and soil conservation and preventative disease control measures are practised.

a *terraced rice fields*

b *lettuces growing using hydroponics*

Figure 3.1 *Two methods used to grow crops*

Food chains and food webs in the natural environment

Living organisms are constantly interacting with each other and the environment in which they live. Certain **terms** are used when talking about these interactions:

- A **habitat** is the place where a particular organism lives.
- A **species** is a group of organisms of common ancestry that closely resemble each other and are normally capable of interbreeding to produce fertile offspring.
- A **population** is composed of all the members of a particular species living together in a particular habitat.
- A **community** is composed of all the populations of different species living together in a particular area.
- An **ecosystem** is a community of living organisms interacting with each other and with their physical (non-living) environment. Examples of ecosystems include a pond, a coral reef, a mangrove swamp and a forest.

Food chains

Organisms within any ecosystem are linked to form **food chains** based on how they obtain **organic food**.

Energy from sunlight enters living organisms through **photosynthesis** occurring in green plants, also known as **producers**. This energy is incorporated into the organic food molecules (carbohydrates, proteins and lipids) produced by the plants and is passed on to **consumers** through food chains. A food chain includes:

- A **producer**, usually a green plant.
- A **primary consumer** that eats the producer.
- A **secondary consumer** that eats the primary consumer.
- A **tertiary consumer** that eats the secondary consumer.

Consumers can also be classified according to what they consume:

- **Herbivores** consume plants or plant material only, e.g. cows, grasshoppers, snails, slugs, parrot fish, sea urchins.
- **Carnivores** consume animals or animal material only, e.g. lizards, toads, spiders, centipedes, eagles, octopuses, sharks.
- **Omnivores** consume both plants and animals, or plant and animal material, e.g. hummingbirds, crickets, humans and crayfish.

Levels of feeding within a food chain are referred to as **trophic levels**.

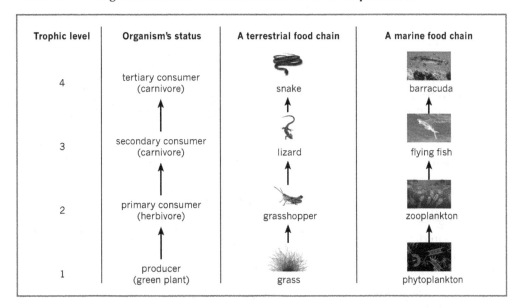

Figure 3.2 *Examples of food chains*

Food webs

Any ecosystem usually has more than one producer, and most consumers have more than one source of food. Consequently, food chains are interrelated to form **food webs**.

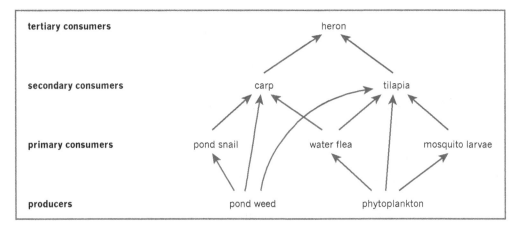

Figure 3.3 *An example of a food web from a freshwater lake*

Decomposers

Decomposers are responsible for **recycling** materials within ecosystems. They are microorganisms, i.e. bacteria and fungi, which feed on dead and waste organic matter causing it to **decompose**. During this process they release **carbon dioxide** and **minerals** into the environment which can be reabsorbed and **re-used** by plants.

The importance of food

The **food** an animal eats is called its **diet**. The human diet must contain the following:

- **Carbohydrates**, **proteins** and **lipids**, also known as **macronutrients**. These are required in relatively large quantities (see Table 3.4, page 38).

- **Vitamins** and **minerals**, also known as **micronutrients**. These are required in relatively small quantities for **healthy growth** and **development**.

- **Water** and **dietary fibre (roughage)**.

To supply the above, the human diet should contain a **variety** of foods selected from each of the **six** different **Caribbean food groups** shown in Figure 3.4. Each group contains foods that supply similar nutrients in similar proportions. The **size** of each sector indicates the **relative amount** of each group that should be eaten daily.

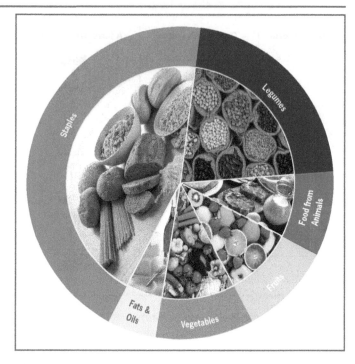

Figure 3.4 *The six Caribbean food groups*

Table 3.2 *Foods in the six Caribbean food groups*

Food group	Examples of foods in the group	Nutrients supplied
Staple foods	Cereals, bread, spaghetti, rice, yam, cassava, eddo, potato, breadfruit, plantain	Carbohydrates (mainly starch), vitamins, minerals, fibre
Legumes and nuts	Peas, beans, lentils, peanuts, cashew nuts	Protein, carbohydrates (mainly starch), vitamins, minerals, fibre
Non-starchy vegetables	Spinach, callaloo, string beans, broccoli, pumpkin, carrots, tomatoes	Vitamins, minerals, fibre
Fruits	Mango, paw paw, guava, West Indian cherry, citrus fruits, bananas	Carbohydrates (mainly sugars), vitamins, minerals, fibre
Foods from animals	Meat, poultry, fish, eggs, cheese	Protein, lipid, vitamins, minerals
Fats and oils	Butter, margarine, vegetable oil, fat on meat	Lipid, vitamins

Carbohydrates, proteins and lipids

Carbohydrates

Carbohydrates are **molecules** composed of carbon, hydrogen and oxygen atoms. Based on their chemical structure, carbohydrates can be classified into **three** groups: **monosaccharides**, **disaccharides** and **polysaccharides**.

- **Monosaccharides** are the simplest carbohydrate molecules; they have the formula $C_6H_{12}O_6$. They include glucose, fructose and galactose.
- **Disaccharides** are formed by chemically joining two monosaccharide molecules together; they have the formula $C_{12}H_{22}O_{11}$. They include maltose, sucrose and lactose.
- **Polysaccharides** are formed by joining many monosaccharide molecules into straight or branched chains. They include starch, cellulose and glycogen (animal starch).

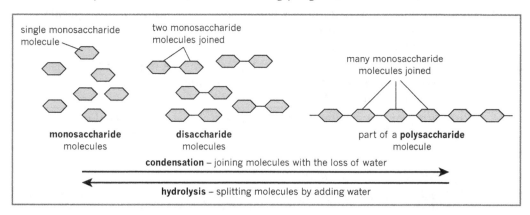

Figure 3.5 *The three types of carbohydrates*

Proteins

Proteins are **molecules** composed of carbon, hydrogen, oxygen, nitrogen, and sometimes sulfur and phosphorus atoms. These atoms form small molecules known as **amino acids.** There are 20 different common amino acids. Hundreds or thousands of amino acid molecules join together in long chains to form protein molecules.

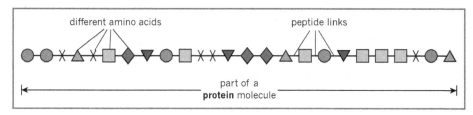

Figure 3.6 *Part of a protein molecule*

Lipids

Lipids are fats and oils. They are **molecules** composed of carbon, hydrogen and oxygen atoms. Each lipid molecule is made up of **four** smaller molecules joined together; three **fatty acid** molecules and one **glycerol** molecule.

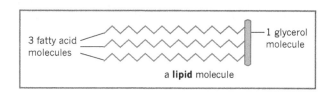

Figure 3.7 *A lipid molecule*

Tests can be performed in the laboratory to identify carbohydrates, proteins and lipids. Apart from the tests for lipids, these are usually carried out on about 2 cm³ of a solution of the test substance in a test tube.

Table 3.3 *Laboratory tests to identify carbohydrates, proteins and lipids*

Food substance	Method	Positive result
Reducing sugars, e.g. glucose and maltose	Add an equal volume of **Benedict's solution** and shake. Heat the mixture.	An **orange-red** precipitate forms.
Non-reducing sugars, e.g. sucrose	Add a few drops of dilute **hydrochloric acid** and heat for 1 minute. Add **sodium hydrogencarbonate** until effervescence stops. Add an equal volume of Benedict's solution, shake and heat.	An **orange-red** precipitate forms.
Starch	Add a few drops of **iodine solution** and shake.	Solution turns **blue-black**.
Proteins – the biuret test	Add an equal volume of **biuret reagent**, or of sodium hydroxide solution followed by drops of copper sulfate solution, and shake.	Solution turns **purple**.
Lipids – the emulsion test	Place 4 cm³ of **ethanol** in a dry test tube. Add 1 drop of test substance and shake. Add an equal volume of **water** and shake.	A **milky-white** emulsion forms.
Lipids – the grease spot test	Rub a drop of test substance onto **absorbent paper**. Leave for 10 minutes.	A **translucent mark** (grease spot) remains.

Table 3.4 *Functions of carbohydrates, proteins and lipids*

Class	Functions
Carbohydrates	• To provide **energy** (16 kJ g⁻¹); energy is easily released when respired. • For **storage**; glycogen granules are stored in many cells.
Proteins	• To make **new cells** for growth and to repair damaged tissues. • To make **enzymes** that speed up reactions in the body. • To make **hormones** that control various processes in the body. • To make **antibodies** to fight disease. • To provide **energy** (17 kJ g⁻¹); used only when stored carbohydrates and lipids have been used up.
Lipids	• To make **cell membranes** of newly formed cells. • To provide **energy** (39 kJ g⁻¹); used after carbohydrates because their metabolism is more complex and takes longer. • For **storage**; fat is stored under the skin and around organs. • For **insulation**; fat under the skin acts as an insulator.

A balanced diet

Humans must consume a **balanced diet** each day. This must contain carbohydrates, proteins, lipids, vitamins, minerals, water and dietary fibre in the **correct proportions** to supply the body with enough **energy** for daily activities and the correct materials for **growth** and **development**, and to keep the body in a **healthy state**.

The amount of **energy** required daily from the diet depends on a person's **age**, **occupation** and **gender (sex)**. In general, daily energy requirements:

- **Increase** as **age increases** up to adulthood. They then remain fairly constant up to old age, when less energy is required daily.
- **Increase** as **activity increases**, e.g. a manual labourer requires more energy than a person working in an office, and a sportsperson requires more energy than someone who never plays any sports.
- Are **higher** in **males** than in females of the same age and occupation.
- **Increase** in a female when she is **pregnant** or **breastfeeding**.

An unbalanced diet

When a person's diet does not contain the right amount of nutrients, it is said to be **unbalanced**. An unbalanced diet may be **lacking** in certain nutrients or certain nutrients may be in **excess**. Both can lead to several serious conditions:

- **Protein-energy malnutrition (PEM)** refers to a group of related disorders that are caused by an inadequate intake of protein or energy. They mainly affect young children in developing countries and include **kwashiorkor**, caused by a severe shortage of **protein**, and **marasmus**, caused by a severe shortage of **protein** and **energy rich foods** such as carbohydrates.

- **Deficiency diseases** are caused by a shortage or lack of a particular vitamin or mineral in the diet. **Night blindness** is caused by a deficiency of vitamin A, **beri-beri** by a deficiency of vitamin B_1, **pellagra** by a deficiency of vitamin B_3, **scurvy** by a deficiency of vitamin C, **rickets** by a deficiency of vitamin D or calcium, and **anaemia** by a deficiency of iron.

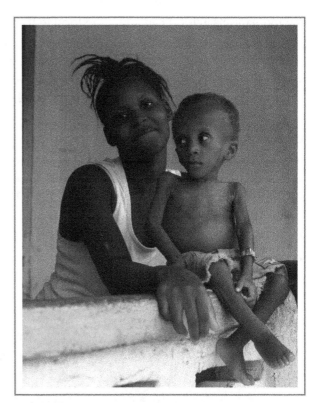

Figure 3.8 *A child with marasmus*

- **Obesity** is generally caused by the excessive consumption of energy rich foods high in **carbohydrates**, especially sugar, and/or **fat**, especially animal fat, and a **lack of physical activity**. It is characterised by an excessive accumulation and storage of **fat** in the body.

- **Diabetes Type II** can be caused by being overweight or obese.

Food additives and their effects on health

Food additives are **chemicals** added to food to prevent it from spoiling, or to improve its colour, flavour or texture. Some people are **sensitive** to certain additives including:

- The **flavour enhancer** monosodium glutamate or MSG.
- **Food colourings** such as tartrazine, cochineal and certain yellow colourings.
- **Preservatives** such as benzoates, nitrates, nitrites and sulfites.
- The **artificial sweetener**, aspartame.

Allergic reactions experienced by persons to these additives may include diarrhoea, colicky pains, hyperactivity, insomnia, irritability, asthma, rhinitis, sinusitis, skin rashes and hives. Some of these additives may also increase a person's risk of developing **cancer**.

The growth of microorganisms in food

Most microorganisms, including bacteria and fungi, need the following **conditions** to grow:

- **Water** or **moisture** so that they can carry out chemical reactions.
- **Oxygen** for aerobic respiration.
- A suitable **temperature** between about 10 °C and 40 °C for enzymes to function (see page 45).
- A suitable **pH** between about 6 and 8 for enzymes to function.

The effects of microorganisms in food

Microorganisms in food can affect the food in the following ways:

- Certain **bacteria** and some **fungi**, mainly **yeasts** and **moulds**, cause food to **spoil**. They feed, grow and reproduce in or on the food, causing changes in its appearance, texture, taste and odour.
- Certain **bacteria**, **viruses**, **parasites** and **moulds** cause food-borne **illnesses** known as **food poisoning** if food containing them is eaten, or if the food consumed contains harmful **toxins** released by them.

Bread mould

If bread mould **spores** in the air land on bread, they germinate and form thread-like structures known as **hyphae**, which grow over the surface of the bread by absorbing moisture and nutrients from the bread. The growth of bread mould can be **slowed** or **prevented** by:

- Sealing the bread in an **air-tight bag** to exclude oxygen and spores.
- Storing the bread in a **cool, dark** place such as a refrigerator.
- **Freezing** the bread.

Figure 3.9 *Bread mould*

Methods of preserving food

Food preservation aims to create conditions that are **unfavourable** for the growth of microorganisms that cause the food to spoil.

Table 3.5 *Methods of preserving food*

Method	Principles of the method
Salting	**Salt** (sodium chloride) is rubbed into the food or the food is placed into a concentrated salt solution (brine). The salt **withdraws water** from the food by **osmosis** so that microorganisms cannot survive and grow, e.g. salt fish and salt pork.
Adding sugar	The food is boiled in a concentrated **sugar** solution, sometimes to the point of crystallisation. The sugar **withdraws water** from the food by **osmosis** so that microorganisms cannot survive and grow, e.g. jams and crystallised fruits.
Drying	The food is **dried** to **remove all water** present so that microorganisms are unable to survive and grow, e.g. sun-dried tomatoes, dried fruits, powdered milk and eggs, and dried meat and fish.
Pickling	The food is placed in **vinegar** (a solution of ethanoic acid). The vinegar **lowers the pH** of the food so that it is too low (too acidic) for microorganisms to grow, e.g. pickled onions and cucumbers.
Heating	Microorganisms are **killed** by high temperatures. Food is **heated** and then **sealed** in airtight containers to prevent microorganisms from re-entering: • **Canning** involves heating food in containers in a steam or boiling water bath at **100 °C** and immediately sealing the containers, e.g. canned vegetables, fish and meat. • **Pasteurisation** involves heating the food to **72 °C** for 15 to 25 seconds and cooling it rapidly. Milk is commonly treated in this way. • **Ultra-high temperature treatment (UHT)** involves heating food to temperatures higher than **135 °C** for 1 to 2 seconds and cooling it rapidly, e.g. UHT milk, soups and baby food.
Refrigeration	The growth of microorganisms is **slowed down** or **inhibited** by low temperatures: • Placing food in a **refrigerator** keeps it at about **4 °C** which **slows** the growth of microorganisms, e.g. fresh meat, fish, fruits and vegetables. • **Freezing** food at temperatures of **–18 °C** and below inhibits the growth of microorganisms, e.g. frozen meat, fish, fruits and vegetables.
Treating with other preservatives	**Preservatives** are chemicals that are added to food to **inhibit** the growth of microorganisms. They include nitrites, nitrates, sulfites, benzoates and sorbates, and they are used to preserve foods such as jams, jellies, dried fruits, soft drinks, wine, cheese and cured meats, e.g. bacon, ham and sausages.

Revision questions

1. **a** Define the term 'photosynthesis'.
    b Give a chemical equation to summarise the process of photosynthesis.
    c Identify FOUR substrates or conditions that plants need to carry out photosynthesis.

2. Briefly describe EACH of the following methods that can be used to produce crops:
    a terracing
    b greenhouse farming
    c organic farming
    d hydroponics
    e contour ploughing
    f rooftop farming

3. Explain what is meant by EACH of the following terms:
    a producer
    b decomposer
    c omnivore
    d population
    e ecosystem

4. Some aphids were observed on the tomato plants in a garden and ladybird beetles were seen feeding on the aphids. The ladybirds were, in turn, being eaten by dragonflies which were, themselves, being fed on by toads. Use this information to draw a food chain for the organisms in the garden.

5. Identify the SIX Caribbean food groups and give ONE example of a food belonging to EACH group.

6. Give TWO functions of EACH of the following macronutrients supplied by the six Caribbean food groups: carbohydrates, proteins and lipids.

7. **a** Distinguish between a balanced diet and an unbalanced diet.
    b Identify THREE factors that affect a person's daily energy requirements and THREE possible consequences of having an unbalanced diet.

8. **a** List FOUR conditions that promote the growth of microorganisms.
    b Outline TWO effects of the presence of microorganisms in food.

9. Explain how EACH of the following methods preserves food:
    a pickling
    b refrigeration
    c salting
    d heating

Digestion in humans

Digestion is the process by which food is **broken down** into simple, soluble food molecules that are useful for body activities. It occurs in the **alimentary canal**, which is a tube 8 to 9 metres long with muscular walls running from the **mouth** to the **anus**. The alimentary canal and its various associated organs, including the liver, gall bladder and pancreas, make up the **digestive system** (see Figure 3.12, page 46).

The digestive process involves:

- **Mechanical digestion**, during which **large pieces** of food are broken down into smaller pieces. Mechanical digestion begins in the **mouth** where food is chewed by the **teeth**, and it continues in the **stomach** where contractions of the stomach walls churn the food.
- **Chemical digestion**, during which large, usually insoluble **food molecules** are broken down into small, soluble food molecules by **enzymes** (see page 45). Chemical digestion begins in the **mouth** and is completed in the **ileum**.

Teeth and mechanical digestion

When food is **chewed** or **masticated**, the teeth break up **large pieces** of food into **smaller pieces**. This is important because:

- It gives the pieces of food a **larger surface area** for digestive enzymes to act on, making chemical digestion quicker and easier.
- It makes food easier to **swallow**.

Types of teeth

Humans have **four** different types of teeth: **incisors**, **canines**, **premolars** and **molars**. An adult has **8** incisors (*i*), **4** canines (*c*), **8** premolars (*pm*) and **12** molars (*m*). The **dental formula** of an adult gives the number of teeth of each kind in one half of the upper and lower jaw as follows:

$$i \frac{2}{2} \; c \frac{1}{1} \; pm \frac{2}{2} \; m \frac{3}{3}$$

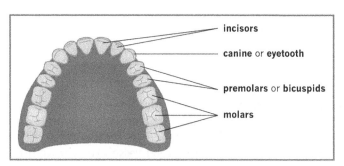

incisors

canine or eyetooth

premolars or bicuspids

molars

Figure 3.10 *Teeth of the upper jaw of an adult human*

Table 3.6 *The different types of teeth in humans*

Type	Position	Shape	Functions
Incisor	At the front of the jaw.	Chisel-shaped with sharp, thin edges. crown — root	• To cut food. • To bite off pieces of food.
Canine (eye tooth)	Next to the incisors.	Cone-shaped and pointed.	• To grip food. • To tear off pieces of food.
Premolar	At the side of the jaw, next to the canines.	Have a fairly broad surface with two pointed cusps. cusp — root	• To crush and grind food.
Molar	At the back of the jaw, next to the premolars.	Have a broad surface with four or five pointed cusps.	• To crush and grind food.

Tooth structure

A tooth is divided into **two** parts: the **crown**, which is the part above the jaw, and the **root**, which is the part embedded in the jawbone. The internal structure of all teeth is similar. The crown is covered with **enamel** and the root with a thin layer of **cement** and the **periodontal membrane**. The bulk of the tooth is composed of **dentine** and the **pulp cavity** occupies the centre. **Nerves** and **blood vessels** run throughout the pulp cavity.

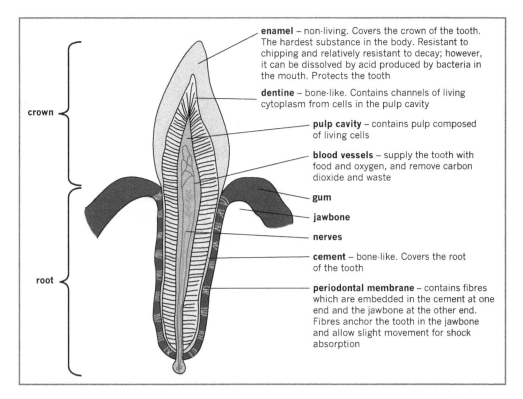

enamel – non-living. Covers the crown of the tooth. The hardest substance in the body. Resistant to chipping and relatively resistant to decay; however, it can be dissolved by acid produced by bacteria in the mouth. Protects the tooth

dentine – bone-like. Contains channels of living cytoplasm from cells in the pulp cavity

pulp cavity – contains pulp composed of living cells

blood vessels – supply the tooth with food and oxygen, and remove carbon dioxide and waste

gum

jawbone

nerves

cement – bone-like. Covers the root of the tooth

periodontal membrane – contains fibres which are embedded in the cement at one end and the jawbone at the other end. Fibres anchor the tooth in the jawbone and allow slight movement for shock absorption

crown

root

Figure 3.11 *A vertical section through a canine tooth showing its internal structure*

Guidelines for the care of teeth

- Brush teeth and gums in the proper way, twice a day.
- Use a fluoride toothpaste and good quality toothbrush when brushing.
- Use dental floss and an interdental brush once a day.
- Use an antibacterial mouthwash after brushing and flossing.
- Avoid eating sugary and starchy foods and drinking sugary drinks, especially between meals and before going to bed.
- Visit a dentist regularly for a check-up and cleaning.

The chemical digestion of food

During **chemical digestion** the large food molecules are broken down into small molecules. Chemical digestion is catalysed (speeded up) by **digestive enzymes** (see page 46).

Enzymes

Enzymes are biological catalysts produced by all living cells. They speed up chemical reactions occurring in living organisms without being changed themselves.

Enzymes are **proteins** that living cells produce from amino acids obtained from food. Without enzymes, chemical reactions would occur too slowly to maintain life. Enzymes are **specific**, meaning that each type of enzyme catalyses only one type of reaction, and they are affected by **temperature** and **pH**:

- Enzymes work best at a particular temperature known as the **optimum temperature**. This is about 37 °C for human enzymes. High temperatures **denature** enzymes, i.e. they are inactivated. Enzymes start to be denatured at about 40 °C to 45 °C.

- Enzymes work best at a particular pH known as the **optimum pH**. This is about pH 7 for most enzymes. Extremes of acidity or alkalinity **denature** most enzymes.

Digestive enzymes

There are **three** categories of **digestive enzymes** and several different enzymes may belong to each category (see Tables 3.7 and 3.8).

Table 3.7 *Categories of digestive enzymes*

Category of digestive enzyme	Food molecules digested	Products of digestion
Carbohydrases	Polysaccharides and disaccharides	Monosaccharides
Proteases	Proteins	Amino acids
Lipases	Lipids	Fatty acids and glycerol

The digestive system and chemical digestion

The process of **chemical digestion** is summarised in Table 3.8.

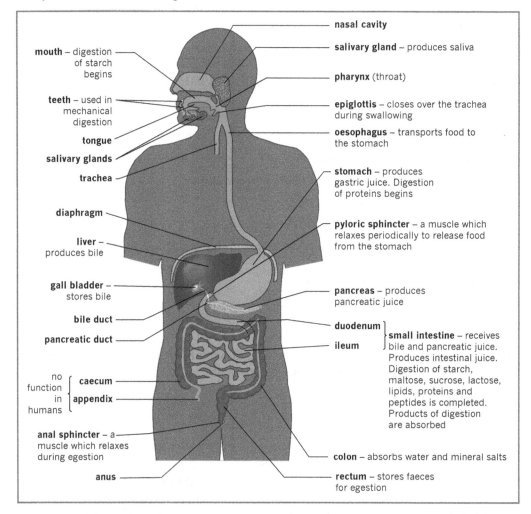

Figure 3.12 *The structures of the human digestive system and their functions*

Table 3.8 *A summary of chemical digestion*

Organ	Digestive juice	Source	Main components	Functions of the components
Mouth	Saliva (pH 7–8)	Salivary glands.	• Water and mucus • **Salivary amylase***	• Moisten and lubricate the food allowing tasting and easy swallowing. • Begins to digest: **starch ⟶ maltose** (a disaccharide)
Stomach	Gastric juice (pH 1–2)	Cells in the stomach wall.	• Hydrochloric acid • **Rennin*** • **Pepsin***	• Maintains an optimum pH of 1–2 for pepsin and rennin, and kills bacteria. • Produced in infants to clot soluble protein in milk so the protein is retained in the stomach. • Begins to digest: **protein ⟶ peptides** (shorter chains of amino acids)
Small intestine (duodenum and ileum)	Bile (pH 7–8)	Cells in the liver. It is stored in the gall bladder and enters the duodenum via the bile duct.	• Bile pigments, e.g. bilirubin • Organic bile salts	• Excretory products from the breakdown of haemoglobin in the liver. Have no function in digestion. • **Emulsify lipids**, i.e. break large lipid droplets into smaller droplets, increasing their surface area for digestion.
	Pancreatic juice (pH 7–8)	Cells in the pancreas. It enters the duodenum via the pancreatic duct.	• **Pancreatic amylase*** • **Trypsin*** • **Pancreatic lipase***	• Continues to digest: **starch ⟶ maltose** • Continues to digest: **protein ⟶ peptides** • Digests: **lipids ⟶ fatty acids** and **glycerol**
	Intestinal juice (pH 7–8)	Cells in the walls of the small intestine.	• **Maltase*** • **Sucrase*** • **Lactase*** • **Peptidase*** (erepsin)	• Digests: **maltose ⟶ glucose** • Digests: **sucrose ⟶ glucose** and **fructose** • Digests: **lactose ⟶ glucose** and **galactose** • Digests: **peptides ⟶ amino acids**

* **digestive enzymes**

Absorption, assimilation and egestion

Absorption

Absorption is the process by which the soluble food molecules, produced in digestion, move into the body fluids and body cells.

Absorption occurs in the **small intestine** and **colon**:

- Monosaccharides, amino acids, fatty acids, glycerol, vitamins, minerals and water are absorbed through the lining of the small intestine, mainly the **ileum**, and into the **blood capillaries** in its walls.
- Water and mineral salts can also be absorbed from any undigested food into the **blood capillaries** in the walls of the **colon**. As this undigested waste moves along the colon to the rectum it becomes progressively more solid as the water is absorbed from it.

Assimilation

*Assimilation is the process by which the body **uses** the soluble food molecules absorbed after digestion.*

- Any non-glucose **monosaccharides** are converted to **glucose** by the liver. The glucose is then used by all body cells in **respiration** to release **energy**. Excess glucose is converted to **glycogen** by **liver** and **muscle** cells and stored, or is converted to **fat** by cells in **fat tissues** and stored under the skin and around organs.
- **Amino acids** are used by body cells to make **proteins** for cell growth and repair. They are also used by cells to make **enzymes**, **hormones** and **antibodies**.
- **Fatty acids** and **glycerol** are used to make **cell membranes** of newly forming cells. They can also be used by body cells in **respiration** and any excess is converted to **fat** and stored in **fat tissue**.

Egestion

*Egestion is the process by which undigested dietary fibre and other materials are **removed** from the body as faeces.*

The almost solid material entering the rectum is called **faeces** and consists of undigested dietary fibre, dead bacteria and intestinal cells, mucus and bile pigments. Faeces is stored in the rectum and **egested** at intervals through the **anus** when the **anal sphincter** relaxes.

10 What happens during digestion?

11 Why are teeth important in the digestive process?

12 Keenan has FOUR types of teeth in his mouth. Identify these and state the function of EACH.

13 Draw a fully labelled diagram of a vertical section through a canine tooth.

14 Melissa develops a cavity in one of her teeth. Suggest FOUR things she should do to prevent cavities forming in her other teeth.

15 What are enzymes and why are they important in digestion?

16 State the function of EACH of the following parts of the digestive system in the digestive process.

a the oesophagus   **b** the liver   **c** the pyloric sphincter

d the colon   **e** the rectum

17 For lunch, Omari consumes a ham sandwich made with two slices of buttered bread and two slices of ham. Describe how the starch, protein and lipid in Omari's sandwich are digested as it passes through his digestive system.

18 When digestion of Omari's sandwich is complete, the products are absorbed and assimilated by his body. What happens during absorption and assimilation?

4 Transport systems

Living organisms need to exchange substances constantly with their environment. They need to take in useful substances and get rid of waste. **Transport systems** provide a means by which these substances are moved between exchange surfaces in the body and body cells.

The need for transport systems in living organisms

The absorption and transport of substances in multicellular organisms is affected by **two** factors:

- Their **surface area to volume ratio**.
- The **limitations of diffusion**.

Large **multicellular organisms** have a **small** surface area to volume ratio. Diffusion through their body surface is not adequate to supply all their body cells with their requirements and remove their waste. In addition, most of their body is too far from its surface for substances to move through it by diffusion. These organisms have developed **transport systems** to carry **useful substances** from specialised organs which absorb them, e.g. the lungs and intestines in humans and roots in plants, to their body cells, and to carry **waste substances** from their body cells to specialised organs which excrete them, e.g. the kidneys in humans.

Transport in plants

Substances are transported around plants by **vascular tissue** composed of **xylem** and **phloem tissue**. Vascular tissue runs throughout roots and stems of plants, and it makes up the mid-rib and veins of leaves.

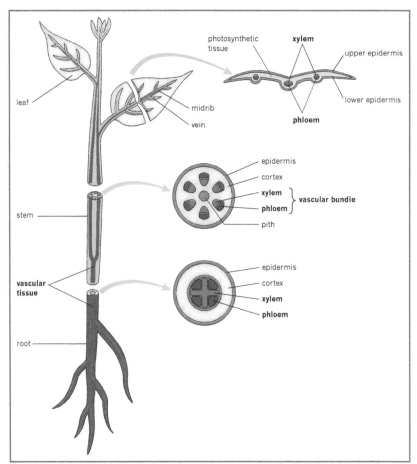

Figure 4.1 *The arrangement of vascular tissue in a flowering plant*

Movement of water and minerals through a plant

Xylem tissue transports **water** and **mineral salts** from roots up to leaves. This tissue is composed of long, extremely narrow, dead, hollow tubes known as **xylem vessels** (see Figure 4.2 below).

Water moves through a plant by a combination of **root pressure**, **transpiration** and **capillarity**:

- The epidermal cells of the **root** absorb water from the soil by **osmosis**. This water moves through the cortex cells of the root by osmosis and this creates a pressure called **root pressure**. This pressure **pushes** the water into and up the xylem vessels in the root and into the xylem vessels in the bottom of the stem.

- The **leaves** of the plant constantly lose water vapour to the atmosphere by a process called **transpiration**. This water vapour is formed by water evaporating from the cells inside the leaf and diffusing out through tiny pores in the underside of the leaf called **stomata**. Transpiration creates a **pull** that draws water from the xylem vessels in the leaves and the xylem vessels in the stem.

- **Capillary action** helps water to move **up** xylem vessels because the vessels are extremely narrow, so they act like **capillary tubes**.

Mineral salts are dissolved in the water in the soil and are absorbed by the roots against a concentration gradient by **active transport**. These dissolved salts then move through the cortex cells of the root and into the xylem vessels in the moving water. The salts are then carried throughout the plant dissolved in the water in the xylem vessels.

Movement of food through a plant – translocation

Phloem tissue transports food, mainly **sucrose** and some **amino acids**, from leaves where it is made, to all other parts of the plant. This tissue is composed of extremely narrow tubes containing living cytoplasm known as **phloem sieve tubes** (see Figure 4.2). Food is moved through the sieve tubes with the help of **active transport.**

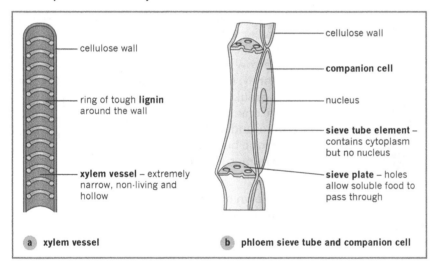

Figure 4.2 *Longitudinal sections through a xylem vessel and phloem sieve tube with companion cell*

The circulatory system in humans

Substances are transported around the human body by the **circulatory system**. The system consists of:

- **Blood**, which serves as the **medium** to transport substances around the body.
- **Blood vessels**, which are **tubes** through which the blood flows to and from all parts of the body.
- The **heart**, which **pumps** the blood through the blood vessels.

Blood

Blood is composed of **three** types of cells:

- **red blood cells**
- **white blood cells**
- **platelets**.

These cells are suspended in a fluid called **plasma.** The cells make up about 45% by volume of the blood and the plasma makes up about 55%.

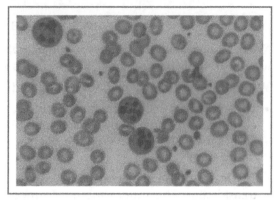

Figure 4.3 *Blood cells under the microscope*

Composition and functions of plasma

Plasma is a yellowish fluid composed of about 90% **water** and 10% **dissolved substances**. The dissolved substances consist of:

- **Products of digestion**, e.g. glucose, amino acids, vitamins and minerals.
- **Waste products**, e.g. carbon dioxide and urea.
- **Hormones**, e.g. insulin and thyroxine.
- **Plasma proteins**, e.g. fibrinogen, prothrombin, albumen and antibodies.

The main **function** of plasma is to **transport** all the substances that it contains around the body.

Blood cells

Table 4.1 *Structure and functions of blood cells*

Cell type and structure	Formation of cells	Functions
Red blood cells (erythrocytes) cell membrane — cytoplasm rich in **haemoglobin**, an iron containing protein - **Biconcave discs** with a thin centre and relatively large surface area to volume ratio so gases easily diffuse in and out. - Have **no nucleus**, therefore they only live for about 3 to 4 months. - Contain the red pigment **haemoglobin**. - Slightly **elastic** allowing them to squeeze through the narrowest capillaries.	- Formed in the red bone marrow found in flat bones, e.g. the pelvis, scapula, ribs, sternum, cranium and vertebrae; and in the ends of long bones, e.g. the humerus and femur. - Broken down mainly in the liver and spleen.	- Transport **oxygen** as **oxyhaemoglobin** from the lungs to body cells. - Transport small amounts of **carbon dioxide** from body cells to the lungs.

Cell type and structure	Formation of cells	Functions
White blood cells (leucocytes) Slightly larger than red blood cells and less numerous; approximately 1 white blood cell to 600 red blood cells. There are two main types; 25% are lymphocytes and 75% are phagocytes. **Lymphocytes** • Have a **rounded** shape. • Have a large, **round nucleus** that controls the production of antibodies. • Have only a small amount of cytoplasm. **Phagocytes** • Have a **variable** shape. • Move by **pseudopodia**; can move out of capillaries through their walls and engulf pathogens using pseudopodia. • Have a **lobed nucleus**.	• Develop from cells in the red bone marrow and mature in other organs, e.g. the lymph nodes, spleen and thymus gland. • Formed in the red bone marrow.	• Produce **antibodies** to destroy disease-causing bacteria and viruses (pathogens). • Produce **antitoxins** to neutralise toxins produced by pathogens. • Engulf and destroy pathogens. • Engulf pathogens destroyed by antibodies.
Platelets (thrombocytes) • Cell **fragments**. • Have **no nucleus** and only live for about 10 days.	• Formed from cells in the red bone marrow.	• Help the blood to **clot** at a cut or wound.

Blood vessels

There are **three** main types of blood vessels:

• **arteries**
• **capillaries**
• **veins**.

Arteries carry blood **away** from the heart. On entering an organ, an artery branches into smaller arteries called **arterioles** which then branch into a network of **capillaries** that run throughout the organ. Capillaries then join into small veins called **venules** which join to form a single **vein** that leads back from the organ **towards** the heart.

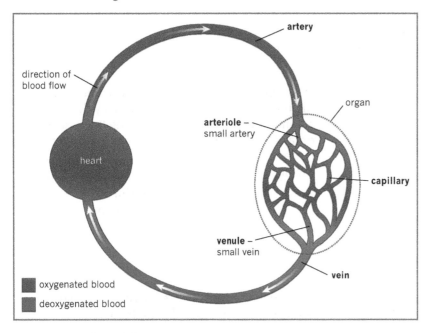

Figure 4.4 *The relationship between the different blood vessels*

Arteries carry blood that is under **high pressure,** therefore they have thick muscular walls to withstand the pressure. **Veins** carry blood that is under **low pressure**, therefore they have **thinner** muscular walls and **valves** to prevent the blood from flowing backwards. **Capillaries** have walls that are **one cell thick** so that food and oxygen can easily pass from the blood into body cells, and carbon dioxide and other waste can pass back into the blood.

The heart

The pumping action of the **heart** maintains a constant circulation of blood around the body. The walls of the heart are composed of **cardiac muscle** which contracts without nerve impulses and does not get tired.

The heart is divided into **four** chambers. The two on the right contain **deoxygenated blood** and are completely separated from the two on the left, which contain **oxygenated blood**, by the **septum.**

- The top two chambers, called **atria,** have thin walls and they collect blood entering the heart from the **anterior** and **posterior vena cavae** and the **pulmonary veins.** Their walls are **thin** because they only have to pump blood a short distance into the ventricles.

- The bottom two chambers, called **ventricles,** have thick walls and they pump blood out of the heart via the **pulmonary artery** and **aorta.** Their walls are **thick** because they have to pump blood longer distances around the body and to the lungs.

Valves are present between each atrium and ventricle, and in the pulmonary artery and aorta as they leave the ventricles, to ensure that blood flows through the heart in **one direction.**

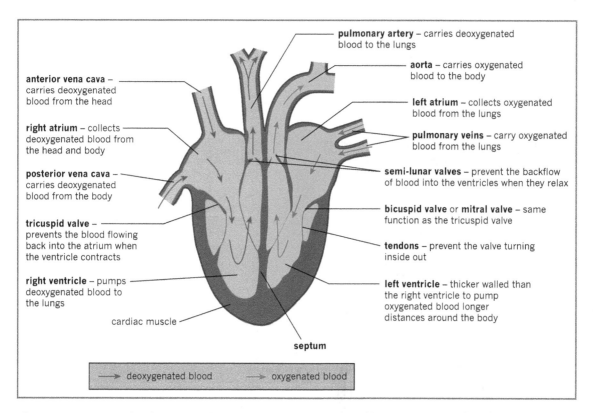

Figure 4.5 *Longitudinal section through the human heart showing the function of the parts*

Heart beat

The atria and ventricles at the two sides of the heart contract and relax together. The **contraction** of a chamber is called **systole** and its **relaxation** is called **diastole**. The heart beats on average 75 times per minute. One **heart beat** or **cardiac cycle** involves the following:

- **Diastole** – the **atria** and **ventricles relax** together, the semi-lunar valves close, the atria fill up with blood from the anterior and posterior vena cavae and pulmonary veins, and the blood flows into the ventricles. This takes 0.4 seconds.

- **Atrial systole** – the **atria contract** together forcing any remaining blood through the tricuspid and bicuspid valves into the ventricles. This takes 0.1 seconds.

- **Ventricular systole** – the **ventricles contract** together, the tricuspid and bicuspid valves close and blood is forced through the semi-lunar valves into the aorta and pulmonary arteries. This takes 0.3 seconds.

Circulation

During one complete circulation around the body, the blood flows through the heart **twice**, therefore, humans have a **double circulation**:

- In the **pulmonary circulation**, blood travels from the **right ventricle** through the **pulmonary arteries** to the **lungs** to pick up oxygen and lose carbon dioxide, i.e. it becomes **oxygenated**. It then travels back via the **pulmonary veins** to the **left atrium**.

- In the **systemic (body) circulation**, blood travels from the **left ventricle** through the **aorta** to the **body** where it gives up oxygen to the body cells and picks up carbon dioxide, i.e. it becomes deoxygenated. It then travels back via the **anterior** or **posterior vena cava** to the **right atrium**.

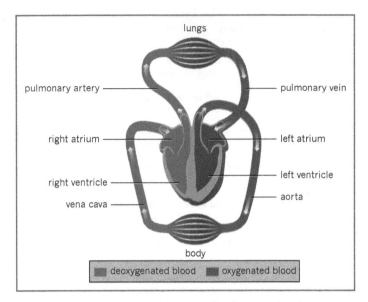

Figure 4.6 *Double circulation in the human body*

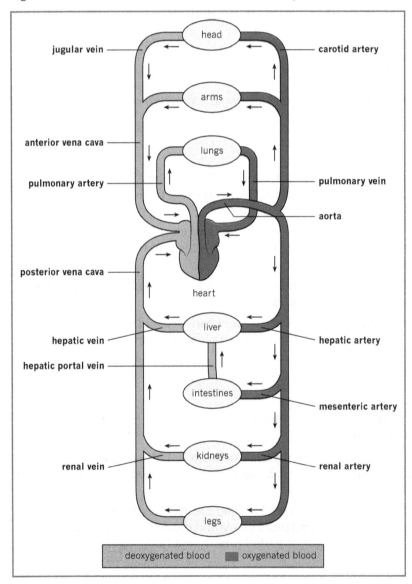

Figure 4.7 *The major blood vessels in the human body*

Blood groups

Blood can be classified into different **blood groups** based on chemicals known as **antigens** present on the surface of red blood cells. There are **two** grouping systems.

The ABO blood group system

The **ABO system** divides blood into **four** groups; group A, group B, group AB and group O. These are determined by the presence or absence of two **antigens** and also two **antibodies** in the plasma.

Table 4.2 *Antigens and antibodies of the ABO blood grouping system*

Blood group	Antigen on the surface of red blood cells	Antibody in the plasma
Group A	A	Anti-B
Group B	B	Anti-A
Group AB	Both A and B	No antibodies
Group O	No antigens	Both anti-A and anti-B

The antibodies in plasma must be different from the antigens on red blood cells. If they were the same, the antibodies would bind to the antigens causing **agglutination** or **clumping** of the red blood cells.

The Rhesus (Rh) blood group system

The **Rhesus** or **Rh system** divides blood into **two** groups; Rh-positive and Rh-negative. These are determined by the presence or absence of an **antigen** known as the **Rh factor.** If the factor is present, the person has **Rh-positive** blood. If the factor is absent, the person has **Rh-negative** blood.

The **Rh factor** poses a risk to a **woman** with **Rh-negative** blood who wishes to have children. If she carries a **baby** with **Rh-positive** blood, a small amount of the baby's blood may enter her bloodstream, especially during labour, causing her to produce **anti-Rh antibodies.** During any **subsequent pregnancies** with Rh-positive babies, these antibodies can pass across the placenta and attack the baby's red blood cells causing anaemia, brain damage and even death. To **prevent** this, the mother is given an injection of a substance called **anti-D** immediately after delivery to stop her from making any anti-Rh antibodies.

Precautions for blood transfusions

During a **blood transfusion**, blood from a healthy person is given to a person who has lost blood. Certain **precautions** have to be followed when handling and transfusing blood.

- Persons handling blood for transfusion must **avoid direct contact** with the blood, e.g. by wearing medical gloves.
- Blood should **not** be taken from a person who is pregnant or has anaemia.
- Donated blood must be **screened** for pathogens, e.g. HIV, hepatitis B and C.
- Blood from the donor must be **cross-matched** with the recipient's blood to ensure that their blood groups are compatible. This prevents **agglutination** of the red blood cells in the **donated** blood. If agglutination occurs, blood vessels may become blocked, and the agglutinated cells **disintegrate**, which can be fatal.

Note that Type **O Rh-negative blood** is known as the **universal donor** type because it has **no A, B or Rh antigens**, so it can be given to anybody. Type **AB Rh-positive blood** is known as the **universal recipient** type because it has **no A, B or Rh antibodies**, so a person with it can receive blood of any type.

Cardiovascular disease

Cardiovascular disease refers to a class of diseases that affect the **heart** and **blood vessels**, including **hypertension**, **heart attack** and **stroke**.

Hypertension

Hypertension (high blood pressure) occurs when the blood pressure in the arteries is consistently high. It is usually caused by artery walls becoming **less elastic** and by fatty deposits containing cholesterol, known as **plaque**, building up around the inside of the walls, making the arteries narrower; a process known as **atherosclerosis**. Risk factors that can lead to hypertension include:

- Being overweight or obese.
- Smoking.
- Too much salt or too much fat in the diet.
- Consumption of too much alcohol.
- Lack of physical exercise.
- Stress.

Heart attack and stroke

One of the main causes of a **heart attack** or a **stroke** is **atherosclerosis**. The plaque in arteries can sometimes rupture and form a **blood clot** that gradually gets larger and starts to block the artery.

- A **heart attack** is caused when a coronary artery supplying the **heart** is blocked by a clot. This results in the death of cells in the region of the heart supplied by the blocked artery. Symptoms of a heart attack include chest pain, upper body pain, shortness of breath and feeling weak or dizzy.

- A **stroke** is caused when an artery supplying the **brain** is blocked by a clot. This results in the death of cells in the region of the brain supplied by the blocked artery. Symptoms of a stroke include drooping of one side of the face, weakness or numbness of one arm, and slurred or garbled speech.

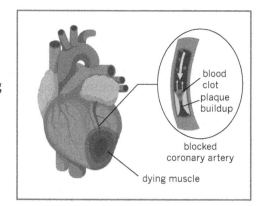

Figure 4.8 *Atherosclerosis in a coronary artery*

Immunity

Immunity is the temporary or permanent resistance to a disease.

There are **two** types of immunity, **natural immunity** and **artificial immunity**.

Natural immunity

Natural immunity results from a person having been exposed to a pathogenic disease caused by a virus or bacterium. **Lymphocytes** bring about this immunity by producing proteins called **antibodies** in response to the presence of foreign substances, known as **antigens**, in the body. Antigens include chemicals, mainly proteins, found in the walls or coats of pathogens. Antigens are **specific** to the type of pathogen and foreign to all other organisms. When a pathogen enters the body, lymphocytes make specific antibodies in response to the pathogen's specific antigens. These **antibodies** destroy the pathogens.

Production of antibodies takes time and the pathogen produces **symptoms** of the disease before being destroyed. Once the person recovers, the antibodies gradually disappear from the blood and some lymphocytes develop into **lymphocyte memory cells** that 'remember' the specific antigen.

When the pathogen enters the body again, the memory lymphocytes recognise the antigen, multiply and **quickly** produce **large quantities** of the specific antibody. The pathogen is destroyed before symptoms of the disease develop. The person has become **immune** to the disease. Depending on the type of pathogen, immunity may last a short time, e.g. against the common cold, to a lifetime, e.g. chicken pox is rarely caught twice.

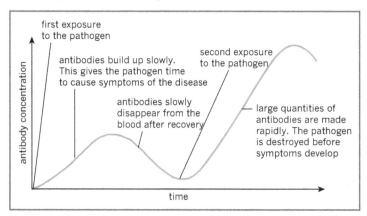

Figure 4.9 *Antibody production during the acquisition of immunity*

A **baby** gains important immunity by receiving antibodies that pass across the **placenta** before birth or from **breast milk** during breastfeeding. Since the baby's lymphocytes have not been involved in producing the antibodies and they gradually disappear from the blood, immunity lasts only a short time.

Artificial immunity

Artificial immunity is acquired by **vaccination** and is used to control the spread of **communicable diseases** (diseases that pass from person to person). A **vaccine** may contain any of the following:

* Live but **weakened** pathogens.
* **Dead** pathogens.
* **Fragments** of the pathogens.
* **Antigens** from the coats of pathogens.

Vaccines do not cause the disease, but lymphocytes still make **antibodies** in response to the specific **antigens** that are present in the vaccine. **Lymphocyte memory cells** are also produced so that an **immune response** is set up whenever the pathogen enters the body. Artificial immunity may last a short time, e.g. against cholera, to a lifetime, e.g. against tuberculosis.

HIV/AIDS and the immune system

Acquired immune deficiency syndrome (AIDS) is caused by the **human immunodeficiency virus (HIV)**. Once in the blood, the virus particles enter specialised white blood cells called **T-helper lymphocyte cells** and begin to make copies of themselves. The new HIV particles burst out of the T-cells, destroying them. The particles then go on to invade more T-cells and this starts to **weaken** the **body's immune system**. When the immune system is weakened to a point that it can no longer destroy invading pathogens, the person becomes ill and develops **AIDS** (see Table 2.6, page 27).

HIV is known as a **retrovirus** because it can replicate (make copies of itself) inside a host cell. **Antiretroviral drugs** are used in the treatment of HIV infection.

Revision questions

1 Explain why multicellular organisms need transport systems within their bodies.

2 Name the TWO tissues that transport substances around plants and identify the substance(s) transported by EACH.

3 a Name the process by which leaves lose water vapour to the atmosphere.

   b Outline how water from the soil moves through a plant and into the air as water vapour.

4 a What is the liquid part of blood known as?

   b Name the THREE types of cells found in blood and state the function(s) of EACH type.

5 Explain the relationship between arteries, capillaries and veins.

6 Name the four chambers of the heart and give a reason why the bottom two chambers have thicker walls than the top two.

7 Distinguish between diastole and systole.

8 Draw a simple flow diagram to show the pathway that a red blood cell takes as it journeys from the lungs around the body and back to the lungs.

9 Name the TWO different blood grouping systems and explain why different blood groups exist.

10 Explain the potential risk to a woman with Rh-negative blood who wishes to have children, and what precaution she must take if she gives birth to a baby with Rh-positive blood.

11 Outline THREE precautions that should be taken when handling and transfusing blood.

12 Suggest THREE factors that could lead to a person developing cardiovascular disease.

13 a Explain how artificial immunity is acquired.

   b Name the sexually transmitted infection that results from damage to the immune system.

Drug use, misuse and abuse

*A **drug** is any chemical substance that affects the functioning of the body.*

Many drugs are used medically to improve health whilst others are illegal. All drugs can be **harmful** If they are **misused** or **abused** (used wrongly or in excessive quantities). Constant misuse and abuse can lead to **addiction**. If the drug is then withdrawn, the user suffers from **withdrawal symptoms**.

Drugs can have both **physiological effects** because they affect the physical functioning of parts of the body and **psychological effects** because they affect the brain and cause changes in behaviour.

Effects of drug misuse and abuse on the body

- **Alcohol** is a **depressant** of the central nervous system. Short-term effects of alcohol use include reduced muscular coordination, impaired mental functioning, slurred speech and memory lapses. Long-term effects include increased blood pressure, stomach ulcers, cirrhosis of the liver and nervous system disorders.

- **Prescription drugs** and **non-prescription** or **over-the-counter drugs** can be misused or abused, and persons can become dependent on them. **Prescription drugs** that may be misused or abused include antibiotics, tranquillisers, painkillers (analgesics), steroids and diet pills (see below). **Non-prescription** drugs that may be misused or abused include painkillers, cough and cold medicines and motion sickness tablets.

- **Illegal drugs** can be extremely harmful and are highly **addictive**. They include:

  - **Cocaine**, which is a **stimulant** of the central nervous system. Its use can cause feelings of power and confidence, bizarre and erratic behaviour, hallucinations, paranoia, other mental disorders and increased breathing and heart rate, and can lead to a heart attack or stroke and sometimes death.

  - **Marijuana (cannabis)**, which alters a person's **perception**. Its use can cause euphoria (a 'high') followed by relaxation and drowsiness, bloodshot eyes, increased appetite and heart rate and difficulty thinking. In the long term it damages the respiratory system, decreases motivation, impairs memory and increases the risk of a heart attack or stroke.

  Other illegal drugs include **LSD (acid)** and **ecstasy** which are **hallucinogens**, and **heroin** which is a **depressant** of the central nervous system.

  Figure 4.10 *Marijuana leaves are dried, rolled into a cigarette and smoked*

- **Steroids** are divided into **two** types. **Corticosteroids** are used to decrease inflammation. **Anabolic steroids** are used to increase muscle mass or reduce body fat, and may be used **illegally** to improve athletic performance or body appearance. Abuse of anabolic steroids can lead to acne, elevated cholesterol and blood pressure, shrinking of testes and growth of breasts in men, increased body hair in females, and liver, heart and kidney damage.

- **Diet pills** are used to help individuals to lose weight. Abuse of diet pills can lead to nervousness, dizziness, anxiety, difficulty sleeping, diarrhoea, stomach pain, high blood pressure, a fast or irregular heart beat, heart palpitations and heart failure.

- **Hormonal injections** can be misused or abused. **Human growth hormone (HGH)** may be used illegally to improve athletic performance and its misuse can lead to swollen joints and joint or muscle pain. **Human chorionic gonadotrophin (HCG)** may be misused as a means to lose weight rapidly. The so-called **HCG diet** combines HCG injections with a considerably reduced food intake and can cause headaches, fatigue, irritability, depression, breast tenderness, and swollen hands and feet.

Blood doping

Blood doping involves increasing the number of **red blood cells** in the bloodstream to improve the blood's ability to carry oxygen. It may be used **illegally** to enhance athletic performance. It can be carried out by injecting a **hormone** to increase production of red blood cells by the red bone marrow, or by giving a **blood transfusion** using blood previously removed from the athlete and stored for a period of time. Blood doping can lead to blood clots forming in blood vessels, a heart attack or stroke.

Social and economic effects of drug abuse

Drug abuse upsets relationships with family and friends, and can lead to personal neglect, automobile accidents, job loss (as the abuser is unable to work), financial problems, increased crime and prostitution (as the abuser has to find money to pay for the drugs), increased demands on health services and a shortened life span for the abuser.

Prostitution exposes abusers to sexually transmitted infections (STIs) and the use of intravenous drugs exposes them to HIV/AIDS and hepatitis A. Crime can lead to arrest and possible imprisonment. Babies born to abusers may have birth defects or be addicted to the drug themselves. Ultimately, standards of living are reduced and human resources are lost.

Physiological effects of exercise

During exercise, **respiration** speeds up in muscles cells, and heart rate and breathing rate increase to supply the muscles with the extra oxygen and glucose they need and to remove the extra carbon dioxide produced. **Exercise** has many benefits:

- It improves the **circulatory system** because it strengthens the heart muscles, increases cardiac output, i.e. the amount of blood pumped by the heart per minute, lowers the resting heart rate, lowers blood pressure and reduces the risk of heart disease.

- It improves the **respiratory system** because it strengthens the diaphragm and intercostal muscles, increases lung capacity and increases the efficiency of gaseous exchange.

- It improves the **musculoskeletal system** because it increases muscle size, strength and endurance, increases bone density which strengthens bones and reduces the risk of osteoporosis, strengthens tendons and ligaments, improves the flexibility of joints and improves muscle tone.

To maintain a **healthy body** it is essential that a person's daily **energy input** from the food eaten balances his or her daily **energy output** as a result of daily activities, including exercise. If energy input exceeds output, the person will **gain weight**. If energy output exceeds energy input, the person will **lose weight**.

Muscle tone

Muscle tone is the unconscious low-level contraction of muscles while they are at rest. Good muscle tone is important because it maintains **balance** and a **good, upright posture**, and it keeps muscles in an **active state** ready for action. **Exercise** is important to improve muscle tone.

The human skeleton

The human skeleton provides the internal framework of the body and is surrounded by muscles. It is composed of 206 bones which are held together at **joints** by tough elastic **ligaments** and it is made from **bone** and **cartilage**.

Functions of the skeleton

The human skeleton has **five** main functions:

- **Movement.** The skeleton is jointed and muscles work across these joints to bring about movement. Most movement is brought about by the **legs** and **arms** whilst the **vertebral column** allows some movement.

- **Protection** for the internal organs and some blood vessels. The **skull** protects the brain and sense organs of the head, i.e. the eyes, ears, nasal cavities and tongue. The **vertebral column** protects the spinal cord. The **rib cage** and **sternum** protect the lungs and heart.

- **Support** for the soft parts of the body. This is mainly carried out by the **vertebral column**, **pelvic girdle** and **legs**.

- **Breathing.** Alternate contractions of the internal and external intercostal muscles between the ribs bring about movements of the **rib cage**, which cause air to be drawn into the lungs and expelled from the lungs (see page 67).

- **Production of blood cells.** Red blood cells, most white blood cells and platelets are produced in the red bone marrow found inside **flat bones**, e.g. the pelvis, scapula, ribs, sternum and cranium, and in the **ends** of **long bones**, e.g. the humerus and femur.

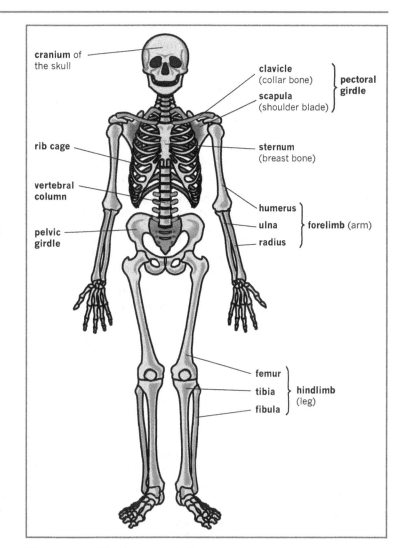

Figure 4.11 *The human skeleton*

Movement

Movement in humans is brought about by **skeletal muscles** working across **joints**. These muscles are attached to the bones of the skeleton by tough, non-elastic **tendons**.

Joints

*A **joint** is formed where two bones meet.*

Most joints allow the rigid skeleton to **move**. There are **three** types of joints:

- **Fixed joints.** The bones are joined together firmly by **fibrous connective tissue** that allows no movement, e.g. the cranium is made of several bones joined by fixed or immovable joints.
- **Partially movable joints.** The bones are separated by **cartilage pads** that allow slight movement, e.g. the vertebrae of the vertebral column are separated by **intervertebral discs** of cartilage.
- **Movable joints** or **synovial joints.** The articulating surfaces of the bones are covered with **cartilage** and **synovial fluid** fills the joint cavity between the bones; both help to reduce friction. The bones are held together by tough, elastic **ligaments**. There are two types of movable joints:
  - **Hinge joints** are formed where the **ends** of the bones meet. They allow movement in **one plane** (direction) only, e.g. the elbow, knee, finger and toe joints.
  - **Ball and socket joints** are formed where a **ball** at the end of one bone fits into a **socket** in the other bone. They allow rotational movement in **all planes,** e.g. the shoulder and hip joints.

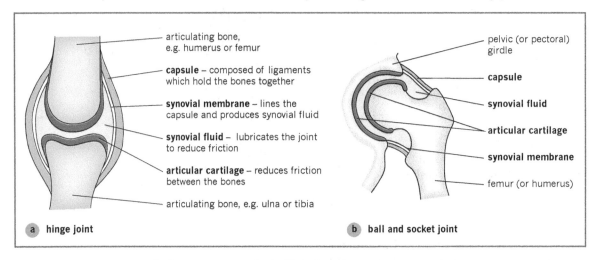

Figure 4.12 *Structure of a hinge joint and a ball and socket joint*

Movement of a limb

When a muscle contracts it exerts a **pull**, but it cannot exert a push when it relaxes. Therefore, **two** muscles, known as an **antagonistic pair**, are always needed to produce movement at a movable joint:

- The **flexor muscle** is the muscle that **bends** the joint when it contracts.
- The **extensor muscle** is the muscle that **straightens** the joint when it contracts.

The muscles that bend and straighten the **elbow joint** are known as the **biceps** and **triceps** muscles:

- The **biceps** is the **flexor** muscle.
- The **triceps** is the **extensor** muscle.

To **bend** the elbow joint, the **biceps contracts** and the triceps relaxes. To **straighten** the elbow joint, the **triceps contracts** and the biceps relaxes.

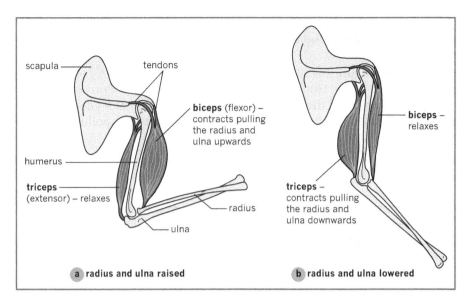

scapula — tendons

biceps (flexor) – contracts pulling the radius and ulna upwards

humerus —

triceps (extensor) – relaxes

radius

ulna

a radius and ulna raised

biceps – relaxes

triceps – contracts pulling the radius and ulna downwards

b radius and ulna lowered

Figure 4.13 *Movement of the elbow joint*

Revision questions

14 What is a drug?

15 Outline some of the effects of the abuse of EACH of the following drugs on the human body:

   a cocaine   **b** alcohol   **c** steroids

16 What happens during blood doping?

17 Name THREE systems in the human body that benefit from a person taking regular exercise.

18 By referring to the different parts of the human skeleton, discuss THREE of its functions.

19 Identify the different types of joints found in the human body and name ONE place where EACH type is found.

20 **a** Why are two muscles needed to bring about movement at a hinge joint?

   b Explain how the muscles of Joe's arm bring about bending and straightening of his elbow joint.

5 Respiration and air pollution

Respiration is the process by which living organisms release the **energy** they need to carry out life processes from the food they consume or make. Humans respire **aerobically**, and gaseous exchange occurring in their **lungs** both supplies the oxygen they need to sustain this process and gets rid of the carbon dioxide produced. The air inhaled into the lungs is often contaminated or **polluted** by harmful substances.

Breathing in humans

Breathing refers to the **movements** that cause air to be moved into and out of the **lungs**, which form part of the **respiratory system**. Breathing must not be confused with respiration, which is the process by which energy is released from food by all living cells (see page 70).

Structure of the human respiratory system

Humans have **two** lungs composed of thousands of air passages called **bronchioles** and millions of swollen air sacs called **alveoli**. Each lung is surrounded by two **pleural membranes** that have **pleural fluid** between them. A single **bronchus** leads into each lung from the **trachea**. The **larynx** (voice box) forms the top part of the trachea and the **nasal cavities** and the **mouth** lead into the **pharynx** (throat), which leads into the larynx.

Each lung receives blood from the heart via a **pulmonary artery** and blood is carried back to the heart via a **pulmonary vein.** The two lungs are surrounded by the **ribs** which form the **chest cavity** or **thorax.** The ribs have **intercostal muscles** between them and a dome-shaped sheet of muscle, the **diaphragm**, stretches across the floor of the thorax.

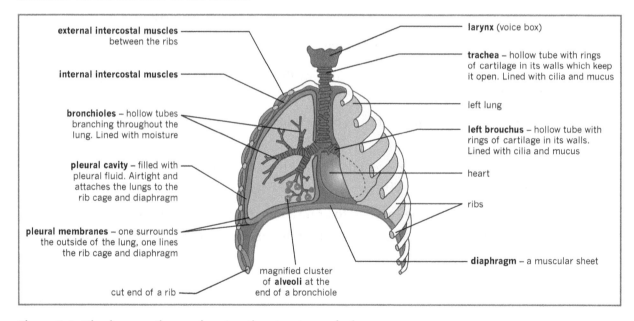

external intercostal muscles between the ribs

internal intercostal muscles

bronchioles – hollow tubes branching throughout the lung. Lined with moisture

pleural cavity – filled with pleural fluid. Airtight and attaches the lungs to the rib cage and diaphragm

pleural membranes – one surrounds the outside of the lung, one lines the rib cage and diaphragm

cut end of a rib

magnified cluster of **alveoli** at the end of a bronchiole

larynx (voice box)

trachea – hollow tube with rings of cartilage in its walls which keep it open. Lined with cilia and mucus

left lung

left brouchus – hollow tube with rings of cartilage in its walls. Lined with cilia and mucus

heart

ribs

diaphragm – a muscular sheet

Figure 5.1 *The human thorax showing the structure of a lung*

The mechanism of breathing

Breathing is brought about by two sets of muscles, the **intercostal muscles** and the **diaphragm.**

Table 5.1 *The mechanism of breathing*

Features		Inhalation (inspiration)	Exhalation (expiration)
1	External intercostal muscles	Contract	Relax
	Internal intercostal muscles	Relax	Contract
	Ribs and sternum	Move upwards and outwards	Move downwards and inwards
2	Diaphragm muscles	Contract	Relax
	Diaphragm	Moves downwards or flattens	Domes upwards
3	Volume inside the thorax and lungs	Increases	Decreases
	Pressure inside the thorax and lungs	Decreases	Increases
4	Movement of air	Air is drawn into the lungs due to the decrease in pressure	Air is pushed out of the lungs due to the increase in pressure

As the air is drawn in during inhalation, it is **warmed** in the nasal passages and **cleaned** and **moistened** by mucus lining the nasal passages and trachea. The air passes through the bronchi and bronchioles and enters the alveoli, where **gaseous exchange** occurs (see pages 68–69).

Table 5.2 *The composition of inhaled and exhaled air*

Component	Inhaled air	Exhaled air	Reason for the differences
Oxygen (O_2)	21%	16%	Oxygen is used by body cells in respiration.
Carbon dioxide (CO_2)	0.04%	4%	Carbon dioxide is produced by body cells during respiration and excreted by the lungs.
Nitrogen (N_2)	78%	78%	Nitrogen is not used by body cells.
Water vapour (H_2O)	Variable	Saturated	Moisture from the respiratory system evaporates into the air being exhaled.

Cardiopulmonary resuscitation (CPR)

CPR is an emergency procedure performed on a person whose heart has stopped beating (cardiac arrest) and/or who has stopped breathing (respiratory arrest). During CPR, the rescuer performs **chest compressions** to maintain circulation so that oxygen can be delivered to vital organs, and **rescue breathing** or **mouth-to mouth resuscitation** to deliver oxygen to the victim's lungs (see pages 136–137).

Gaseous exchange

*Gaseous exchange is the process by which oxygen **diffuses** into the blood and carbon dioxide diffuses out of the blood through a **respiratory surface**.*

Respiratory surfaces are surfaces through which gases are exchanged and they have several **adaptations** to make them as **efficient** as possible:

- They have a **large surface area** so that large quantities of gases can be exchanged.
- They are very **thin** so that gases can diffuse through them rapidly.
- They are **moist** so that gases can dissolve before they diffuse through the surface.
- They have a **rich blood supply** (if the organism has blood) to quickly transport gases between the surface and the body cells.

Gaseous exchange in humans

The **walls** of the **alveoli** form the respiratory surface in humans. **Oxygen** in inhaled air dissolves in moisture lining the alveoli and diffuses into the blood, whilst **carbon dioxide** diffuses out of the blood into the air in the alveoli and is exhaled.

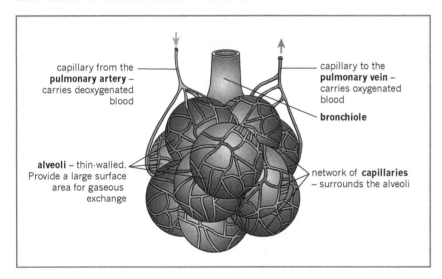

capillary from the
pulmonary artery –
carries deoxygenated
blood

capillary to the
pulmonary vein –
carries oxygenated
blood

bronchiole

alveoli – thin-walled.
Provide a large surface
area for gaseous
exchange

network of **capillaries**
– surrounds the alveoli

Figure 5.2 *Surface view of a cluster of alveoli showing the blood supply*

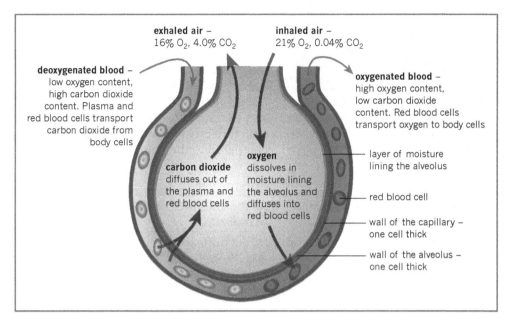

Figure 5.3 *Gaseous exchange in an alveolus*

Gaseous exchange in plants

The **walls** of all the **cells** inside leaves, stems and roots form the respiratory surface in plants, and gaseous exchange occurs by **direct diffusion** between these cells and the air spaces between them. Gases diffuse into and out of the air spaces in **leaves** through small holes, known as **stomata** (singular stoma), which are mainly in their undersurface. Leaves carry out **two** processes:

* **Respiration**, which uses oxygen and produces carbon dioxide, and occurs throughout the day and night.
* **Photosynthesis**, which uses carbon dioxide and produces oxygen, and occurs during the day only.

Movement of gases into and out of **leaves** depends on the time of day:

* During the **night** only **respiration** occurs. **Oxygen** diffuses **in** and **carbon dioxide** diffuses **out**.
* During the **day** the rate of **photosynthesis** is greater than the rate of respiration. **Carbon dioxide** diffuses **in** and **oxygen** diffuses **out**.

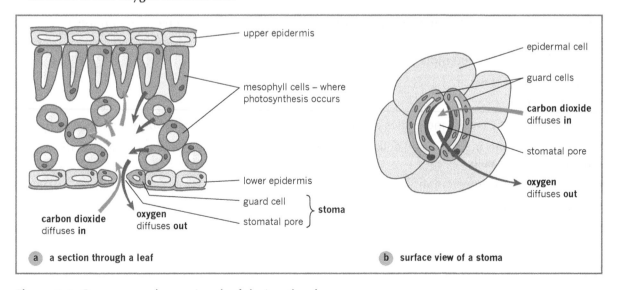

Figure 5.4 *Gaseous exchange in a leaf during the day*

Table 5.3 *A summary of the adaptations of the respiratory surfaces in humans and plants*

Adaptation of the respiratory surface	Organism	
	Human	Flowering plant
Large surface area	Each alveolus has a pocket shape and a human has two lungs, each with over 350 million alveoli giving a total surface area of about 90 m².	Leaves are broad, thin and numerous, and stems and roots have a branching structure creating a large surface area compared to the volume.
Thin	The walls of the alveoli are only one cell thick.	Cell walls and membranes are extremely thin.
Moist	The walls of the alveoli are lined with a thin layer of moisture.	All the cells are covered with a thin layer of moisture.
Transport system	A network of capillaries surrounds each alveolus.	Direct diffusion occurs between the air and the cells due to the large surface area to volume ratio.

Revision questions

1. What is meant by the term 'breathing'?

2. Describe the structure of a human lung.

3. Explain the mechanism by which air is drawn into the lungs.

4. **a** What does CPR stand for?

   b Outline what happens when a person performs CPR.

5. Identify the respiratory surface in a human and in a plant, and state THREE features that are common to the two surfaces identified.

Respiration

Respiration is the process by which energy is released from food by all living cells.

Respiration is catalysed by **enzymes** and occurs slowly in a large number of stages. The energy released is then **used**:

- To help maintain a constant **body temperature** (37 °C in humans) since some of the energy is released as **heat** energy.
- To **manufacture** important molecules, e.g. proteins and DNA.
- For **cell growth** and **repair**.
- For **cell division**.
- In **active transport** to move molecules and ions into and out of the cells through their membranes.
- For **special functions** in specialised cells, e.g. contraction of muscle cells and transmission of impulses in nerve cells.

There are **two** types of respiration:

- **aerobic respiration**
- **anaerobic respiration**.

Aerobic respiration

Aerobic respiration is the process by which energy is released from food by living cells using oxygen.

Aerobic respiration occurs in most cells. It **uses oxygen** and takes place in the **mitochondria.** It always produces **carbon dioxide, water** and **energy.** The amount of energy produced depends on the type of food molecules respired, known as the **respiratory substrate.**

Table 5.4 *Amount of energy produced by different respiratory substrates*

Respiratory substrate	Energy produced / kJ g^{-1}
Carbohydrate	16
Lipid	39
Protein	17

The main respiratory substrate used by cells is **glucose:**

$$\text{glucose} + \text{oxygen} \xrightarrow{\text{enzymes in mitochondria}} \text{carbon dioxide} + \text{water} + \text{energy}$$

or

$$C_6H_{12}O_6 + 6O_2 \xrightarrow{\text{enzymes in mitochondria}} 6CO_2 + 6H_2O + \text{energy}$$

Anaerobic respiration

Anaerobic respiration is the process by which energy is released from food by living cells without the use of oxygen.

Anaerobic respiration occurs in some cells. It takes place **without oxygen** in the **cytoplasm** of the cells. The products of anaerobic respiration **vary** and it produces considerably **less energy** per molecule of glucose than aerobic respiration. Yeast cells, certain bacteria and muscle cells are capable of carrying out anaerobic respiration.

The importance of anaerobic respiration

Making bread and alcoholic beverages

Yeast cells carry out anaerobic respiration known as **fermentation.** It produces **ethanol, carbon dioxide** and a small amount of **energy:**

$$\text{glucose} \xrightarrow{\text{enzymes in cytoplasm}} \text{ethanol} + \text{carbon dioxide} + \text{energy}$$

When **making bread,** the yeast ferments sugars present in dough. The **carbon dioxide** produced forms **bubbles** in the dough that cause it to rise. When the bread is baked, heat from the oven causes the bubbles to expand, kills the yeast and evaporates the ethanol.

When making **alcoholic beverages** such as beer, wine, rum and other spirits, the yeast ferments sugars present in grains, fruits or molasses. Fermentation stops when the **ethanol** concentration reaches about 14–16% because it kills yeast cells, so the ethanol content of beer and wine is always below about 16%. Spirits are made by **distillation** of the fermentation mixture.

In muscle cells during strenuous exercise

During **strenuous exercise**, if oxygen cannot be delivered to the muscle cells quickly enough for the demands of aerobic respiration, the cells begin to respire **anaerobically**. This produces **lactic acid** and a small amount of **energy**:

$$\text{glucose} \xrightarrow[\text{cytoplasm}]{\text{enzymes in}} \text{lactic acid} + \text{energy}$$

Lactic acid builds up in the muscle cells and begins to harm them, causing fatigue and eventually collapse as they stop contracting. The muscle cells are said to have built up an **oxygen debt**. This debt must be **repaid** directly after exercise by resting and breathing deeply so that the lactic acid can be removed by respiring it **aerobically**.

Air pollution

Pollution is the contamination of the natural environment by the release of unpleasant and harmful substances into the environment.

Air pollution results from the release of harmful substances into the **atmosphere**. Many human activities and certain natural activities contribute to air pollution.

Table 5.5 *The main air pollutants, their sources and effects*

Air pollutant	Sources in the environment	Harmful effects
Sulfur dioxide (SO$_2$)	• Burning fossil fuels, especially coal and oil, in industry and power stations. • Volcanic eruptions.	• Causes **respiratory disorders**, e.g. bronchitis and asthma, and reduces the growth of plants. • Dissolves in rainwater forming **acid rain**. Acid rain decreases the pH of the soil, damages plants, harms animals, corrodes buildings and causes lakes, streams and rivers to become acidic and unsuitable for aquatic organisms. • Combines with water vapour, smoke and other air pollutants to form **smog**, which causes **respiratory disorders**, e.g. bronchitis, asthma, lung disease, emphysema and lung cancer.
Carbon dioxide (CO$_2$)	• Burning fossil fuels, e.g. in industry, power stations, motor vehicles and aeroplanes.	• Builds up in the upper atmosphere, enhancing the **greenhouse effect** and **global warming**, which is causing polar ice caps and glaciers to melt, sea levels to rise, low-lying coastal areas to flood, changes in global climate, and more severe weather patterns and natural hazards.
Methane (CH$_4$)	• Extraction, processing and transportation of fossil fuels, mainly natural gas. • Livestock farming, rice agriculture and landfills.	• Builds up in the upper atmosphere enhancing the **greenhouse effect** and **global warming** (see above).
Carbon monoxide (CO)	• Burning fossil fuels, mainly in motor vehicles.	• Binds with **haemoglobin** in place of oxygen. This reduces the amount of oxygen reaching body tissues which reduces respiration and affects mental awareness. It causes dizziness, headaches and visual impairment, and can lead to unconsciousness and death.

Air pollutant	Sources in the environment	Harmful effects
Lead	• Mining of lead ores and extraction of lead from its ores. • Car exhaust fumes when using unleaded petrol in some countries.	• Damages various body tissues and organs including the kidneys, liver, bones and nervous system, particularly the brain. • Particularly harmful to **young children** because it reduces IQ and causes behavioural problems and learning disorders.
Carbon particles (C) in smoke, and other particulate matter	• Burning fossil fuels, e.g. in industry. • Wild fires and cigarette smoke. • Mining and quarrying.	• Cause **respiratory disorders**, e.g. bronchitis, asthma, lung disease, emphysema and lung cancer. • Coat the leaves of plants and **block stomata**, both of which reduce photosynthesis and plant growth. • Contribute to the formation of **smog** (see earlier in the table).

The effects of smoking on the respiratory system

When a person smokes **cigarettes** made from tobacco, **smoke** containing several thousand different chemicals, including **nicotine**, **tar** and **carbon monoxide**, is inhaled into the respiratory system. Smoking can lead to **nicotine addiction** and can **harm** the respiratory system in several ways:

Reduced oxygen carrying capacity of the blood

Carbon monoxide combines more readily with haemoglobin than oxygen does, which reduces the amount of oxygen carried to body cells. This reduces respiration and the smoker's ability to exercise. In a pregnant woman it deprives the foetus of oxygen, reducing its growth and development.

Lung damage

Cigarette smoke **damages** lungs:

• It causes **mucus** production to increase and paralyses the **cilia**, which stops them from beating so the mucus is not removed. The person then develops a **persistent cough**, which is the body's way of trying to remove the mucus.

• It irritates and inflames the walls of the **bronchi** and **bronchioles**. This, together with the increased mucus production and paralysis of the cilia, causes the airways to become **obstructed**, making breathing difficult and leading to **chronic bronchitis**.

• It causes the walls of the **alveoli** to become less elastic and the walls between the alveoli to break down which decreases their surface area. This reduces gaseous exchange, makes exhaling difficult and causes air to remain trapped in the lungs, a condition known as **emphysema**.

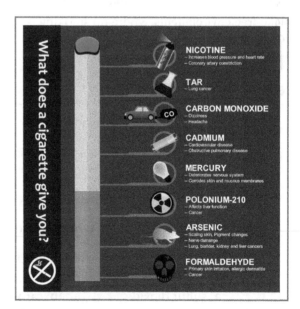

Figure 5.5 *Some components of cigarette smoke*

Note that chronic bronchitis and emphysema are two types of **chronic obstructive pulmonary disease** or **COPD**.

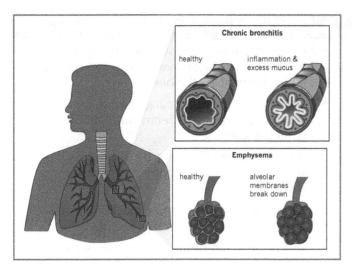

Figure 5.6 *Chronic obstructive pulmonary disease (COPD)*

Cancer of the mouth, throat, oesophagus or lungs

Some components of **tar** and many other chemicals in cigarette smoke are **carcinogenic**. These cause **mutations** (changes) in cells in different regions of the respiratory system. This leads to the development of **cancerous tumours** that replace normal, healthy tissue in these regions.

Secondhand smoke and smoke-free environments

Secondhand smoke consists of smoke exhaled by smokers and smoke from the lit ends of cigarettes. This smoke contains the same chemicals that the smoker inhales in mainstream smoke, but it has a higher concentration of **cancer-causing agents** and smaller particles, and is **more toxic** than mainstream smoke. It increases a non-smoker's risk of asthma, cancer, heart attack and stroke.

Smoke-free environments, where no smoking is allowed, protect individuals against exposure to secondhand smoke. They also aim to reduce smoking in general and to help people to stop smoking all together, and they contribute to improved air quality.

Revision questions

6 Define the term 'respiration'.

7 Distinguish between aerobic respiration and anaerobic respiration and write the chemical equation to summarise aerobic respiration.

8 Explain how Kendra makes use of anaerobic respiration when she makes bread.

9 What is meant by the term 'pollution'?

10 Outline some of the harmful effects of the following pollutants, which are produced by burning fossil fuels in industry:

  a sulfur dioxide   **b** carbon monoxide

11 Name the TWO main greenhouse gases that are produced by human activity and discuss the consequences of these gases building up in the upper atmosphere.

12 **a** Name the THREE main components of cigarette smoke.

  b Outline how smoking cigarettes damages the lungs.

13 What are smoke-free environments and why are they important?

6 Excretion

Chemical reactions occurring in living organisms constantly produce **waste** and **harmful** substances. The body gets rid of these substances by a process known as **excretion**.

Excretion and egestion

Excretion is the process by which waste and harmful substances produced by the body's metabolism (the chemical reactions occurring inside body cells) are removed from the body.

Excretion is **important** because:

- It prevents **toxic** metabolic waste substances from building up in the body and damaging or killing cells.
- It helps to keep the environment within the body **constant**, e.g. by maintaining the concentration of body fluids.

Egestion is the process by which undigested dietary fibre and other materials are removed from the body as faeces.

Egestion must **not** be confused with excretion. The dietary fibre removed during egestion is not produced in the body's metabolism, so its removal cannot be classed as excretion.

Metabolic waste excreted by humans

Humans produce several **waste substances** during metabolism.

Table 6.1 *Metabolic waste produced by humans*

Metabolic waste product	Metabolic reaction producing the waste
Carbon dioxide	Respiration in all body cells.
Water	Respiration in all body cells.
Urea (nitrogenous waste)	The breakdown of excess amino acids in the diet by the liver.
Bile pigments	The breakdown of haemoglobin from red blood cells by the liver.
Heat	General metabolism, especially respiration.

Excretory organs in humans

Humans have several **organs** that excrete waste products.

Table 6.2 *Excretory organs in humans*

Excretory organ	Products excreted
Kidneys	Water, urea and salts as **urine**.
Lungs	Carbon dioxide and water vapour during **exhalation** (see page 67).
Skin	Water, urea and salts as **sweat**. It also excretes heat.
Liver	Bile pigments. It also makes urea.

The human kidneys

Humans have two **kidneys** which form part of the **urinary system**. The kidneys have **two** functions:

- To **excrete** metabolic waste, mainly urea, from the body.
- To **regulate** the volume and concentration of blood plasma and body fluids by regulating the amount of water they contain, a process known as **osmoregulation**.

The kidneys and excretion in humans

Each kidney is divided into three regions: an outer region called the **cortex**, an inner region called the **medulla** and a central hollow region called the **pelvis**. A **renal artery** carries blood to each kidney and a **renal vein** carries blood away.

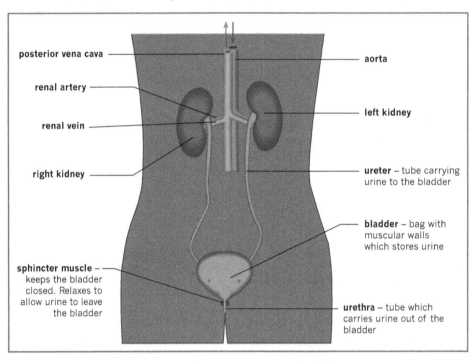

Figure 6.1 *Structure of the urinary system in a human*

Each kidney is composed of thousands of **kidney tubules** or **nephrons** that produce urine. Each nephron begins with a cup-shaped **Bowman's capsule** in the cortex which surrounds an intertwined cluster of capillaries called a **glomerulus**. After the Bowman's capsule, each nephron is divided into **three** sections:

- The **first convoluted (coiled) tubule** in the cortex.
- The **loop of Henle** in the medulla.
- The **second convoluted (coiled) tubule** in the cortex.

An arteriole, which branches from the renal artery, leads into each glomerulus. A capillary leads out of each glomerulus and branches to form a **network of capillaries** that wrap around each nephron and then join into a venule that leads into the renal vein. Nephrons join into **collecting ducts** in the cortex and these ducts lead through the medulla and out into the pelvis.

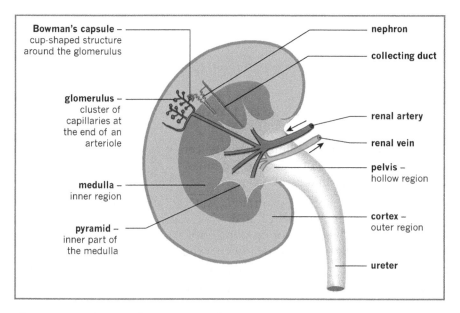

Figure 6.2 *A longitudinal section through a kidney showing the position of a nephron*

Urine is produced in the nephrons by **two** processes:

- **Ultra-filtration** or **pressure filtration**
- **Selective reabsorption**

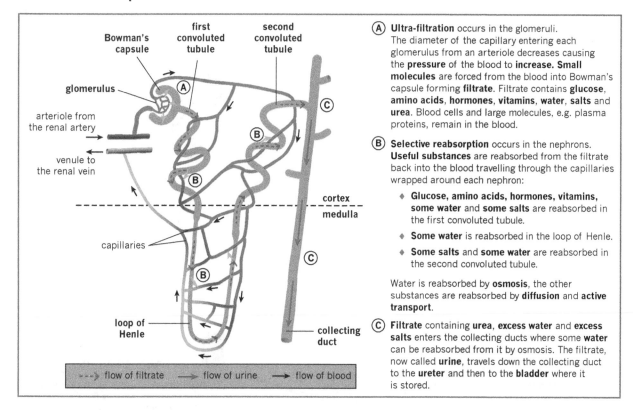

(A) **Ultra-filtration** occurs in the glomeruli. The diameter of the capillary entering each glomerulus from an arteriole decreases causing the **pressure** of the blood to **increase**. **Small molecules** are forced from the blood into Bowman's capsule forming **filtrate**. Filtrate contains **glucose**, **amino acids**, **hormones**, **vitamins**, **water**, **salts** and **urea**. Blood cells and large molecules, e.g. plasma proteins, remain in the blood.

(B) **Selective reabsorption** occurs in the nephrons. **Useful substances** are reabsorbed from the filtrate back into the blood travelling through the capillaries wrapped around each nephron:

- ◆ **Glucose, amino acids, hormones, vitamins, some water** and **some salts** are reabsorbed in the first convoluted tubule.
- ◆ **Some water** is reabsorbed in the loop of Henle.
- ◆ **Some salts** and **some water** are reabsorbed in the second convoluted tubule.

Water is reabsorbed by **osmosis**, the other substances are reabsorbed by **diffusion** and **active transport**.

(C) **Filtrate** containing **urea, excess water** and **excess salts** enters the collecting ducts where some **water** can be reabsorbed from it by osmosis. The filtrate, now called **urine**, travels down the collecting duct to the **ureter** and then to the **bladder** where it is stored.

Figure 6.3 *Detailed structure of a nephron explaining how urine is produced*

The kidneys and osmoregulation in humans

Osmoregulation is the regulation of the water content (concentration) of blood plasma and body fluids.

The water content of blood plasma and body fluids must be kept constant to prevent water moving into and out of body cells unnecessarily.

- If body fluids contain **too much water** (become too dilute), water will **enter** body cells by osmosis. The cells will swell and may burst. Drinking a lot of liquid or sweating very little, e.g. in cold weather, can cause body fluids to become **too dilute**.

- If body fluids contain **too little water** (become too concentrated), water will **leave** body cells by osmosis. The cells shrink and the body becomes **dehydrated**. If too much water leaves cells, metabolic reactions cannot take place and cells die. Not drinking enough, excessive sweating or eating a lot of salty foods can cause body fluids to become **too concentrated**.

The **kidneys** regulate the water content of body fluids by controlling how much **water** is reabsorbed into the blood plasma during **selective reabsorption**. This determines how much water is lost in urine. Osmoregulation involves:

- The **hypothalamus** of the brain, which detects changes in the concentration of blood plasma.
- The **antidiuretic hormone (ADH)**, which is produced by the **pituitary gland** at the base of brain in response to messages from the hypothalamus.

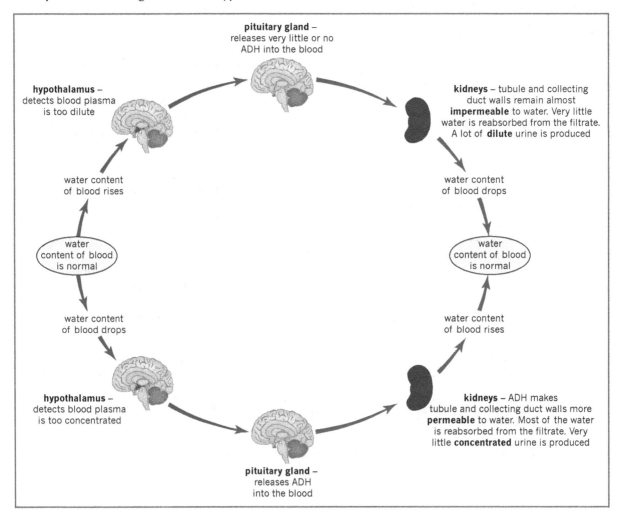

Figure 6.4 *Osmoregulation*

Kidney failure and renal dialysis

When nephrons stop functioning properly so that they are unable to remove waste from the blood and regulate the volume and composition of blood plasma and body fluids, **kidney failure** occurs. Harmful waste, especially urea, builds up in the blood and can reach toxic levels, resulting in death. Kidney failure can be treated by **renal dialysis**.

During **dialysis**, blood from a vein, usually in the arm, flows through a **dialysis machine** and is returned to the body. In the machine, **waste products**, mainly **urea**, together with **excess water** and **excess salts** are removed from the blood. Dialysis must occur at regular intervals. Most people require three sessions a week, each lasting 4 hours.

The human skin

The **skin** is the largest organ in the human body. It is made up of **three** layers:

- The **epidermis** – the outermost layer.
- The **dermis** – below the epidermis.
- The **subcutaneous layer** – the bottom layer made up mainly of fat cells.

The skin has several functions including **excretion** and **regulation of body temperature**.

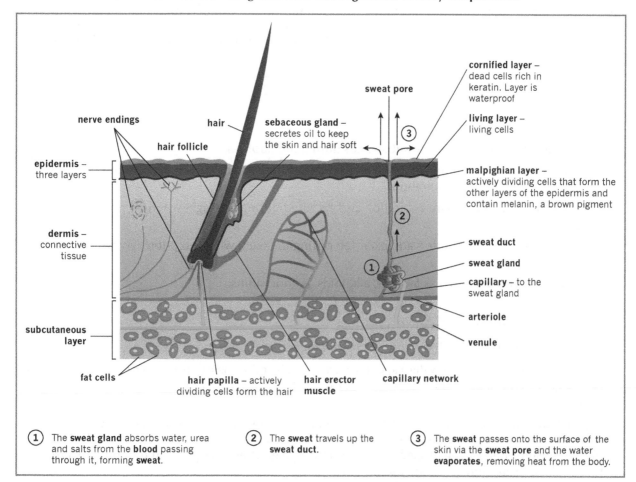

Figure 6.5 *A section through the human skin showing its structure and the mechanism of sweat formation*

Regulation of body temperature

Humans must maintain a constant internal body temperature of **37 °C** for **enzymes** to function correctly. Most heat is **gained** from **metabolic processes**, mainly respiration, and the blood carries this heat around the body. Heat is **lost** mainly by conduction, convection and radiation through the skin, and also by evaporation of water during sweating. The **hypothalamus** in the brain detects changes in the temperature of the blood and sends messages to the appropriate structures in the skin, causing them to respond.

Table 6.3 *How the skin helps to maintain a constant body temperature*

Body temperature rises above 37 °C	Body temperature drops below 37 °C
Sweating occurs: water in the sweat **evaporates** and removes heat from the body.	**Sweating stops**: there is no water to evaporate and remove heat from the body.
Vasodilation occurs: arterioles supplying the capillaries in the dermis of the skin **dilate** so that more blood flows through them and more heat is lost to the environment from the blood.	**Vasoconstriction occurs**: arterioles supplying the capillaries in the dermis of the skin **constrict** so that very little blood flows through them and very little heat is lost. The heat is retained by the blood flowing through vessels deeper in the body.
Hair erector muscles relax: this causes the hairs to **lie flat** so no insulating layer of air is created.	**Hair erector muscles contract**: this causes the hairs to **stand up** and trap a layer of air next to the skin, which acts as insulation. This is important in hairy mammals and creates 'goose bumps' in humans.

Excretion and osmoregulation in plants

Metabolic waste excreted by plants

Plants produce the following waste substances during metabolism:

- **Oxygen** – produced in photosynthesis and excreted during the **day** when the rate of photosynthesis is higher than the rate of respiration.
- **Carbon dioxide** – produced in respiration and excreted during the **night** when no photosynthesis is occurring.
- **Water** – produced in respiration and excreted during the **night** when no photosynthesis is occurring.
- **Organic waste products** such as tannins, alkaloids, anthocyanins.

Mechanisms of excretion in plants

Plants, unlike animals, do not have any specialised excretory organs.

- **Oxygen, carbon dioxide** and **water vapour** are excreted by **diffusing** out through the **stomata** of leaves (see page 69) and small regions of loosely packed cells in bark-covered stems and roots, known as **lenticels**.
- **Organic waste products** can be converted to **insoluble** substances, e.g. oils or insoluble crystals. In this insoluble form they can be stored in the cells of leaves, bark, petals, fruits and seeds. They are then removed when the plant **sheds** these structures, e.g. when **bark peels off** the trunk of a tree and **leaves fall off** in autumn or during the dry season.

Osmoregulation in plants

Plants have developed adaptations to control how they obtain, store and lose water in order to **regulate** their water content, and these depend on the **environment** in which they live:

- **Halophytes** live in **salty** conditions, e.g. in mangrove swamps. Their roots can filter out some salt as they take in water, while special glands in their leaves excrete salt.
- **Mesophytes** live on **land** and usually have enough water available. Their leaves have waxy cuticles to prevent excess water loss by evaporation and their stomata can almost close when water supplies in the soil are low.
- **Xerophytes** live in **dry** regions, e.g. in deserts. They have developed adaptations to conserve water, mainly by **reducing transpiration**, which is the loss of water vapour from the surface of leaves.

Table 6.4 *Methods by which plants, especially xerophytes, can conserve water*

Method	Adaptations
Reducing the rate of transpiration	• Leaves have extra-thick, waxy cuticles. • Leaves have reduced numbers of stomata. • Stomata are grouped together in sunken pits that trap water vapour. • Stomata almost close in the daytime and open at night when it is cooler. • The surface area of leaves is reduced, e.g. in the needle-shaped leaves of conifers, spines of cacti and scales of casuarina. • Leaves are shed in the dry season or winter months.
Storing water	• Leaves or stems of many succulent plants store water, e.g. the leaves of aloe and stems of cacti. • Roots of some plants store water, e.g. some members of the pumpkin family.
Increasing the uptake of water	• Plants have very long, deep tap roots to absorb water from deep in the soil. • Plants have shallow, widespread root systems to absorb surface water from a wide area.

Revision questions

1. Distinguish between excretion and egestion.

2. List the different excretory organs in the human body and state what EACH excretes.

3. Outline how urine is produced in Mario's kidneys.

4. **a** Name the process by which the water content of body fluids is regulated.

   b Tamesha plays tennis all day in the hot Sun and drinks very little. What effect will her behaviour have on the quantity and concentration of her urine? Explain your answer.

5. A person suffering from kidney failure can be treated using dialysis. Explain why this treatment must occur at regular intervals.

6. Explain the changes that occur in a person's skin if their body temperature rises above 37 °C.

7. Explain how plants excrete their metabolic waste.

8. Plants living in regions where water supplies in the soil are low develop various adaptations to aid in their survival. Suggest FOUR of these adaptations.

7 Sense organs and coordination

Humans must constantly monitor their environment and **respond** appropriately to any changes in this environment to help them survive. To do this, two systems are involved: the **nervous system** and the **endocrine (hormonal) system**.

Some important definitions

Stimulus is a change in the internal or external environment of an organism that initiates a response.

Response is a change in an organism or part of an organism which is brought about by a stimulus.

Receptor is the part of an organism that **detects** a stimulus.

Effector is the part of an organism that **responds** to a stimulus.

Sense organs in humans

Sense organs contain specialised cells, known as **receptor cells**, which detect **stimuli**. The cells turn these stimuli into **electrical impulses** or **nerve impulses** that travel along nerve cells to the **brain**. The brain then interprets these messages as sensations of seeing, hearing, smelling, tasting and touching.

Table 7.1 *Sense organs in the human body*

Sense organ	Stimuli detected
Eyes	• Light.
Ears	• Sound waves. • Position of the head.
Nose	• Chemicals in the air.
Tongue	• Chemicals in food. Four main tastes are detected; sweet, sour, salty and bitter.
Skin	• Touch and texture. • Pressure. • Pain and itching. • Temperature.

The eye

The **eye** detects **light** that has been reflected from an object and converts it into **nerve impulses**. The impulses are transmitted along the **optic nerve** to the brain, which translates them into a precise picture of the object.

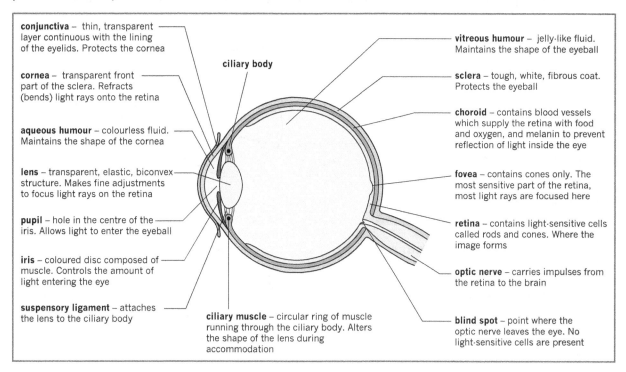

conjunctiva – thin, transparent layer continuous with the lining of the eyelids. Protects the cornea

cornea – transparent front part of the sclera. Refracts (bends) light rays onto the retina

aqueous humour – colourless fluid. Maintains the shape of the cornea

lens – transparent, elastic, biconvex structure. Makes fine adjustments to focus light rays on the retina

pupil – hole in the centre of the iris. Allows light to enter the eyeball

iris – coloured disc composed of muscle. Controls the amount of light entering the eye

suspensory ligament – attaches the lens to the ciliary body

ciliary body

ciliary muscle – circular ring of muscle running through the ciliary body. Alters the shape of the lens during accommodation

vitreous humour – jelly-like fluid. Maintains the shape of the eyeball

sclera – tough, white, fibrous coat. Protects the eyeball

choroid – contains blood vessels which supply the retina with food and oxygen, and melanin to prevent reflection of light inside the eye

fovea – contains cones only. The most sensitive part of the retina, most light rays are focused here

retina – contains light-sensitive cells called rods and cones. Where the image forms

optic nerve – carries impulses from the retina to the brain

blind spot – point where the optic nerve leaves the eye. No light-sensitive cells are present

Figure 7.1 *Structure and functions of the parts of the human eye as seen in longitudinal section*

Forming an image

In order to see, light rays from an object must be **refracted** (bent) as they enter the eye so that they form a clear **image** of the object on the receptor cells of the retina. Being **convex** in shape, both the **cornea** and the **lens** refract the light rays.

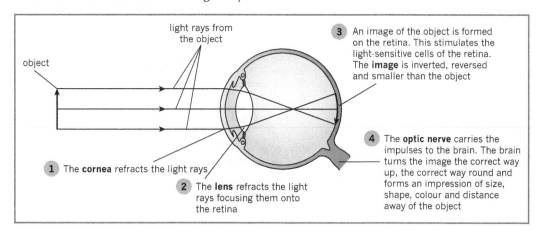

object

light rays from the object

3 An image of the object is formed on the retina. This stimulates the light-sensitive cells of the retina. The **image** is inverted, reversed and smaller than the object

1 The **cornea** refracts the light rays

2 The **lens** refracts the light rays focusing them onto the retina

4 The **optic nerve** carries the impulses to the brain. The brain turns the image the correct way up, the correct way round and forms an impression of size, shape, colour and distance away of the object

Figure 7.2 *Formation of an image in the eye*

Focusing light onto the retina – accommodation

Accommodation is the process by which the shape of the lens is changed to focus light coming from different distances onto the retina.

By changing shape, the **lens** makes fine adjustments to focus the light rays onto the retina. This is brought about by the **ciliary muscles** in the ciliary body.

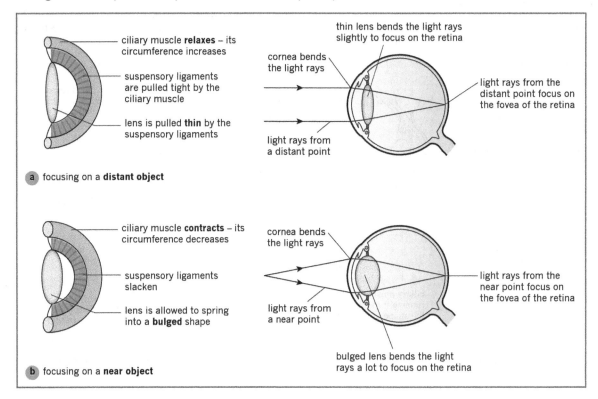

Figure 7.3 *Accommodation*

Controlling the amount of light entering the eye

The size of the **pupil** controls the amount of light entering the eye. Muscles of the **iris** control the pupil size.

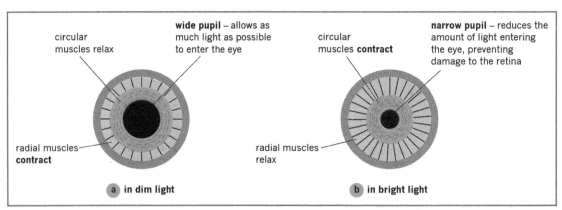

Figure 7.4 *Controlling the amount of light entering the eye*

Sight defects and their corrections

Short-sightedness

A person with **short sight** can see **near** objects clearly, but distant objects are out of focus. Light rays from near objects focus on the retina; light rays from **distant** objects focus **in front** of the retina. It is caused by the eyeball being too **long** from front to back or the lens being too **curved** (thick). It is corrected by wearing **diverging (concave) lenses** as spectacles or contact lenses.

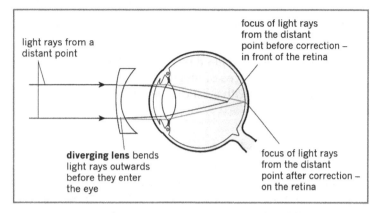

Figure 7.5 *The cause and correction of short sight (myopia)*

Long-sightedness

A person with **long sight** can see **distant** objects clearly, but near objects are out of focus. Light rays from distant objects focus on the retina; light rays from **near** objects focus **behind** the retina. It is caused by the eyeball being too **short** from front to back or the lens being too **flat** (thin). It is corrected by wearing **converging (convex) lenses** as spectacles or contact lenses.

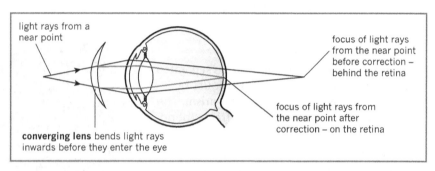

Figure 7.6 *The cause and correction of long sight (hypermetropia)*

Glaucoma

Glaucoma is a condition in which the **pressure** of the fluid within the eye increases due to the flow of aqueous humour from the eye being blocked. If left untreated, the optic nerve becomes damaged and it can lead to **blindness**. The most common type develops slowly and causes a gradual loss of peripheral (side) vision. Glaucoma is treated with **eye drops** to reduce fluid production or improve the flow of fluid from the eye, or by **laser treatment** or **surgery** to open the drainage channels.

Cataract

A **cataract** is a **cloudy** area that forms in the lens. It develops slowly and as it increases in size it leads to cloudy or blurred vision, halos forming around lights, colours appearing faded, and difficulty seeing in bright light and at night. It is usually caused by **ageing** and is usually corrected by **surgery** to remove the clouded lens and to replace it with an **artificial lens**.

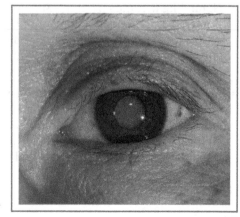

Figure 7.7 *An eye with a cataract*

Damage to the eyes

Staring directly at the **Sun** or very **bright lights** can damage the **retina** at the back of the eye and cause blind spots to develop. Extended exposure to **ultraviolet light** from the Sun can lead to **cataracts** developing and can also damage the **cornea** or the **retina**. Damage to the retina may lead to **blindness**.

Eyes can be **physically injured** by being poked, e.g. with a stick or finger, by flying objects getting into the eye, e.g. small pieces of metal or sand, by being hit by a sports ball, e.g. a cricket, tennis or squash ball, or by being hit with a fist during a fistfight.

Light

Light is **electromagnetic radiation.** It forms the part of the electromagnetic spectrum that is visible to the human eye and is responsible for the sense of **sight.** This **visible spectrum** is composed of a range of colours that have different wavelengths from **red**, which has the longest wavelength, through orange, yellow, green, blue and indigo to **violet**, which has the shortest wavelength. These are the colours of the rainbow. When mixed together, they form **white light.**

The **colour** of an object depends on the part of the visible spectrum it **reflects**, e.g. if an object reflects green light, it appears green. If an object reflects all the colours, it appears white. If an object absorbs all the colours, it appears black.

Dispersion of light

A narrow beam of **white light** can be **separated** or **dispersed** into its component colours by passing it through a **triangular glass prism**. The glass slows down the light and refracts (bends) it slightly:

- **Red light**, with the longest wavelength, is slowed down the least, so is refracted the least.
- **Violet light**, with the shortest wavelength, is slowed down the most, so is refracted the most.

Water droplets can also disperse light, e.g. when raindrops disperse sunlight, a **rainbow** is formed.

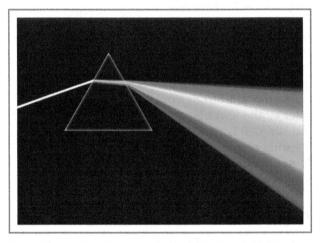

Figure 7.8 *The dispersion of white light into its component colours*

Natural and artificial lighting

Light sources can be either **natural** or **artificial**:

- **Natural light** comes from the **Sun**. It is only available between sunrise and sunset and the quantity, duration and intensity of it cannot be controlled. It contains **all** the colours of the visible spectrum, so it is ideal for plants to carry out **photosynthesis**. It also contains ultraviolet rays and infrared rays and has several **health benefits** to humans, e.g. it helps the skin to produce vitamin D. It can also be **harmful**, e.g. ultraviolet rays can cause **skin cancer** and **cataracts**.
- **Artificial light** is **man-made**. Kerosene lamps, incandescent light bulbs, fluorescent lights and light-emitting diodes (LEDs) all generate artificial light. It is the only light available between sunset and sunrise, and the quantity, duration and intensity of it can be controlled. It does **not** usually contain all the colours of the visible spectrum, so it is not ideal for plants to carry out photosynthesis. It also has limited health benefits and the colours of objects often appear **different** in artificial light.

Transparent, translucent and opaque materials

Materials can be classified into **transparent**, **translucent** and **opaque** based on the quantity of light that can **pass through** them:

- **Transparent materials** allow light to pass through completely. Objects at the other side are clearly visible. The materials are see-through, e.g. glass, water and air.

- **Translucent materials** scatter light, allowing some to pass through. Objects at the other side can be seen to some extent, though they usually appear blurry and unclear. The materials are partially see-through, e.g. frosted glass and wax paper.

- **Opaque materials** do not allow any light to pass through. Objects at the other side cannot be seen. The materials are not see-through, e.g. metal, wood and cardboard.

The ear

The **ear** detects **sound waves** and converts them into **nerve impulses**. The impulses are transmitted along the **auditory nerve** to the brain, which interprets them as **sound**. The ear also detects the position and movement of the head, which helps to control **balance**.

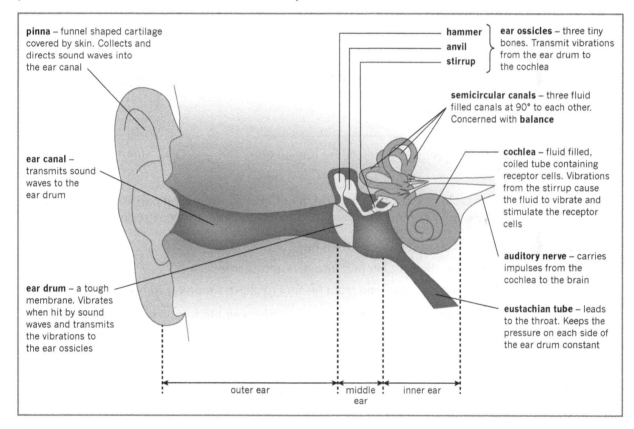

Figure 7.9 *Structure and functions of the parts of the human ear*

Sound

Sounds are pressure waves created by vibrating objects. **Sound waves** travelling through the air are made of areas of high pressure alternating with areas of low pressure.

- The **loudness** of a sound depends on the **amplitude** of the sound wave. The greater the amplitude, the louder the sound. Loudness is measured in **decibels** or **dB**. Very loud sounds exceeding **120 dB** can cause an eardrum to burst or can damage the receptor cells in the cochlea, which can lead to hearing loss.

- The **pitch** of a sound depends on the **frequency** of the sound waves, i.e. the number of waves per second. The higher the frequency, the higher the pitch. Frequency is measured in **hertz** or **Hz**. The approximate range of human hearing is **20 Hz** to **20 000 Hz**. As a person **ages**, this range decreases and it often becomes more difficult to hear high-pitched sounds.

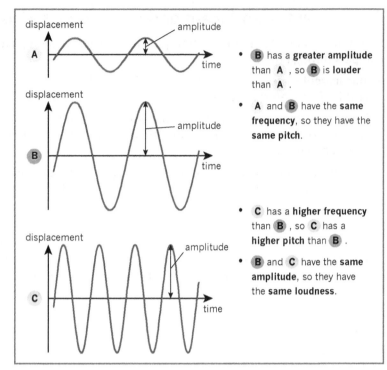

- **B** has a **greater amplitude** than **A**, so **B** is **louder** than **A**.

- **A** and **B** have the **same frequency**, so they have the **same pitch**.

- **C** has a **higher frequency** than **B**, so **C** has a **higher pitch** than **B**.

- **B** and **C** have the **same amplitude**, so they have the **same loudness**.

Figure 7.10 *Sound waves with different amplitudes and frequencies*

Revision questions

1. Make a list of the sense organs of the human body and give ONE stimulus detected by EACH.

2. Construct a table to show the function of EACH of the following parts of the eye: the cornea, the pupil, the lens, the choroid, the optic nerve and the vitreous humour.

3. Explain how Jason's eyes adjust when he:

   a walks from his dimly lit kitchen into his sunny garden.

   b watches his dog, Gizmo, run from his feet to chase a monkey in his garden.

4. Nia has her eyes tested and is told that she is short sighted. Explain the possible cause of her sight defect and how it can be corrected.

5. What is a cataract and how can it be treated?

6. Describe how white light can be separated into its component colours and list these colours.

7. a Distinguish between natural lighting and artificial lighting.

   b Differentiate between transparent, translucent and opaque materials and give ONE example of EACH.

8. Construct a table to give the function of EACH of the following structures of the human ear: the pinna, the ear drum, the ear ossicles, the cochlea and the eustachian tube.

9. a What does the loudness of a sound depend on?

   b What is the approximate frequency range that a human can hear?

The nervous system

The **nervous system** is composed of **neurones** or **nerve cells** which transmit messages called **nerve impulses** to help **coordinate** the body's activities. The human nervous system is divided into **two** parts:

- The **central nervous system (CNS)**, which consists of the **brain** and the **spinal cord**.

- The **peripheral nervous system (PNS)**, which consists of **cranial** and **spinal nerves** that connect the central nervous system to all parts of the body.

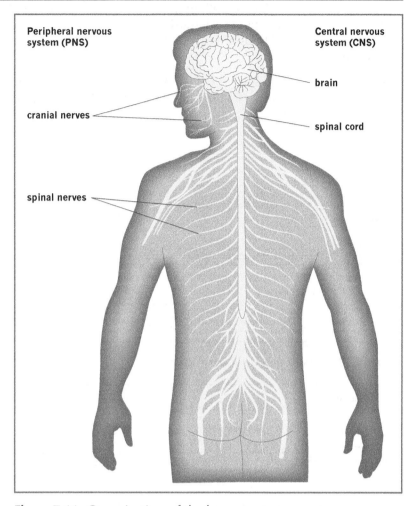

Figure 7.11 *Organisation of the human nervous system*

The brain

The **human brain** is an extremely complex organ. It has **five** main parts, each concerned with different functions.

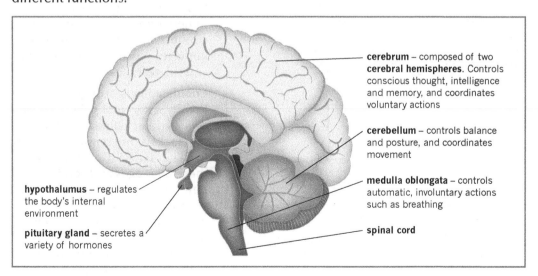

Figure 7.12 *Functions of the main parts of the human brain as seen in longitudinal section*

Neurones

All neurones have a **cell body** with thin fibres of cytoplasm extending from it called **nerve fibres**. Nerve fibres that carry impulses **towards** the cell body are called **dendrites**. Nerve fibres that carry impulses **from** the cell body are called **axons**; each neurone has only one axon. There are **three** types of neurones:

- **Sensory neurones** that transmit impulses from **receptors** to the **CNS**.
- **Motor neurones** that transmit impulses from the **CNS** to **effectors**.
- **Relay** or **intermediate neurones** that transmit impulses throughout the **CNS**. They link sensory and motor neurones.

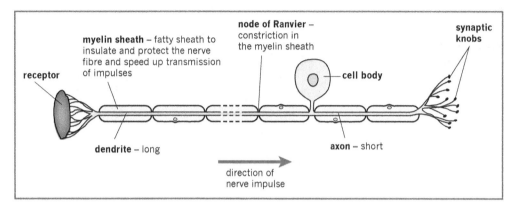

Figure 7.13 *Structure of a sensory neurone*

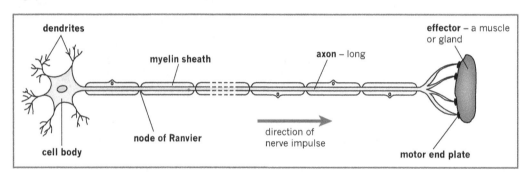

Figure 7.14 *Structure of a motor neurone*

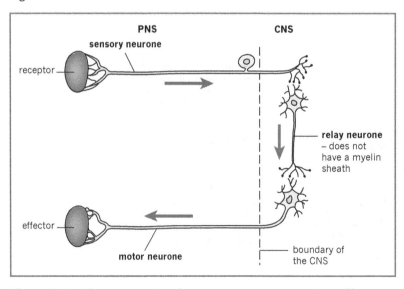

Figure 7.15 *The connection between a receptor and an effector*

Nerves are cordlike bundles of nerve fibres surrounded by connective tissue through which impulses pass between the CNS and the rest of the body.

Coordination is brought about by the CNS. **Receptor cells** in sense organs detect stimuli and send messages along **sensory neurones** to the CNS. The CNS **processes** these messages and sends new messages out along **motor neurones** to **effectors** so that the most appropriate action is taken. Messages are passed between sensory and motor neurones in the brain and spinal cord by **relay neurones**.

Voluntary and involuntary actions

- A **voluntary action** is an action that is consciously controlled by the **brain**. Examples include eating, walking, running, clapping and reading a book.

- An **involuntary action** is an action that occurs without conscious thought. Examples include breathing, digestion, heart beat and reflex actions such as the withdrawal reflex, the knee jerk reflex, blinking, sneezing, coughing, saliva production and the pupil reflex.

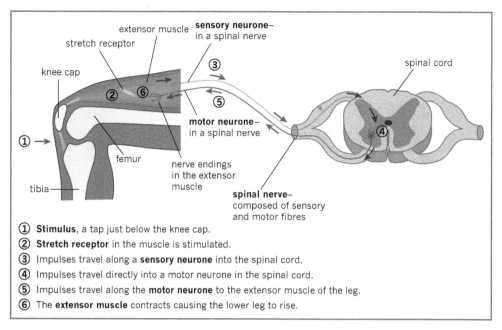

1. **Stimulus**, a tap just below the knee cap.
2. **Stretch receptor** in the muscle is stimulated.
3. Impulses travel along a **sensory neurone** into the spinal cord.
4. Impulses travel directly into a motor neurone in the spinal cord.
5. Impulses travel along the **motor neurone** to the extensor muscle of the leg.
6. The **extensor muscle** contracts causing the lower leg to rise.

Figure 7.16 *The knee jerk reflex arc*

Note that a **relay neurone** connects the sensory and motor neurones in most reflex arcs.

Malfunctions of the nervous system

Paralysis occurs when a person loses control of one or more muscles. The muscles stop being able to contract and bring about movement due to messages not passing from the CNS to them. Paralysis is mainly caused by injury to the spinal cord or by a stroke.

Physical disabilities affect a person's physical abilities and/or mobility. They can be caused by **injuries** to the brain or spinal cord, e.g. visual impairment, or by **conditions** or **diseases** that affect the brain such as cerbral palsy, the spinal cord such as spina bifida, or the motor neurones such as motor neurone disease. Damage to the **cerebrum** of the brain can also affect a person's mental ability, memory and personality.

The endocrine system

The **endocrine system** is composed of **endocrine glands** or **ductless glands** that secrete **hormones** directly into the blood to help coordinate the body's activities. Hormones are referred to as **chemical messengers**.

Table 7.2 *Control by the nervous and endocrine system compared*

	Nervous system	Endocrine system
How messages are transmitted	As **electrical impulses** along **neurones** in the **CNS** and **nerves**.	By **chemical messengers (hormones)** in the **blood**.
Transmission and effects	• Transmission is **rapid**. • Affects **precise** places in the body. • Effects are **immediate**. • Effects are **short-lasting**.	• Transmission is **slow**. • Affects **generalised** regions of the body. • Effects are usually **slow**. • Effects are usually **long-lasting**.

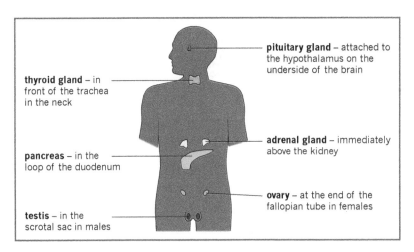

Figure 7.17 *The position of the main endocrine glands*

Table 7.3 *Hormones of the main endocrine glands and their functions*

Endocrine gland	Hormone(s)	Function(s)
Pituitary gland	**Antidiuretic hormone (ADH)**	Controls the **water content** of blood plasma and body fluids by controlling water reabsorption in the kidney (see page 78).
	Growth hormone (GH)	• In **children**: stimulates **growth** by stimulating the production of protein in cells and bone growth. • In **adults**: helps maintain healthy **bone** and **muscle** masses.
	Follicle stimulating hormone (FSH)	• In **females**: helps regulate the **menstrual cycle** by stimulating the development and maturation of the **follicles** and **ova** in the ovaries and stimulating the ovaries to produce **oestrogen** (see page 21). • In **males**: helps control production of **sperm** in the testes.
	Luteinising hormone (LH)	• In **females**: helps regulate the **menstrual cycle** by stimulating **ovulation** and the development of the **corpus luteum** in the ovaries (see page 21). • In **males**: stimulates the production of **testosterone** by the testes.
Thyroid gland	**Thyroxine**	Controls the **rate of metabolism** and energy production in cells, and physical **growth** and **mental development**, especially in children.

Endocrine gland	Hormone(s)	Function(s)
Adrenal glands	Adrenaline (flight, fright or fight hormone)	Released in large amounts when frightened, excited or anxious. Speeds up **metabolism**, mainly respiration, and increases blood sugar levels, heart beat, breathing rate and blood supply to muscles, i.e. it triggers the **fight-or-flight response** and gives the feeling of **fear**.
Pancreas	Insulin and glucagon	Regulate **blood glucose** levels: • **Insulin** is secreted when blood glucose levels rise; it stimulates body cells to absorb glucose for respiration and liver cells to convert excess glucose to glycogen (animal starch). • **Glucagon** is secreted when blood glucose levels drop; it stimulates liver cells to convert stored glycogen to glucose.
Ovaries	Oestrogen (produced by the Graafian follicle)	Controls the development of female **secondary sexual characteristics** at puberty: the development of breasts, a broad pelvis, pubic and underarm hair. Helps regulate the **menstrual cycle** by stimulating the **uterus lining** to thicken each month after menstruation (see page 21).
	Progesterone (produced by the corpus luteum)	Helps regulate the **menstrual cycle** by maintaining a thick **uterus lining** after ovulation each month (see page 21).
Testes	Testosterone	Controls the development of male **reproductive organs** and **secondary sexual characteristics** at puberty: the development of a deep voice, facial and body hair, muscles and broad shoulders. Controls **sperm** production in the testes.

Revision questions

10. Describe the main divisions of the human nervous system.

11. Construct a table to give the functions of the following regions of the brain: the hypothalamus, the cerebrum, the cerebellum and the medulla oblongata.

12. Draw a labelled diagram to show the structure of a motor neurone.

13. Explain the difference between a voluntary action and an involuntary action, and give TWO examples of EACH.

14. Fabian is involved in a car crash and his right leg is paralysed. Explain the possible cause of this paralysis.

15. For EACH of the following endocrine glands, identify where the gland is located in the body, name the hormone it produces and outline the functions of the hormone:

    a the thyroid gland   b the adrenal glands   c the testes

8 Health and sanitation

According to the World Health Organisation (WHO), **health** is a state of complete physical, mental and social well-being, and not merely the absence of disease and infirmity. **Sanitation** is the practice of maintaining good health and preventing disease by maintaining health-enhancing conditions through good personal and community hygiene.

Good personal and community hygiene

Personal hygiene

Personal hygiene refers to the practice of keeping oneself **clean** and **well-groomed** in order to promote good overall health and well-being. Maintaining personal hygiene is **important** because it helps to:

- Eliminate body odours.
- Promote social acceptance.
- Prevent infections.
- Prevent dental caries.
- Ensure good health.

Good personal hygiene **practices** include:

- Regular washing of the **body** and the **hair** and applying deodorant daily.
- Regular washing of **hands**, especially after visiting the toilet and before preparing food.
- Keeping the **genitals** clean, especially during menstruation in females.
- Keeping **nails** trimmed and clean.
- Regular brushing and flossing of **teeth**.
- Frequent changing and washing of **clothes**.

Community hygiene

Community hygiene refers to the practice of keeping one's living area **clean** in order to promote overall health and well-being. Many human activities produce **waste** that must be treated and disposed of properly. This waste includes **sewage** and **garbage**:

- **Sewage** consists of human faeces and urine, household wastewater, wastewater from some industries and rainwater. Communities must have adequate **toilet facilities** to ensure that faeces and urine enter sewage systems and do not enter the environment. Sewage must then be **treated** in sewage treatment plants to make it harmless and therefore prevent **infectious diseases** from spreading, **vectors** of disease from breeding, water supplies from becoming **contaminated** and aquatic environments from becoming **polluted,** all of which can occur if sewage is released directly into the environment.

- **Garbage** consists of **solid waste**, including plastics, paper, glass, metal, and food and garden waste. Regular **collection** of garbage and its proper **disposal** are essential to prevent **vectors** from breeding and spreading disease, **pollution** of the environment, and the garbage from piling up and creating an **eyesore** and unpleasant odours. Disposal in landfills, incineration, composting and recycling are some of the main ways to dispose of garbage.

Figure 8.1 *Uncollected garbage is an eyesore*

Pests, parasites and pathogens

*A **pest** is a plant or animal that has a harmful effect on humans, their food or their living conditions.*

Household pests invade homes and can damage structures, deposit faecal pellets, eat human food and bite or sting humans. Many of these pests are also **vectors of disease** because they carry **pathogens** in or on their bodies. Household pests include **cockroaches** and **flies** which can carry gastroenteritis, cholera, typhoid and dysentery, **rats** and **mice** which can carry leptospirosis and the plague, and **mosquitoes** which can carry malaria, yellow fever, dengue, chikungunya and zika.

*A **parasite** is an organism that lives in or on another living organism known as its **host**.*

Parasites obtain their **food** from their host and they usually harm their host to varying extents. Parasites include tapeworms, hookworms, ticks, fleas and lice.

*A **pathogen** is a parasitic microorganism that causes **disease** in its host.*

Pathogens damage their host's health. Pathogens include **viruses** such as dengue, **bacteria** such as cholera, **fungi** such as ringworm and **protozoans** such as those causing malaria.

Conditions that encourage breeding of household pests and pathogens

Conditions that encourage the **breeding** of pests and pathogens include:

- Faeces, dead animals or animal waste left lying around.
- Pools of standing water caused by leaking taps and water-holding containers left lying around.
- Uncovered or overflowing drains.
- Garbage, including food waste, left lying around.
- Unclean toilets.
- Food left uncovered.
- Unclean tables, work surfaces, cupboards, shelves and floors in kitchens.

The life cycle of a mosquito

During its life cycle, a mosquito passes through **four** distinct **stages:**

- **Egg:** the adult female lays eggs in standing water. The eggs float on the surface of the water.
- **Larva:** the larva hatches from the egg. Larvae live in the water where they hang from the surface and breathe air through breathing tubes. They **feed** on microorganisms and organic matter in the water, enabling them to **grow.**
- **Pupa:** the pupa develops from the larva. Pupae live in the water, where they hang from the surface and breathe air through two breathing tubes. **Larval tissue re-organises** into adult tissue in the pupa.
- **Adult** or **imago:** the adult emerges from the pupa. Adults rest in cool, dark places around human residences during the day, and they fly and feed on nectar and sugars from plants in the evenings. After mating, the female requires a **blood meal** to mature her eggs before she lays them. She usually obtains the blood from a human and can transmit any pathogens she is carrying whilst feeding.

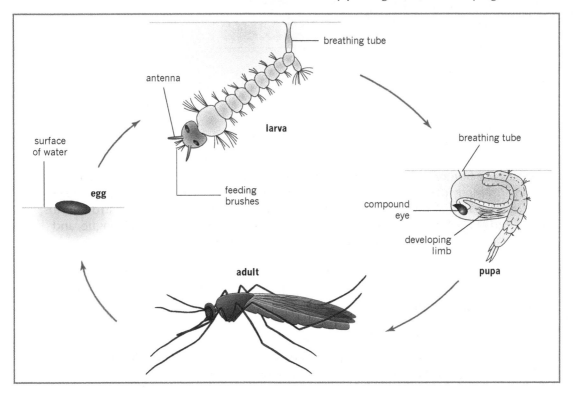

Figure 8.2 *The life cycle of a mosquito*

Note that the **housefly** also passes through four distinct stages during its life cycle; egg, larva or maggot, pupa and adult.

The control of mosquitoes and other pests

Mosquitoes and other pests can be controlled by **four** main methods:

- **Chemical control:** involves killing pests using chemicals, e.g. insecticides and poisoned baits.
- **Biological control:** involves killing pests using natural enemies of pests, e.g. predators.
- **Mechanical control:** involves deterring pests using physical means, e.g. barriers and traps.
- **Sanitary control:** involves removing conditions that attract pests, e.g. removing all garbage.

Table 8.1 *Methods used to control pests*

Pest	Methods of control
Mosquitoes	To control mosquito **larvae** and **pupae**: • Add **insecticides** to breeding areas to kill larvae and pupae. • Introduce **fish** such as *Tilapia* into breeding areas to feed on larvae and pupae. • **Drain** all areas of standing water and remove all containers that collect water. • Spray **oil**, **kerosene** or non-toxic **lecithins** onto still-water breeding areas to prevent larvae and pupae from breathing.
	To control **adult** mosquitoes: • Spray with **insecticides** to kill adults. • Remove **dense vegetation** to reduce protection for adults during daylight hours. • Place **mosquito screens** over windows and doors to prevent adults entering buildings, and place **mosquito nets** over beds at night.
Flies	• Spray adults with **insecticides** to kill them. • Use **fly traps** to kill adults. • **Dispose** of all human and animal waste properly. • **Treat** all sewage. • **Cover** food so that adults cannot land on it.
Rats and mice	• Use **rat** or **mouse bait** to kill them. • Introduce **cats** or other animals that prey on them. • Use **rat** or **mouse traps** to trap and kill them. • **Rodent-proof** buildings.
Cockroaches	• Spray with **insecticides** to kill them. • Use **cockroach bait** to kill them. • **Cover** all food and do not leave food scraps lying around.

Food contamination and its consequences

Food can be **contaminated** by **pathogens**, **chemicals** and **foreign objects** such as hair, finger nails and dirt at any stage from its production to its preparation and consumption.

Table 8.2 *Some ways in which food can be contaminated*

Contaminants	Examples of ways in which the contaminants enter food
Pathogens – mainly bacteria and some viruses	• By poultry eating **rodent droppings** that contain *Salmonella* bacteria, their meat and eggs can be contaminated by *Salmonella*. • By faecal bacteria on animals' hides during **slaughtering** contaminating the meat. • From unclean surfaces during the **processing** of food. • By washing food in **contaminated water**. • From a person's **hands** when handling food. • By a person **coughing** or **sneezing** when handling food. • From **improperly cleaned** food preparation surfaces, or cooking and eating utensils. • By **flies** landing on food.
Chemicals	• By crops being sprayed with **pesticides**, especially close to harvest time, the crops can be contaminated by the pesticides. • By large fish, such as tuna, accumulating **pollutants**, such as mercury, in their bodies from the food they eat and their environment. • By cattle being given **growth hormones** to increase meat and milk production, their meat and milk can be contaminated by the hormones.
Foreign objects	• By a person not following correct hygiene procedures when **handling** food, e.g. by not wearing a hair net, not keeping his or her nails trimmed, or not washing fruit and vegetables thoroughly to remove dirt.

Consequences of eating contaminated food

Consuming **contaminated food**, especially food contaminated with **pathogens**, can lead to **food poisoning**. Symptoms of food poisoning include:

- an upset stomach, nausea and vomiting
- abdominal cramps
- diarrhoea
- fever
- dehydration.

Practising **proper food hygiene** when preparing food can help to **prevent** contamination of food, especially by pathogens:

- **Wash** hands, utensils and food preparation surfaces regularly, especially after being in contact with uncooked meat, poultry or fish.
- **Wash** fruit and vegetables thoroughly in uncontaminated water before eating or cooking.
- Keep uncooked foods, especially meat, poultry and fish, **separate** from ready-to-eat foods.
- **Cook** food thoroughly, especially meat, poultry and fish.
- **Defrost** frozen food thoroughly and safely in a refrigerator before cooking.

Waste produced by humans

Waste produced by humans can be divided into **five** categories:

- **Domestic waste** is produced by households. It includes **sewage** and **garbage** (see page 94).

- **Industrial waste** is generated by **industrial activity**, including manufacturing, mining, food and construction industries. Its components depend on the industry producing it.

- **Biological waste** contains, or has been contaminated by, potentially **hazardous biological materials**, e.g. bacteria, viruses and human cells. This is called biohazardous waste. The waste usually comes from hospitals and laboratories and can contain human blood, blood products, tissues and organs, surgical dressings and gloves, syringes, needles, blood vials, culture dishes and scalpels.

- **Chemical waste** contains potentially **harmful chemicals** produced mainly by factories. It can contain mineral oils, cyanides, acids and alkalis, solvents, expired drugs, **radioactive waste** and compounds of heavy metals such as mercury and lead.

- **Electronic waste** or **e-waste** consists of discarded **electrical** or **electronic devices**, e.g. computers, tablets, mobile phones and televisions, with components that contain potentially harmful chemicals, e.g. lead, cadmium and mercury.

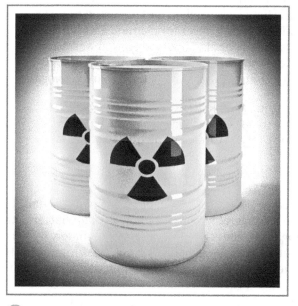

a *biohazardous waste*   **b** *radioactive waste*

Figure 8.3 *Two types of hazardous waste*

Biodegradable and non-biodegradable waste

Waste can also be categorised as **biodegradable** and **non-biodegradable**.

- **Biodegradable waste** can be broken down by living organisms, mainly bacteria and fungi, into harmless materials that can be recycled into the environment. It includes food waste, most paper, garden and farmyard waste, and some plastics.

- **Non-biodegradable waste** cannot be broken down by living organisms so it remains in the environment. It includes metal, glass, rubber and most plastics.

Reduce, reuse, recycle

The amount of **waste** that has to be disposed of can be decreased by practising the **3R's** of waste management: **reduce**, **reuse** and **recycle**.

- **Reduce** means to **cut down** on what is produced and what is used. If this is achieved, then there should be less waste to reuse and recycle. For example, the manufacture and use of disposable plates, cutlery, glasses, napkins, diapers, bags and excessive packaging materials should be reduced to a minimum.

- **Reuse** means to **use** the same item **again**, preferably many times, for the same purpose or a different purpose. Glass bottles, cloth shopping bags, old tyres and old newspapers can all be reused.

- **Recycle** means to **reprocess** materials back into new raw materials that can then be used to make new products. **Paper** can be repulped and reused to make new paper, **glass** and **metal** can be melted and recast, and some **plastics** can be melted and reformed to make plastic wood, fibres for clothing and other useful materials. Food and garden waste can be **composted** to make soil conditioner and agricultural waste can be used to make **biogas**.

Practising the 3R's of waste management also helps to **conserve** valuable **natural resources**, many of which are running out.

Figure 8.4 *The 3R's of waste management*

Biogas production

Organic waste such as manure and other agricultural waste, garden waste and food waste, is placed into an **anaerobic digester** where certain **bacteria** break it down anaerobically (without oxygen) into **biogas**. Biogas is a mixture of approximately **60% methane (CH_4)**, **40% carbon dioxide** and traces of other gases, e.g. hydrogen sulfide. Biogas can then be used as a **fuel** for cooking, heating and generating electricity, and the leftover residue from the digester can be used as a soil conditioner.

The impact of waste on the environment

If waste, particularly **solid waste**, is not disposed of properly it creates **unsanitary conditions** which lead to the spread of **disease**, and it becomes a threat to the environment:

- **Pathogens** and intestinal **parasites** or their eggs which are present in human faeces, untreated sewage and solid waste can enter water supplies and contaminate **potable** (drinkable) water. This leads to the spread of **diseases** such as cholera, gastroenteritis, typhoid and dysentery, and **parasites** such as *Giardia* that causes diarrhoea.

- Solid waste provides a **breeding ground** for **pests**. This causes their populations to increase, which in turn increases the spread of **diseases** such as leptospirosis, gastroenteritis, dengue, yellow fever and malaria.

- **Toxic chemicals** from solid waste can leach out and contaminate the soil, aquatic environments (see pages 203–204) and sources of potable water.

- **Unpleasant** and **harmful gases** can be released into the atmosphere and cause air pollution (see pages 72–73).

- Solid waste creates an **eyesore** and **unpleasant odours**.

Revision questions

1. What is the main reason for practising good personal and community hygiene?

2. Suggest FOUR measures Franchero can take to maintain good personal hygiene.

3. Distinguish between sewage and garbage, and explain why it is important that EACH type of waste is disposed of correctly.

4. a Differentiate between a pest, a parasite and a pathogen.

   b State FOUR conditions that encourage household pests and pathogens to breed.

5. a What is the difference between chemical and biological control of pests?

   b Suggest the most appropriate methods to control the different stages in the life cycle of a mosquito.

6. a Identify FIVE different ways in which food can become contaminated.

   b Discuss some of the consequences of eating contaminated food.

7. List FIVE different categories of waste produced by humans.

8. Distinguish between biodegradable waste and non-biodegradable waste, and give TWO examples of EACH type.

9. Explain EACH of the following as it relates to waste management:

   a reduce   b reuse   c recycle

10. Discuss the impact of waste, particularly solid waste, on the environment.

Exam-style questions – Chapters 1 to 8

Structured questions

1 **a)** Figure 1 shows how the three states of matter can be changed from one form to another. The letters A and B represent two of the processes that bring about the changes.

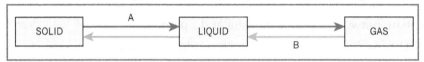

Figure 1 *Changing state*

    i) Name the processes taking place at A and B. **(2 marks)**

    ii) Using a circle to represent ONE particle, draw nine particles to show how they would be arranged in the solid state. **(2 marks)**

b) Figure 2 shows an unspecialised plant cell.

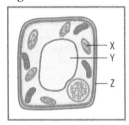

Figure 2 *An unspecialised plant cell*

    i) Identify the structures labelled X and Y. **(2 marks)**

    ii) State ONE function of X and ONE function of Y. **(2 marks)**

    iii) In what way does the property of Z differ from the cell membrane? **(2 marks)**

    iv) Name the cell structures that contain genetic information. **(1 mark)**

c) i) Distinguish between 'diffusion' and 'osmosis'. **(2 marks)**

    ii) Jessica was advised to soak her wilted romaine lettuce leaves in water before making a salad with them. On following the advice, she noticed that the leaves became crisp and firm. Explain what happened to make Jessica's lettuce leaves firm. **(2 marks)**

Total 15 marks

2 **a)** Figure 3 shows the structure of a flower from a flowering plant.

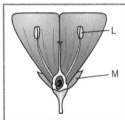

Figure 3 *Structure of a flower*

    i) Name the parts labelled L and M. **(2 marks)**

    ii) Outline how the flowering plant reproduces sexually. **(3 marks)**

    iii) Suggest ONE method Nathan could use to propagate the same plant asexually. **(1 mark)**

    iv) Give ONE advantage and ONE disadvantage of asexual reproduction to plants. **(2 marks)**

b) Figure 4 shows some stages in the germination of a seed.

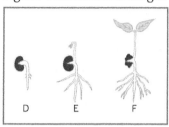

Figure 4 *Stages in the germination of a seed*

  i) Identify ONE condition that must be present for the seed to germinate. **(1 mark)**

  ii) At which stage, D, E or F, do you think that the overall mass will be increasing? Give a reason for your answer. **(2 marks)**

c) i) Overpopulation is a problem encountered in several developing countries. Suggest TWO ways in which governments or individuals can work towards overcoming the problem. **(2 marks)**

  ii) Suggest TWO likely consequences to these countries if they do not work towards controlling their populations. **(2 marks)**

Total 15 marks

3 **a)** Figure 5 summarises the process of photosynthesis.

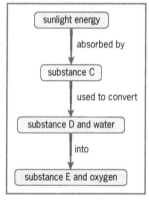

Figure 5 *The process of photosynthesis*

  i) Identify substances C, D and E. **(3 marks)**

  ii) During photosynthesis, light energy is converted into another form of energy. What form is this? **(1 mark)**

b) Table 1 shows the food sources of several organisms found in the ocean.

Table 1 *Food sources of some organisms found in the ocean*

Organism	Food source
zooplankton	phytoplankton
shrimp	phytoplankton
jellyfish	zooplankton and shrimp
crab	shrimp
sea turtle	crab and jellyfish

  i) Using only the information contained in Table 1, construct a food web for the organisms. **(2 marks)**

  ii) Identify from the food web ONE herbivore and ONE secondary consumer. **(2 marks)**

iii) Decomposers are not usually shown in food webs; however, they are essential in any ecosystem. What are decomposers and what is their role within an ecosystem? **(2 marks)**

c) Aaron, a farmer, and Katy, a gardener, both grow a variety of food crops.

    i) Name TWO different Caribbean food groups that might contain foods grown by Aaron and Katy. **(2 marks)**

    ii) Katy has limited outdoor space available to grow her lettuces and tomatoes. Suggest TWO different methods that she could use to maximise her yields. **(2 marks)**

    iii) Suggest ONE advantage that Aaron would gain if he practised crop rotation in his fields. **(1 mark)**

Total 15 marks

4   **a)** Figure 6 is a diagram of the human skeleton.

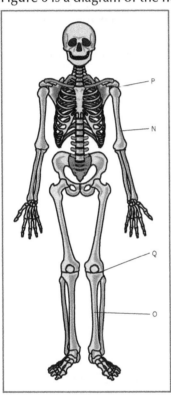

Figure 6 *The human skeleton*

    i) Name the bones labelled N and O. **(2 marks)**

    ii) Identify the types of joints labelled P and Q. **(2 marks)**

    iii) Why does joint Q require two muscles for movement to occur? **(2 marks)**

    iv) The veins of a leaf are often referred to as the skeleton of the leaf. Name the two types of transporting tissues that are found in these veins. **(2 marks)**

  b) **i)** Discuss the physiological effects of exercise on the circulatory system. **(3 marks)**

    ii) Marcus drives to and from his office job each day, eats his lunch sitting at his desk and spends his evenings sitting watching TV. Suggest ONE possible consequence of Marcus's behaviour. **(1 mark)**

  c) **i)** What is a drug? **(1 mark)**

    ii) Name TWO illegal drugs that are the most commonly abused in the Caribbean. **(2 marks)**

Total 15 marks

5 **a)** Distinguish between respiration and breathing. **(2 marks)**

b) Figure 7 shows part of the respiratory system.

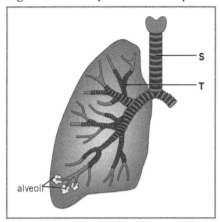

Figure 7 *Part of the human respiratory system*

  i)   Name the structures labelled S and T. **(2 marks)**

  ii) Identify TWO features of the alveoli that make them efficient in carrying out gaseous exchange. **(2 marks)**

c) A study was carried out into the link between smoking levels and lung cancer. The researchers recorded the number of deaths from lung cancer per 100 000 individuals in the population and the smoking levels of each person dying. The results for men aged 60 to 69 years are given in Table 2.

Table 2 *Death rates from lung cancer among men aged 60 to 69 years related to smoking levels*

Level of smoking		Death rate per 100 000 population
Never smoked		12
Smoked 20 cigarettes per day for:	30 years	234
	40 years	487
Smoked 40 cigarettes per day for:	30 years	576
	40 years	608

  i)   Which individuals are most at risk of dying from lung cancer? **(1 mark)**

  ii) Give TWO conclusions that the researchers could have drawn from the results. **(2 marks)**

d) Laila used to be a very good sprinter; however, she started to smoke heavily and now finds that whenever she tries to run she quickly becomes breathless and at times she even collapses.

  i)   Name the substance that builds up in Laila's muscles and causes her to collapse. **(1 mark)**

  ii) Other than lung cancer, suggest TWO ways in which Laila's heavy smoking contributes to her breathlessness. **(2 marks)**

e) Tyler moves from the countryside into an industrial town that has several large coal-burning factories and an oil-burning power plant and he becomes concerned about the harmful effects that the burning of the coal and oil could have on himself and his community.

  i)   Identify ONE likely air pollutant that Tyler could be concerned about. **(1 mark)**

  ii) Outline TWO different harmful effects that the pollutant identified in **e) i)** above could have on Tyler and his community. **(2 marks)**

Total 15 marks

6 **a) i)** What is meant by the term 'excretion'?   (2 marks)

   ii) Name ONE excretory organ, other than the kidney, found in the human
            body and identify ONE substance that it excretes.   (2 marks)

   b) Figure 8 is a diagram of a nephron found in a human kidney.

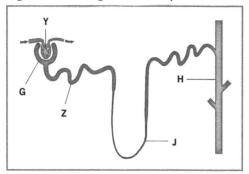

Figure 8 *Diagram of a nephron*

   i) Identify the structures labelled G, H and J in Figure 8.   (3 marks)

   ii) Briefly describe the process that takes place in EACH of the structures
            labelled Y and Z.   (4 marks)

   c) Table 3 shows the composition of Andrew's urine one hour after he drank two large glasses
        of water and again one hour after he played a 90-minute game of football in the heat of the
        day without drinking.

Table 3 *Composition of Andrew's urine*

Component	% in Andrew's urine after drinking	% in Andrew's urine after playing football
Urea	2.0	6.0
Salt	0.3	1.0
Water	95	90

   i) Which activity caused Andrew's urine to have the HIGHEST concentration?   (1 mark)

   ii) Name the hormone secreted by Andrew's pituitary gland when there is
            not enough water in his body fluids.   (1 mark)

   iii) Explain how the hormone named in **c) ii)** above functioned to prevent
            Andrew losing too much water in his urine when his body fluids became
            too concentrated.   (2 marks)

                                                                              Total 15 marks

7 **a) i)** State the function of EACH of the following parts of Ariel's ear:

            - the pinna
            - the ear drum
            - the cochlea.   (3 marks)

ii) Figure 9 shows three displacement–time graphs representing three sound waves, A, B and C.

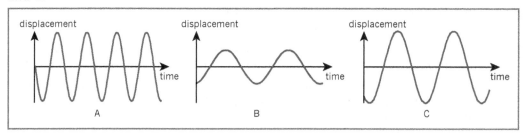

Figure 9 *Different sound waves*

Which sound wave would:

- be the quietest

- have the highest pitch? **(2 marks)**

iii) Would Xavier be able to hear a sound with a frequency of 25 000 Hz? Give a reason for your answer. **(1 mark)**

b) Complete Table 4, which gives information about three different regions of the brain.

Table 4 *Functions of three regions of the brain*

Region of the brain	One function
Medulla oblongata	•
	• Controls conscious thought
Cerebellum	•

(3 marks)

c) i) What are hormones often referred to as? **(1 mark)**

ii) Identify the hormone that is released in large quantities when a person is frightened. **(1 mark)**

iii) Jamal is found to have developed an underactive pituitary gland. By referring to TWO different hormones produced by Jamal's pituitary gland, explain how this reduced activity could affect his body. **(4 marks)**

Total 15 marks

8 a) i) Distinguish between personal hygiene and community hygiene. **(2 marks)**

ii) Give TWO reasons why it is important to practise good personal hygiene. **(2 marks)**

b) i) Mr Scruffy always has a pile of garbage outside his house. Name TWO household pests that might be present in the garbage. **(2 marks)**

ii) Suggest ONE way in which EITHER of the pests named in b) i) above could affect Mr Scruffy and his family. **(1 mark)**

iii) Other than the garbage pile, suggest TWO other conditions that could encourage pests to breed around Mr Scruffy's house. **(2 marks)**

c) i) Waste can be classified as biodegradable and non-biodegradable. What is meant by the term 'biodegradable'? **(1 mark)**

ii) Give ONE example of a waste material that is biodegradable and ONE example of a waste material that is non-biodegradable. **(2 marks)**

iii) Outline TWO potential consequences to the population of your country if its waste is not disposed of properly. **(2 marks)**

iv) What measure can the population of your country put in place to reduce the amount of waste to be disposed of? **(1 mark)**

Total 15 marks

Structured essay questions

9 **a) i)** Describe the events taking place in Chantal's ovaries and uterus during one complete menstrual cycle. **(4 marks)**

ii) Name TWO hormones, other than those secreted by Chantal's pituitary gland, that control her menstrual cycle and outline the role played by EACH. **(4 marks)**

b) Chantal misses her period and decides to go to the doctor because she thinks she might be pregnant. Her doctor confirms her suspicions. Outline the role that the placenta, umbilical cord and amniotic fluid play in the development of Chantal's baby during her pregnancy. **(7 marks)**

Total 15 marks

10 **a) i)** Explain why his mother's breast milk is considered to be a complete food for baby Allan. **(2 marks)**

ii) Describe how his mother's milk is digested as it passes through baby Allan's digestive system. **(6 marks)**

b) i) Why is it necessary to preserve food? **(1 mark)**

ii) By referring to THREE different methods, discuss the principles used in food preservation. **(6 marks)**

Total 15 marks

11 **a)** Describe, in detail, what happens during one complete heart beat. **(8 marks)**

b) Sara contracted chicken pox when she was a child and her son, Noah, recently contracted the disease. Explain how Sara remained healthy despite her close contact with Noah throughout his illness. **(7 marks)**

Total 15 marks

12 **a)** Ben finds it difficult to see the words in his Integrated Science text book clearly and his optician tells him that he is long sighted. With the aid of TWO diagrams explain the possible cause of Ben's long-sightedness and how it can be corrected. **(8 marks)**

b) i) Distinguish between a voluntary action and an involuntary action. **(2 marks)**

ii) When Asher's doctor tapped her knee just below her knee cap to test her reflexes, her lower leg moved upwards. Explain the events occurring in Asher's nervous system that brought about this response. **(5 marks)**

Total 15 marks

Section B – The home and workplace

9 Temperature control and ventilation

Heat energy flows from places of higher temperature to places of lower temperature. By controlling this **transfer** we are able to use the energy for purposes such as cooking or drying, or to remove it when we need to for purposes such as refrigerating or air conditioning.

Methods of heat transfer and their applications

Conduction is the process of heat transfer through a medium by the relaying of energy between particles colliding with each other.

Convection is the process of heat transfer in a medium by the movement of its particles between regions of different density.

Radiation is the process of heat transfer by means of electromagnetic waves.

Table 9.1 *Heat transfer through solids, liquids, gases and a vacuum*

Conduction	Occurs mainly in solids; to a greater extent in metals than in non-metals; less through liquids, and very poorly through gases; cannot occur through a vacuum.
Convection	Occurs mainly in liquids and gases (fluids); cannot occur through a vacuum.
Radiation	Occurs mainly through gases and through a vacuum.

Conduction

- **Non-metals** – When one end of a non-metallic bar is warmed, the particles present (atoms or molecules) absorb the heat energy. They then **vibrate and collide** more vigorously with their neighbouring particles, passing on the increased vibration along the bar. The temperature of a substance increases with the speed of its particles and therefore the temperature at the cooler end of the bar gradually increases.

- **Metals** – Vibrating particles in metals transfer the energy in a similar way to those in non-metals. However, metals contain freely moving **electrons** that also absorb some energy when heated and transfer it quickly to the vibrating particles by collisions. Metals are therefore better **conductors** of heat.

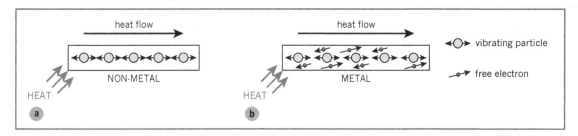

Figure 9.1 *Conduction in non-metals and metals*

Consider a copper rod and a wooden rod, both initially covered in wax, being heated by a water bath as shown in Figure 9.2a. The wax quickly melts from the copper and very slowly from the wood, indicating that copper is a very good **conductor**, but wood is a good **insulator** (poor conductor).

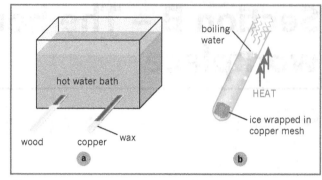

Figure 9.2b shows a piece of ice wrapped in copper mesh so that it sinks to the bottom of a test tube of water. The water, heated at the top to **avoid convection**, rapidly comes to a boil, but the ice remains solid for some time. This demonstrates that **water is a very poor conductor of heat.**

Figure 9.2 *Demonstrating conduction*

Convection

When a liquid or gas is warmed from below, the molecules at the bottom move more vigorously and take up more space. The heated region becomes **less dense** and **rises**, allowing cooler molecules from denser regions to fall and take their place.

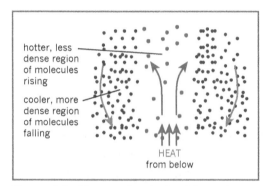

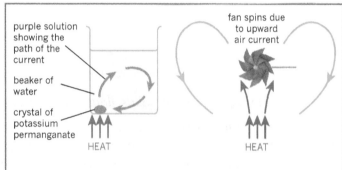

Figure 9.3 *Convection in liquids and gases* **Figure 9.4** *Demonstrating convection*

Radiation

All bodies absorb and emit **thermal radiation** in the form of **infrared waves**, a form of **electromagnetic radiation** (see page 86). Our bodies detect infrared radiation as **warmth**. Electromagnetic radiation can readily transfer energy through **gases** and even through a **vacuum**. It is how we obtain our energy from the Sun through the vacuum of space.

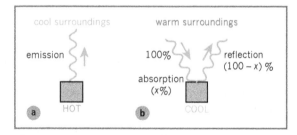

Figure 9.5 *Emitters and absorbers of radiation*

Table 9.2 *Physical properties affecting absorption and emission of radiation*

Matt /dull / rough / black	Shiny / smooth / polished / silver (or white)
Good absorbers (poor reflectors)	Poor absorbers (good reflectors)
Good emitters	Poor emitters

Examples

* An oven is a net **emitter** since it is **hotter** than its surroundings (see Figure 9.5a).
  Painting it **shiny white** makes it a poor emitter, preventing heat from leaving.

* A refrigerator is a net **absorber** since it is **cooler** than its surroundings (see Figure 9.5b).
  Painting it **shiny white** makes it a poor absorber (good reflector), preventing heat from entering.

Land and sea breezes

- **During the day** – The Sun's **radiation** warms the land at a higher rate than it warms the sea. Air in contact with the land is warmed by **conduction** and then rises by **convection**, allowing a breeze of cool air from over the sea to take its place. Coastal regions therefore do not experience very high temperatures during the day.

- **During the night** – **Radiation** from the land occurs at a higher rate that it does from the sea. Air in contact with the sea is warmed by **conduction** and then rises by **convection**, pulling a cool breeze from over the land to take its place. Coastal regions therefore do not experience very low temperatures during the night.

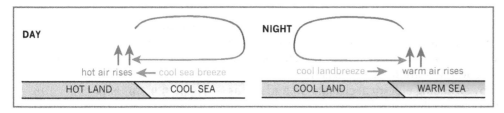

Figure 9.6 *Land and sea breezes*

Applications of heat transfer

- **Air conditioners** are placed at high levels in rooms. The air they cool becomes denser and falls, allowing warmer air to rise and be cooled.

- **Heaters** are placed near to the floor. The air they heat becomes less dense and rises, allowing cooler, denser air to fall and be heated.

- **Saucepans** have copper bottoms to conduct heat rapidly to the food being cooked. They also have insulating plastic handles to prevent conduction to the persons holding them.

- **Concrete blocks** have poor conducting air pockets to reduce heat flow through them.

- **Vacuum flask** – see Figure 9.7.

- **Solar water heater** – see Figure 9.8.

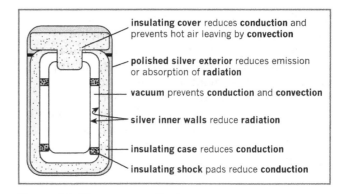

Figure 9.7 *The vacuum flask*

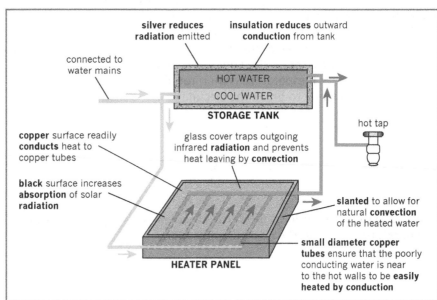

Figure 9.8 *The solar water heater*

Thermostatic control

*An **electric thermostat** is a device that regulates temperature by switching an electrical circuit on or off when it becomes too hot or too cold.*

- For ovens, the thermostat will switch the heater off when the temperature is **above** a certain value.
- For air conditioners and refrigerators, the thermostat will switch the motor off when the temperature is **below** a certain value.

The bimetallic strip

This consists of two metal strips riveted together, e.g. brass and iron. **Brass expands more than iron** when heated and so the straight strip bends such that brass is on the outer side of the curve. Brass also **contracts** more on cooling. Bimetallic strips can be used to regulate temperature by **switching** electrical circuits on and off, as explained in the thermostat applications below.

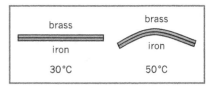

Figure 9.9 *The bimetallic strip*

Electric thermostat used in an oven

With the switch on, the heater warms and the bimetallic strip bends outwards, causing the sliding contacts to separate and break the heating circuit. The oven then cools, the bimetallic strip straightens, the contacts reconnect and the process repeats. To control the temperature, an adjusting screw can be advanced so that it forces the sliding contacts further over each other. The bimetallic strip must then bend more in order to break the circuit.

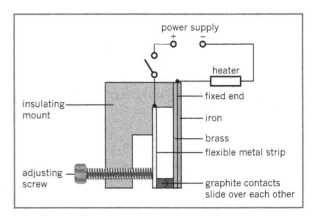

Figure 9.10 *Thermostat in an oven*

Electric thermostat used in an electric iron

As the heater warms, the bimetallic strip bends downwards, separating the sliding contacts and breaking the circuit. The heater then cools, the bimetallic strip straightens and the contacts reconnect, restarting the heating process. By advancing the control screw, the contacts slide further over each other. A higher temperature is then required before the strip bends sufficiently to break the circuit.

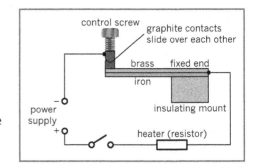

Figure 9.11 *Thermostat in an electric iron*

Temperature and thermometers

Temperature is a measure of the degree of hotness of a body.

The SI unit of temperature is the **kelvin (K)**. However, **degrees Celsius (°C)**, is commonly used. Temperature is measured using a **thermometer**.

Liquid-in-glass thermometers

Some thermometers contain a liquid in an enclosed glass tube. The reservoir of liquid is in the **bulb**. The liquid **expands** when heated and moves through a narrow capillary (**bore**), which has a **scale** alongside it. **Mercury** or alcohol is commonly used as the liquid in such a thermometer.

Laboratory mercury thermometer

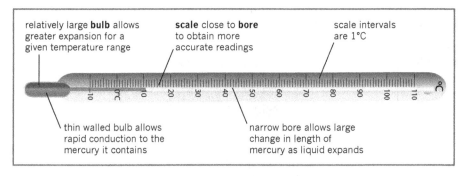

relatively large **bulb** allows greater expansion for a given temperature range

scale close to **bore** to obtain more accurate readings

scale intervals are 1°C

thin walled bulb allows rapid conduction to the mercury it contains

narrow bore allows large change in length of mercury as liquid expands

Figure 9.12 *Liquid-in-glass laboratory mercury thermometer*

Advantages of using mercury instead of alcohol

- Mercury conducts heat better than alcohol and therefore responds faster to the temperature being measured.
- The boiling point of mercury is higher than that of alcohol and so it can measure higher temperatures.
- Mercury is bright silver and easily seen, whereas alcohol is colourless and must be tinted.

Disadvantages of using mercury instead of alcohol

- The freezing point of mercury is not as low as that of alcohol. Alcohol can therefore measure colder temperatures.
- Mercury is more expensive than alcohol.
- Mercury is very poisonous. Alcohol is less harmful.

Clinical mercury thermometer

The **clinical thermometer** is designed to measure the temperature of a **living person**.

- The scale ranges from **35 °C to 43 °C**. The **normal body temperature** of a living human is **37 °C**.
- The interval between markings on the scale is **0.1 °C** so that a very **precise** reading is obtained.
- There is a narrow **constriction** in the bore. When the thermometer is removed from the patient, the sudden change in temperature causes a rapid contraction of the mercury. As the mercury rushes towards the bulb, it breaks at the constriction, leaving the **thread** above it to be read. The thermometer can then be **shaken** to send the mercury back to the bulb for its next use.

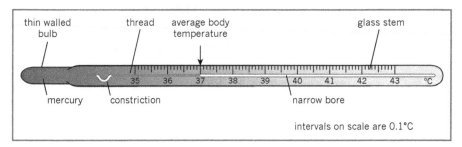

thin walled bulb

thread

average body temperature

glass stem

mercury

constriction

narrow bore

intervals on scale are 0.1°C

Figure 9.13 *Liquid-in-glass clinical thermometer*

Maximum and minimum thermometer

A maximum and minimum thermometer is used to measure the maximum and minimum temperatures reached in a particular place over a period of time.

- **As the temperature increases**, alcohol in the left tube expands **through** the left steel index and presses on the mercury, causing it to force the right steel index upwards.

- The indexes have a light spring that holds them against the tube.

- **As the temperature decreases**, alcohol in the left tube contracts, pulling the mercury with it. If the mercury reaches the left index, it forces it upwards. Alcohol in the right tube flows **through** the index.

- The **highest and lowest temperatures** of the period can be read from the bottom of the indexes.

- The **current temperature** can be read from the mercury level in either scale.

- After reading the scales, a **magnet is used to return the indexes** so they touch the mercury.

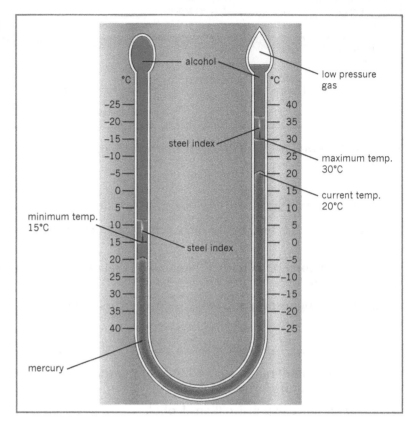

Figure 9.14 *Maximum and minimum thermometer*

Digital thermometers

There are several types of digital thermometers with temperature-sensing abilities that depend on different physical principles.

- These thermometers have **sensors** that produce currents dependent on the temperature. The sensors are connected to a **digital display**, which shows the temperature.

- They can be placed in a furnace, or even underground to measure the temperature of the soil. Long electrical wires can lead from the sensor to the digital display for easy reading.

- They are used in furnaces and freezers since they can measure very high and very low temperatures.

- Since they respond quickly and do not contain toxic mercury, they are rapidly replacing **clinical mercury thermometers**.

Cooling effects of evaporation

*Evaporation is the escape of molecules from the **surface** of a liquid.*

Cooling due to evaporation

During evaporation, the more **energetic** molecules escape from the surface of the liquid at a rate dependent on its temperature. To do so, they **absorb heat energy** from other molecules of the liquid so that they can overcome the attractive forces existing between them. This energy is known as **latent heat of vaporisation.** The temperature of the liquid **falls** since the more energetic molecules have escaped.

During condensation, latent heat of vaporisation is **released** and the attractive forces are no longer overcome. The temperature of the surroundings therefore **rises**.

Sweating and metabolic rate

Chemical reactions constantly occur in our bodies. These reactions are necessary to maintain life and are called **metabolic processes** or metabolism. The **metabolic rate** is a measure of the amount of energy used by the body per unit time to sustain itself and carry out all its activities.

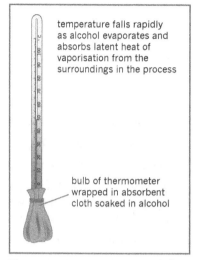

temperature falls rapidly as alcohol evaporates and absorbs latent heat of vaporisation from the surroundings in the process

bulb of thermometer wrapped in absorbent cloth soaked in alcohol

Figure 9.15 *Evaporative cooling*

This energy is provided by the process of **respiration**. As metabolic reactions take place, heat energy is released by respiring cells and we become hotter. Our **sweat glands** then release **perspiration** (sweat which, **on evaporation**, removes heat and helps us to feel cooler (see page 79)).

Factors affecting the rate of evaporation

- **Temperature:** Molecules move faster at higher temperatures and so have a better chance of overcoming the attractive forces of neighbouring molecules and escaping as a gas.
- **Humidity:** If the humidity is high, molecules escaping from the surface are more likely to crash into other molecules and rebound to the liquid, reducing the rate of evaporation.
- **Wind:** This removes molecules from above the surface, allowing evaporating molecules to have a better chance of escaping without colliding and rebounding to the liquid.
- **Surface area:** A large surface area allows more molecules to escape from it, thus increasing the rate of evaporation.

Ventilation

Ventilation is the process by which clean air is intentionally provided to a space and stale air is removed from it.

In order to keep us **healthy** and **comfortable**, the air around us should have the following properties:
- Have an adequate oxygen level.
- Have an adequate humidity level.
- Be at an adequate temperature.
- Be free of dust, pollen and toxic contaminants.
- Be free of mould and bacteria.

Problems of inadequate ventilation of enclosed spaces

- As we breathe, **oxygen levels fall** and **carbon dioxide levels rise**, making respiration difficult.
- Exhaled **water vapour** causes increased humidity, **reducing the cooling effect** of evaporation.
- **Microorganisms** (such as mould) rapidly multiply in warm, humid environments, creating an **unhealthy, musty odour**.
- **Toxins** and **dust** can **interact negatively** with our bodies.

Providing adequate ventilation

- **Windows on different sides of a room** allow **clean** air to enter and **stale** air to move out.
- An open **window on a high level** allows warm air to exit by convection as **cool, fresh** air enters below.
- **Fans** cool us by replacing warm, moist air from around our bodies with **cooler, less humid** air.
- **Air conditioners** pull warm, moist air from a room and replace it with **cool, less humid** air. The heat that is extracted from the warm air is released to the outdoor environment. Air conditioners also act as **dehumidifiers**, since water is removed from the air as it is cooled.
- **Dehumidifiers** should be used in highly humid rooms such as cellars (see 'Effects of high humidity').
- **Humidifiers** should be used in rooms where the air is very dry (see 'Effects of low humidity').

Effects of high humidity

The Caribbean region is generally humid since the high temperatures close to the equator result in excessive evaporation from the surrounding sea. Effects of high humidity are outlined below:

- Leads to **early decay of building materials**, such as wooden structures.
- Promotes the development of **fungi**, including **mould**, which produce **distasteful odours** and can lead to **allergic reactions** in humans.
- Promotes the development of **bacteria** and **viruses** and encourages the growth of **dust-mites**.
- On a hot day, especially if we are engaged in active physical work or exercise, our body temperature can rise significantly, causing the production of excessive sweat that is unable to evaporate. This can lead to **dehydration** and **heatstroke** since our **higher metabolic rate** will further increase our body temperature. A range of symptoms may result, including nausea and vomiting, headaches and dizziness, gasping for breath, seizures, kidney failure, and even a state of unconsciousness.

Effects of low humidity

- **Mucous membranes** in the nose and throat can become **dehydrated**, making breathing difficult.
- Materials may shrink or become **brittle and crack**.

1 **a** Describe conduction of heat in non-metals.

   b Why is conduction of heat faster in metals than in non-metals?

2 Explain why a sea breeze blows towards a coastal region during the day.

3 Two cans are made from the same material into the same size and shape. One is painted black and the other is painted silver. They are both filled with hot water and left in the shade. State and explain which will cool faster.

4 **a** Explain why there is a constriction in the bore of a clinical liquid-in-glass thermometer.

   b Why does a nurse or doctor shake the thermometer before and after using it?

5 State the type of thermometer that is suitable for determining:

   a the highest temperature reached in your bedroom during the week.

   b the temperature in a pottery kiln or furnace.

   c the temperature of boiling water in your school laboratory.

6 **a** State what is meant by the term 'evaporation'.

   b Explain, in terms of molecules and energy, why a liquid becomes cooler as it evaporates.

   c List FOUR factors that increase the rate of evaporation.

7 **a** State what is meant by the term 'ventilation'.

   b List THREE properties of the air that are necessary to keep us comfortable and healthy.

   c List THREE negative effects of high levels of humidity.

10 Conservation of energy

Bodies need **energy** in order to do **work**. Energy exists in different forms that are **interchangeable** and can be **transferred** from one body to another in different ways.

The concept of energy

Work is done when a force moves an object through a distance in the direction of the force. **Energy** is needed to make this change.

Energy is the ability to do work (that is, the ability to make a change).

Calculating work and energy

work or energy = force × distance moved **in the direction of the force**

$$\therefore\ W = F \times d \quad \text{or} \quad E = F \times d$$

The SI unit of work or energy is the **joule, J.**

1 joule is the work done or energy used when a force of 1 newton moves an object through a distance of 1 metre in the direction of the force.

Therefore, 1 joule is equal to 1 newton metre (N m).

Example

A block has a weight of 50 N. Asabi pushes it with a horizontal force of 20 N through a distance of 25 m across a floor. Determine: **a** the work done and **b** the energy used.

a $W = F \times d$ **b** $E = 500\,\text{J}$
$W = 20\,\text{N} \times 25\,\text{m}$
$W = 500\,\text{J}$

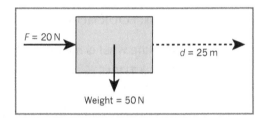

Figure 10.1

The weight of the block **is not used** since it acts **perpendicularly** to the distance across the floor. Recall that work = force × distance moved **in the direction of the force**. The energy used is equivalent to the work done.

Some types of energy

Table 10.1 *Some types of energy*

Energy type	Description
Gravitational potential energy	Energy **stored** by a body due to its position in a gravitational force field.
	It increases as the body rises above the Earth's surface.
Elastic potential energy	Energy **stored** by a body due to its position in an elastic force field.
	It increases as the body is stretched or compressed.
Nuclear energy	Energy **stored** in an atomic nucleus due to its physical state.
Chemical energy	Energy **stored** by a body due to its chemical state.
Kinetic energy	Energy possessed by a body due to its **motion.**
Thermal energy	Energy possessed by a body due to the **motion of its particles** (atoms, molecules, ions). Increased temperature produces increased motion.

Energy type	Description
Heat energy	**Thermal energy transferred** from hotter to cooler bodies.
Sound energy	Energy **transported** as particle **vibrations** through a material in the form of a wave.
Electrical energy	Energy **transferred** by **charged particles**; e.g. electrons in metal wires.
Electromagnetic energy	Energy **transported** in the form of **waves** as electric and magnetic field vibrations (radio, TV, microwaves, infrared, visible light, ultraviolet, X-rays, gamma rays).

Interconversion of energy

The principle of conservation of energy states that energy cannot be created or destroyed but can be transformed from one type to another.

For example, **chemical energy** stored in batteries, and **gravitational potential energy** stored in water behind a river dam, can be transformed into **electrical energy** as needed.

Whenever **energy is transformed**, an equal amount of **work is done.** This work can put objects into motion if the transformation is to **kinetic energy,** or it can move objects upwards if the transformation is to **gravitational potential energy.** If the work is done against **friction**, the transformation is to **heat and sound energy.** Several examples of energy transformations are outlined below.

Main energy transformations occurring during various situations

- **Coconut falling to the ground**

- **Vehicle driving over bump**

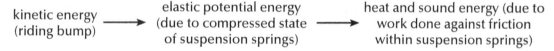

- **Gasoline-fuelled car accelerating on a level road**

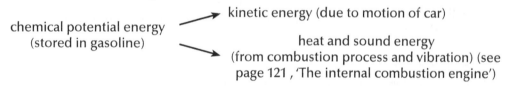

- **Aircraft taking off**

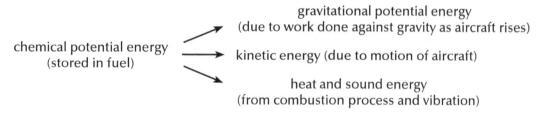

- **Charging a battery**

    electrical energy ⟶ chemical potential energy (stored in battery)

- **Electrical motor lifting a load**

    electrical energy ⟶ gravitational potential energy (due to work done against gravity)

- **Solar calculator or solar powered laptop computer**

    light energy ⟶ electrical energy (generated by solar panel) ⟶ light energy (from display screen)

    ⟶ heat energy (small amount due to electrical resistance)

- **Filament lamp**

    electrical energy ⟶ heat energy and light energy (due to work done against the electrical resistance of the hot filament)

- **Hydro-electric power station**

    gravitational potential energy (due to height through which water falls) ⟶ kinetic energy (moving water spins turbine connected to generator) ⟶ electrical energy (from generator)

- **Diesel-electric power station**

    chemical potential energy (stored in diesel) ⟶ heat energy (from combustion; boils water to produce steam) ⟶ kinetic energy (moving steam spins turbine connected to generator) ⟶ electrical energy (from generator)

- **Nuclear power station**

    nuclear potential energy (stored in uranium) ⟶ heat energy (from nuclear emissions; boils water to produce steam) ⟶ kinetic energy (moving steam spins turbine connected to generator) ⟶ electrical energy (from generator)

- **Photosynthesis**

    light energy (from Sun) ⟶ chemical energy (stored in carbohydrate molecules of green plants) (see page 32)

Gravitational potential energy at A ⟶ Kinetic energy at B ⟶ Gravitational potential energy at C ⟶ ......

At A and C: $E_K = 0$ since the ball is momentarily at rest.
E_{GP} is maximum since it is at its maximum height.

At B: E_K is maximum since the ball moves fastest.
E_{GP} is minimum since it is at its lowest position.

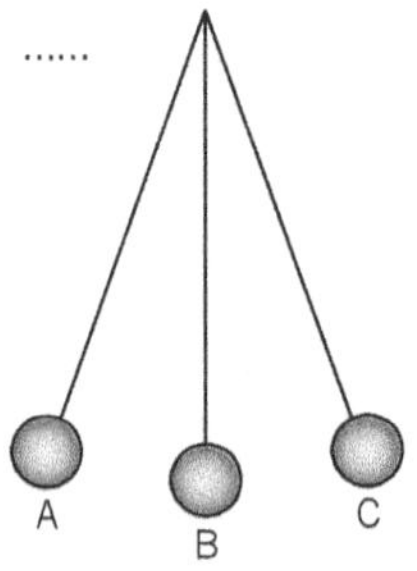

A   B   C

Figure 10.2 *Energy transformation of a swinging pendulum*

The internal combustion engine

Most motor vehicles in the Caribbean are powered by an **internal combustion engine**. Inside this engine, a **fuel** and **air** mixture is **burned** to release energy. The process releases **harmful exhaust** containing a mixture of carbon monoxide, oxides of nitrogen, particulate matter and unburnt hydrocarbons. Methods used to save energy supply to vehicles and to reduce the negative effects of internal combustion engines are outlined in Table 10.2.

Table 10.2 *Saving energy and reducing the negative effects of the internal combustion engine*

Methods used	Effect of use
Catalytic converters	Convert toxic gases to less harmful ones in the exhaust system.
Government regulations	Ensure that air quality is monitored to meet certain standards.
Solar-electric cells	Make us less dependent on fossil fuels. Vehicles now also have solar cells.
Public transportation, carpooling and bicycles	Reduce fuel required per person transported.
Well-tuned vehicles	Fewer toxins emitted and less fuel used.
Improved vehicles	• Streamlined designs offer minimum air resistance. • 'Idle off' systems save fuel by switching off the engine when the car stops. • Smaller, more efficient engines produce the same power. • Energy efficient air conditioners and LED lighting reduce energy use. • New suspension systems generate electricity by absorbing energy whenever a vehicle accelerates, decelerates or encounters a bump. • New cooling systems re-use the heat energy produced by the engine.

Mass converting to energy

*Nuclear fission is the splitting of a **large** atomic nucleus into smaller atomic nuclei, resulting in a large output of energy and a small loss in mass.*

- The '**atomic bomb**' is a weapon that utilises a violent nuclear fission reaction.
- **Nuclear power plants** produce electricity in **nuclear reactors** by a controlled nuclear fission reaction of **uranium.**

*Nuclear fusion is the joining of **small** atomic nuclei to form a larger atomic nucleus, resulting in a large output of energy and a small loss in mass.*

- The '**hydrogen bomb**' is a weapon that utilises a violent nuclear fusion reaction.
- **Radiant energy from the Sun** is produced when hydrogen atoms join to form helium atoms.

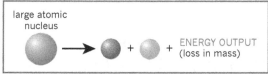

Figure 10.3 *Nuclear fission*

Figure 10.4 *Nuclear fusion*

Energy supplies for use in space

Suitable: solar cells and **nuclear devices** can be small, portable, durable and reliable for long periods.

Unsuitable: fossil fuels are non-renewable, cause pollution and harm the environment. **Chemical batteries** are short-lived and are hazardous when disposed of.

Transport and transfer of energy

Energy can be transported from one point to another in several ways.

- **Conduction:** As atoms or molecules collide with their neighbours, they transfer energy among themselves and, in so doing, transport it to some other point in the material.

- **Collision:** A swinging cricket bat transfers kinetic energy to a ball when they collide. The ball then transports the energy to a fielder and transfers it to his palms when he catches it. A moving vehicle will transfer kinetic energy to a stationary one as it collides with it.

- **Convection:** During convection, energy is transported upwards by particles moving from a warm region that is less dense than its cooler surroundings.

- **Waves:** Energy of a vibration can be transferred between particles of **a sound wave** as it is transported through a medium. **Water waves** transport energy across the ocean and **electromagnetic waves**, such as light, can transport energy through glass, water, air and even through a vacuum!

Transfer of energy by waves

Waves are produced by **vibrations** and may be either **transverse** or **longitudinal**.

Transverse waves

Transverse waves have **crests** and **troughs** and transfer energy **perpendicular to the direction of vibration** of their source. Examples are water waves, electromagnetic waves and the wave on a rope vibrated perpendicularly to its length from one end.

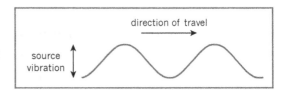

Figure 10.5 *Transverse wave in a rope*

Electromagnetic waves (listed below) are transverse waves that, unlike other types of waves, can also travel through a vacuum.

- **Radio and TV** waves transfer energy so we can listen to or watch the news and movies.

- **Microwaves** transfer messages between our cell phones and transfer heat to our food.

- **Infrared, visible light** and **ultraviolet** waves bring us solar energy through the vacuum of space.

- **X-rays** transfer energy through our flesh to form images on photographic material.

- **Gamma rays**, emitted during a nuclear reaction, carry energy through our flesh just like X-rays.

Longitudinal waves

Longitudinal waves have regions of **high pressure** (H) and of **low pressure** (L). They transfer energy **parallel to the direction of vibration** of their source. Examples are sound waves and the wave on a slinky vibrated parallel to its length from one end.

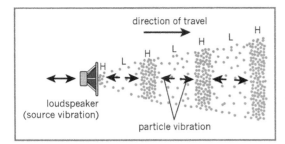

Figure 10.6 *Sound wave in air*

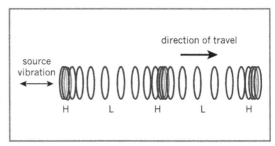

Figure 10.7 *Longitudinal wave in slinky*

Reflection and focusing of waves

Curved reflectors can be used to focus radio and TV waves onto a **receiver aerial** or to focus a beam of solar radiation to boil a pot of water. They can also produce a concentrated beam from the headlamps of vehicles and a wide-angled view from rear-view mirrors.

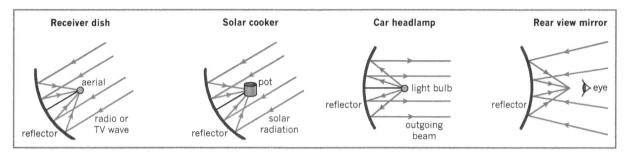

Figure 10.8 *Curved reflectors*

Momentum and its conservation

*The **velocity** of a body is its speed in a particular direction.*

The SI unit of velocity is the **metre per second (m s⁻¹).**

*The **momentum** of a body is the product of its mass and velocity.*

$$p = m \times v$$

The SI unit of momentum is the **kilogram metre per second (kg m s⁻¹).**

Velocity and momentum are quantities with **directions** that must be considered in calculations. Along a straight line, we take one direction as positive and the other as negative.

Example 1

Determine the momentum of a shell of mass 0.25 kg moving at 300 m s⁻¹.

$p = m \times v = 0.25 \text{ kg} \times 300 \text{ m s}^{-1} = 75 \text{ kg m s}^{-1}$

Example 2

Car A of mass 1000 kg moves east at 20 m s⁻¹ and car B of mass 1200 kg moves west at the same speed. What is their total momentum?

Since the cars move in opposite directions, we can designate **east as positive and west as negative.**

$p = (m_A \times v_A) + (m_B \times v_B)$

$p = (1000 \text{ kg} \times 20 \text{ m s}^{-1}) + (1200 \text{ kg} \times - 20 \text{ m s}^{-1})$

$p = 20\,000 \text{ kg m s}^{-1} - 24\,000 \text{ kg m s}^{-1}$

$p = - 4000 \text{ kg m s}^{-1}$

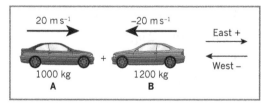

Figure 10.9

The total momentum is 4000 kg m s⁻¹ directed to the **west.**

Note that we drop the negative sign since it simply means west.

Conservation of momentum

The principle of conservation of linear momentum states that for a system of colliding objects, their total momentum immediately before the collision is equal to their total momentum immediately after the collision.

Example

Car A of mass 2 kg and velocity 4 m s^{-1} collides head-on with car B of mass 2 kg, which is initially stationary. Determine the following:

a The total momentum before the collision.

b The total momentum after the collision.

c The magnitude (size) of their common velocity after the collision if they stick together.

d The magnitude (size) of the velocity of car B after the collision if car A becomes stationary.

a Total momentum before the collision

$$p = (m_A \times v_A) + (m_B \times v_B)$$
$$p = (2\,\text{kg} \times 4\,\text{m s}^{-1}) + (2\,\text{kg} \times 0\,\text{m s}^{-1})$$
$$p = 8\,\text{kg m s}^{-1} + 0\,\text{kg m s}^{-1}$$
$$p = 8\,\text{kg m s}^{-1}$$

b From the principle of conservation of linear momentum, the total momentum after the collision must also be 8 kg m s^{-1}.

c After the collision, the cars are **stuck together** and therefore have **the same velocity, v.**

$$p = (m_A + m_B)\,v$$
$$8\,\text{kg m s}^{-1} = (2\,\text{kg} + 2\,\text{kg})\,v$$
$$8\,\text{kg m s}^{-1} = (4\,\text{kg})\,v$$
$$v = \frac{8\,\text{kg m s}^{-1}}{4\,\text{kg}}$$
$$v = 2\,\text{m s}^{-1}$$

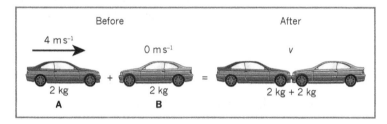

Figure 10.10

d After the collision, **car A becomes stationary.**

$$p = (m_A \times v_A) + (m_B \times v_B)$$
$$8\,\text{kg m s}^{-1} = (2\,\text{kg} \times 0\,\text{m s}^{-1}) + (2\,\text{kg} \times v)$$
$$8\,\text{kg m s}^{-1} = 0 + (2\,\text{kg} \times v)$$
$$8\,\text{kg m s}^{-1} = (2\,\text{kg} \times v)$$
$$v = \frac{8\,\text{kg m s}^{-1}}{2\,\text{kg}}$$
$$v = 4\,\text{m s}^{-1}$$

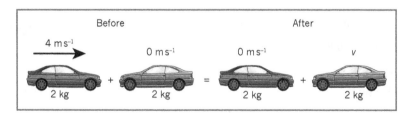

Figure 10.11

Revision questions

1. Define energy and state its SI unit.

2. Kwame pushes a block through a distance of 20 m by using a force of 50 N. Calculate:
   a the energy converted   b the work done

3. Define each of the following terms:
   a gravitational potential energy   b chemical energy
   c kinetic energy

4. a State the principle of conservation of energy.
   b Use arrow diagrams to show the energy conversions occurring during each of the following:
      i A stone falling from a cliff and crashing to the ground.
      ii A diesel-electric power station producing electricity.

5. a What is meant by each of the following?
      i Nuclear fission.
      ii Nuclear fusion.
   b Which of the two processes in part a is used to produce:
      i electricity in nuclear power plants?
      ii energy obtained from the Sun?
   c What happens to the mass of a substance that undergoes a nuclear reaction?

6. State THREE ways of reducing the energy used by vehicles.

7. a Draw a diagram showing a transverse wave on the surface of the ocean. Your diagram should indicate the direction of vibration of the water particles and the direction in which the energy is transferred.
   b Electromagnetic waves are transverse waves. Name THREE types of electromagnetic waves.
   c Draw a ray diagram to show how solar energy can be focused to boil a pot of water.

8. a Calculate the momentum of body X of mass 40 kg and velocity $2\,m\,s^{-1}$.
   b Body X collides with a stationary body Y and comes to rest. What is the total momentum after the collision?
   c Determine the magnitude of the common velocity (i.e. the speed) of the bodies after the collision if they stick together and have the same mass.

11 Electricity and lighting

Electricity is a very important part of everyday life. It is used in **homes** and **workplaces** for many purposes including lighting, heating, cooling and entertainment. Care has to be exercised when using electricity as serious accidents can occur.

Conductors, semiconductors and insulators

Conductors of electricity are materials containing electric charges which can flow freely.

Good conductors of electricity include:

- **Metals** – They contain free electrons that have broken away from their orbits around the nucleus.
- **Graphite** (a form of carbon) – This is a non-metal but it also contains free electrons and is therefore a good conductor.
- **Solutions of ionic substances** (electrolytes) such as table salt – They have freely moving positive and negative electric charges (**ions**) that travel in opposite directions when connected in an electrical circuit.
- **Molten ionic substances** – They also contain freely moving ions.

Insulators (or poor conductors) are materials in which electrical charges do not flow freely.

Poor conductors of electricity include:

- **Non-metallic materials** (excluding graphite) – Most of these substances do not contain free charges.

Semiconductors are materials with conductivity between that of good conductors and insulators.

Table 11.1 *Examples of conductors, semiconductors and insulators*

Good conductors	Semiconductors	Insulators
Silver, gold, copper, aluminium, graphite, body fluids containing ions, salt solution	Silicon, germanium	Glass, wood, quartz, rubber, plastic

Table 11.2 *Uses of conductors, semiconductors and insulators*

Material	Uses

Conductors	• **Electrical wires:**
	  ♦ **Copper** is commonly used because it is an excellent electrical conductor.
	  ♦ **Aluminium** is also a good conductor. It is used to transmit electricity through power lines, as it is cheaper per gram and it is less dense than copper.
	  ♦ **Silver** conducts electricity better than copper but is expensive and is only used for special circuits.
	• **Electrical contacts:** Graphite is used for '**make and break**' contacts in electrical circuits. Unlike metals which make a poor connection, graphite wears to a smooth surface with good contact connection.

Semi-conductors	• **Electronic components:** Semiconductors are used in the manufacture of light and heat sensors, light-emitting diodes (LEDs) and several components found in computers and other modern devices. • **Photovoltaic cells:** Solar panels that convert light into electrical energy are made of semiconducting materials, the most popular being **silicon**.
Insulators	• **To cover electrical wires and to encase certain appliances:** Rubber and plastics are used to provide insulation and prevent electrical shock.

An **electric circuit** is a **complete path** or loop through which electrons can flow from a **source** and then return to the source. Electrons will not flow if this path is incomplete. Table 11.3 shows various circuit symbols used in representing an electric circuit.

Table 11.3 *Electrical circuit symbols*

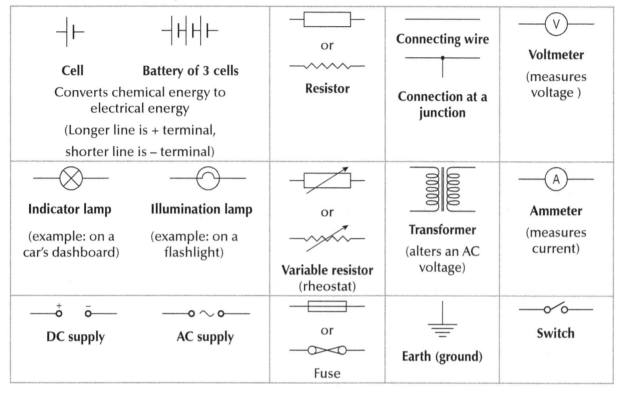

Cell **Battery of 3 cells** Converts chemical energy to electrical energy (Longer line is + terminal, shorter line is – terminal)	or **Resistor**	**Connecting wire** **Connection at a junction**	**Voltmeter** (measures voltage)
Indicator lamp (example: on a car's dashboard) **Illumination lamp** (example: on a flashlight)	or **Variable resistor** (rheostat)	**Transformer** (alters an AC voltage)	**Ammeter** (measures current)
DC supply **AC supply**	or **Fuse**	**Earth (ground)**	**Switch**

Using a circuit to investigate good and poor conductors

The circuit shown in Figure 11.1 is set up. The bulb used should glow brightly if connected directly to the cell. Small pieces of various materials such as copper, iron, graphite, plastic, wood, cloth, rubber, glass and paper are, in turn, connected between the points X and Y. Liquids such as water and cooking oil, and solutions such as dilute acids, and salt water, can also be connected between X and Y by the use of electrodes (conducting strips) as shown in Figure 11.1b.

If the bulb glows brightly, the material is a very good conductor. If the bulb is dim, the material is not a good conductor and if the bulb does not glow at all, the material is an insulator.

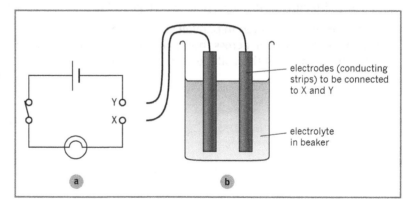

Figure 11.1 *Investigating good and poor conductors*

Voltage, current, resistance and power in circuits

Cells and batteries behave as electrical **pumps.** When connected to components in a circuit, they provide a **voltage** that forces a **current** through them.

Table 11.4 *Important electrical quantities and their SI units*

Quantity	Definition	SI unit
Voltage (V)	*Electrical energy per unit charge used in driving the electrons through a circuit.*	volt (V)
Current (I)	*Rate of flow of electrical charge through a circuit.*	ampere (A)
Resistance (R)	*The opposition to the flow of electrical current through a material.*	ohm (Ω)
Power (P)	*The rate of using energy (the rate of doing work).*	watt (W)

Appliances are generally labelled with their **power rating.** This indicates the rate at which they can **do** work or **use** electrical energy. If an appliance is labelled 1500 W, 110 V, this indicates that when a voltage of 110 V is placed across it, the appliance will use (consume) electrical power of 1500 W.

Direct current (DC) flows in **one direction** only. Batteries produce DC.

Alternating current (AC) **repeatedly reverses direction**. The electric company delivers AC to our homes.

Three useful equations

voltage = current × resistance   power = voltage × current   power = $\frac{\text{energy}}{\text{time}}$

$$V = I \times R \qquad\qquad P = V \times I \qquad\qquad P = \frac{E}{t}$$

The first equation is known as Ohm's law.

Ohm's law states that at constant temperature, the current through a conductor is proportional to the voltage across it.

Setting up circuits with ammeters and voltmeters

- **Ammeters** are connected in **series** with components to measure the current **through** them (see Figure 11.2).

- **Voltmeters** are connected in **parallel** with components to measure the voltage **across** them. Figure 11.2 shows a voltmeter measuring the voltage across resistor X.

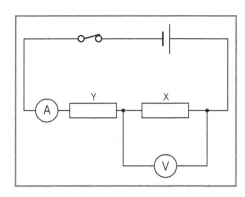

Figure 11.2 *Connecting ammeters and voltmeters*

Series circuits

All components in a series circuit are connected in **one complete loop** so that the current can only travel along one pathway.

Example

Each cell in the circuit shown produces a voltage of 9 V, therefore the total voltage produced by the battery of two cells is 18 V. The variable resistor (rheostat) is adjusted to a value of 6 Ω and the switch is turned on.

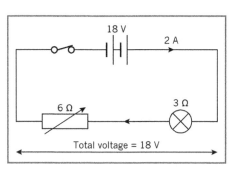

Figure 11.3

a What is the voltage across each of the following?

  i) The indicator lamp.

  ii) The variable resistor (rheostat).

b What is the power used by each of the following?

  i) The indicator lamp.

  ii) The variable resistor (rheostat).

c What is the power delivered by the battery?

Note the following by examining the diagram.

- The voltage of 18 V from the battery is divided between the variable resistor and lamp.
- Current is the same at all points in a series circuit.

a i $V = IR$

$V = 2\,A \times 3\,\Omega$

$V = 6\,V$

Using current through lamp and resistance of lamp

ii $V = IR$

$V = 2\,A \times 6\,\Omega$

$V = 12\,V$

Using current through rheostat and resistance of rheostat

b i $P = VI$

$P = 6\,V \times 2\,A$

$P = 12\,W$

Using voltage across lamp and current through lamp

ii $P = VI$

$P = 12\,V \times 2\,A$

$P = 24\,W$

Using voltage across rheostat and current through rheostat

c The power **delivered** by the battery is the power **used** by the total resistance so we can simply sum the powers calculated in **b**:

12 W + 24 W = 36 W

Or since the battery provides the power used by the resistors, apply the calculation directly to the battery using the voltage and current it produces:

$P = VI = 18\,V \times 2\,A = 36\,W$

Sometimes the power relation $P = V\,I$ is written as W (for Watts) $= V\,I$ or $I = \frac{W}{V}$

Parallel circuits

Components in a parallel circuit are connected in **different branches** of the circuit. This means that the current can travel along more than one pathway around the circuit.

Example 1

a Determine the resistance of the resistor R in Figure 11.4.

b Calculate the electrical power used by each of the following:

i) the lamp

ii) the resistor.

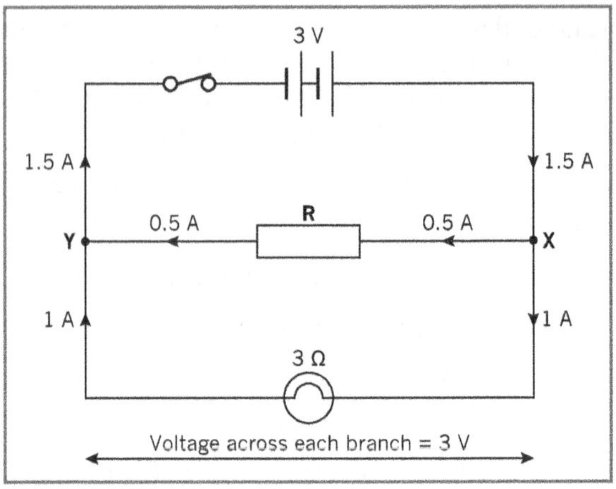

Examine Figure 11.4 and note the following:

- **Voltage** across components **in parallel is always the same**, so that voltage across R = 3 V and voltage across lamp = 3 V.

- **The sum of the currents in the branches is equal to the total current outside the branch.**
  The current of 1.5 A splits at junction X to go through the resistor, R, and the lamp. These currents join at junction Y to 1.5 A before returning to the battery.

Figure 11.4

a $V = I \times R$

$\frac{V}{I} = R$

$\therefore \frac{3\,V}{0.5\,A} = R$

$6\,\Omega = R$

b i) $P = VI$

$P = 3\,V \times 1\,A$

$P = 3\,W$

ii) $P = VI$

$P = 3\,V \times 0.5\,A$

$P = 1.5\,W$

Example 2

A device is rated at 550 W, 110 V. Calculate the following:

a The current flowing in the device when a 110 V supply is connected across it.

b The resistance of the device.

c The energy consumption in 5 minutes.

a $P = VI$

$\frac{P}{V} = I$

$\frac{550\,W}{110\,V} = I$

$5\,A = I$

b $V = IR$

$\frac{V}{I} = R$

$\frac{110\,V}{5\,A} = R$

$22\,\Omega = R$

c $P = \frac{E}{t}$

$E = P \times t$

$E = 550\,W \times (5 \times 60\,s)$

$E = 165\,000\,J$ or $165\,kJ$

Note that we must convert time from minutes to the SI unit seconds.

Advantages of parallel connection of appliances in domestic wiring

- Appliances can **operate on the same voltage**. This is about 115 V in Trinidad and Barbados and 110 V in Jamaica. If connected in series, each appliance will only obtain a part of this voltage (see Figure 11.3).

- Appliances can be **controlled by individual switches** (See Figure 11.7).

- Appliances **can draw different currents** from the constant voltage (see Figure 11.4).

Fuses and domestic wiring

Fuses

*A **fuse** is a short wire that melts and breaks a circuit when the current exceeds a certain value.*

A fuse placed **in series** with a device can therefore **protect** it from excessive currents that could overheat the circuit and cause an electrical fire.

An appropriate fuse should melt ('blow') at a current slightly greater than that which the circuit takes under normal operation. This value is known as the **current rating** of the fuse.

Example

A vacuum cleaner rated at 1200 W is to be used on a 120 V supply.

a Calculate the amperage (current in A) that it takes.

b State, with reasons, which of the following fuses would be suitable to protect the device:

3 A, 5 A, 13 A, 20 A

c How much energy is consumed by the vacuum cleaner if it works for 30 minutes?

a $P = V I$ $\qquad \therefore I = \frac{P}{V} = \frac{1200\ W}{120\ V} = 10$ A

b The 13 A fuse is most suitable since its current rating is just above the normal current of 10 A. The lower rated fuses will 'blow' as soon as the device is switched on. The 20 A fuse can allow a much larger current to flow than is necessary, which can result in damage due to overheating and may produce an electrical fire.

c $P = \frac{E}{t}$ $\qquad \therefore E = P \times t = 1200\ W \times (30 \times 60\ s) = 2\,160\,000$ J

Three-core flex used in domestic wiring

Appliances are generally connected to the electrical mains supply by means of a flexible cable known as a **flex**. A **three-core flex** comprises three individually insulated wires known as the **live wire**, the **neutral wire** and the **earth wire**. These wires are connected to the electrical mains supply by means of a **three-pin plug**. Their conventional colour code is as follows:

Europe and UK: **live wire** – brown   **neutral wire** – blue   **earth wire** – green (or green/yellow striped)

Live and neutral wires

These wires are **connected to the terminals of the appliance** and carry the current under **normal operation.** No current then flows in the **earth wire** (see Figure 11.5).

Earth wire and short circuits

Figure 11.6 shows how the case of a device can become electrified if it is a conductor and is accidentally connected to the circuit by means of a piece of conducting material. If no earth wire was connected and someone then touches the case, they can receive an **electrical shock.**

As a safety precaution, many appliances are fitted with an **earth wire connected to the case** and with a **fuse connected in the live wire.**

As soon as the **short circuit** occurs, current flows in the **live and earth wires** instead of in **the live and neutral wires.** This current is higher as most of the resistance is bypassed, causing the fuse to 'blow' and the **circuit to break.**

- The circuit is therefore protected from damage by the high current.

- We are protected from the danger of an electrical shock.

If the case of the device is not a conductor, the earth wire is not usually required.

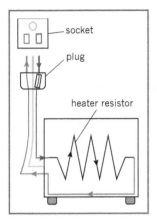

Figure 11.5 *Current flow during normal operation*

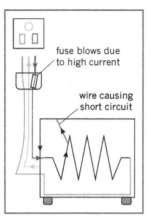

Figure 11.6 *Current flow during short circuit*

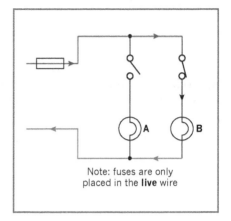

Note: fuses are only placed in the **live** wire

Figure 11.7 *Lighting circuit*

Thick wires prevent overloading of circuits

Thick wires have less resistance and therefore provide less chance of overheating, destroying insulation and causing electrical fires. The following devices use high currents and should have thick wires:

- **Heavy-duty appliances**, e.g. water heaters, refrigerators, electric stoves and washing machines.
- **Circuits connected to several appliances** that may be drawing currents at the same time.
- **Overhead cables** used for long-distance power transmission from power stations.

Wiring a three-pin plug

1. Cut off about **4 cm** of the flex casing.
2. Strip **1 cm** of the insulation from each of the three coloured cables using a wire stripper.
3. Tightly twist the strands of each cable.
4. The terminals on the plug should be marked L, N, E. One by one, twirl each cable in a **clockwise** direction around its correct terminal, ensuring that there are **no exposed strands** and then tighten the screw to hold it firmly.

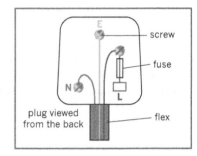

plug viewed from the back

Figure 11.8 *Wiring a three-pin plug*

Electrical energy consumption in our homes

We need to measure and control the amount of electricity we consume. Heating devices such as clothes irons, hair dryers and electric stoves can be particularly costly to operate.

Calculating the energy we use in kilowatt-hours

Energy consumption in the home is measured in **kilowatt-hours** instead of in **joules**.

$1 \, kWh = 1 \, kW \times 1 \, h = 1000 \, W \times (60 \times 60 \, s) = 3\,600\,000 \, J$

Example

Calculate the total weekly energy used in a home in kW h, given the following information about appliance use:

- One 1500 W kettle used for 30 minutes on a daily basis.
- Four 60 W lamps used for 5 hours each night.
- One 160 W refrigerator always in use.

Appliance	Power (kW)	Time (h)	Energy (kW h)
One kettle	1 × 1.5	7 × 0.5	5.25
Four lamps	4 × 0.060	7 × 5	8.40
One refrigerator	1 × 0.160	7 × 24	26.88
TOTAL			40.53

- Power must be represented in kW and time in h.
- The value for each appliance in column 4 is obtained by multiplying the values of columns 2 and 3.

Calculating electricity bills

Electric meters are usually read monthly and the energy used within the period is found by subtracting the previous reading from the current reading.

Analogue meters

- The hands on the dials rotate alternately **clockwise and anti-clockwise**.
- The dials are read from **left to right**.
- The digits chosen are those at which the hands point or have just passed.
- The reading shown in Figure 11.9 is 05358 kW h.

Figure 11.9 *Analogue electric meter*

Figure 11.10 *Digital electric meter*

Digital meters

- These are much easier to read, as shown in Figure 11.10.

Charges on our electricity bills

- **Energy charge:** This may be either on a fixed rate or a variable rate.
  - **Fixed** or **flat rate:** For example, $0.25 per kW h charged for all electricity used.
  - **Variable** or **block rate:** For example, the first 100 kW h may be charged at $0.80 per kW h, and further charges may only be at $0.50 per kW h.
- **Fixed charge:** A fixed charge may be applied **to cover administrative cost** and/or **meter rental**.
- **Fuel adjustment charge:** A charge per kW h **to cover fluctuating fuel costs**.

Example

On 28 July, a customer's meter reading was 25 224 kW h and on 24 August it was 25 375 kW h. Calculate the electricity bill for the period given the following information:

- Energy is charged on a **block rate**. The first 100 kW h is charged at a rate of $0.40 per kW h and any additional usage is charged at $0.30 per kW h.
- There is also a fuel **adjustment charge** of $0.008 per kW h and a **rental fee** of $12.00.

First find the energy used: 25 375 kW h – 25 224 kW h = 151 kW h

Then find the costs:

- Energy (variable rate) (first 100 kW h) $100 \text{ kW h} \times 0.40 \frac{\$}{\text{kW h}} = \$40.00$

  (Remaining 51 kW h) $51 \text{ kW h} \times 0.30 \frac{\$}{\text{kW h}} = \$15.30$

- Fuel adjustment $151 \text{ kW h} \times 0.008 \frac{\$}{\text{kW h}} = \$1.21$

- Rental $= \$12.00$

TOTAL CHARGE $68.51

========

Conserving electrical energy

Most of our electricity is obtained by **burning fossil fuels**, which introduce **harmful pollutants** to our environment. The supply of this non-renewable resource is becoming depleted at the same time as the demand for energy is increasing.

Ways to reduce energy consumption in the home

- Install high efficiency, certified appliances.
- Use energy-efficient lighting such as LED or fluorescent bulbs.
- Use **LED–LCD** (light-emitting diode–liquid crystal display) or **plasma** TV screens since they are more energy efficient than the old **CRT** (cathode ray tube) screens. LED–LCD is the most efficient.
- Install photovoltaic (PV) systems to produce electricity from sunlight.
- Install solar water heaters.
- Switch off electrical appliances when not in use.
- Cook with covered saucepans to prevent wastage of heat energy to the air.
- When boiling, adjust the heat source to the minimum required to maintain boiling.
- Wash only full loads in the washing machine.
- Use clothes lines or racks for drying instead of electric dryers.
- Avoid frequent opening of the refrigerator door and ensure that its rubber gasket is not worn.
- **Ensure that your home is designed for efficiency** so the air conditioner is needed less by using:
  - Double-glazed windows, especially in rooms that are air conditioned.
  - Proper insulation of roofs and ceilings.
  - Walls built with hollow blocks (air is a poor conductor).
  - Curtains and awnings or hoods at windows to block solar radiation.
  - Outer walls painted white to reflect radiation.

Energy wastage due to faulty electrical appliances

- Circuits can sometimes have current leakages due to the **corrosion** of parts.
- **Poor lubrication** of moving parts can lead to energy loss as heat due to friction.
- **Faulty thermostats** cause overheating of heaters and excessive cooling of refrigerators and air conditioners.

Filament lamps, fluorescent tubes and LED lamps

Filament (incandescent) lamps consist of a high resistance coil made of the metal tungsten kept in a sealed glass enclosure containing an inert gas or vacuum. An electrical current through the filament heats it to about 2500 °C, causing it to emit **heat** and a **yellowish light**.

Fluorescent tubes are sealed tubes containing mercury vapour at low pressure. Electrons, pulled by a voltage through the vapour, strike the mercury atoms causing them to release ultraviolet radiation (UV). A white phosphor coating on the inner wall of the tube absorbs the UV and emits a **bluish-white light** or a light similar to **daylight**.

Compact fluorescent lamps (CFLs) operate on the same principle as the fluorescent tubes and are now replacing the less efficient filament lamps, since they are designed to fit into the same fixtures.

Light-emitting diodes (LEDs) emit light when a current passes through them. They convert electrical energy very efficiently to light energy and can produce **coloured lighting, soft white lighting** or **'daylight-type'** lighting.

Table 11.5 *Comparison of lamps used for lighting*

	Filament lamp	Fluorescent tube	LED
Approximate lifetime/ hours	1000	7 000–15 000	50 000
Efficiency	Poor	High	Very high
Relative operational cost	Low	Lower	Lowest
Relative cost of device	Reasonable	Reasonable	Expensive
Shadow characteristic	Sharp, since the source is small	Diffused, since the source is extended	Sharp, since the source is small
Brightness control	Easily controlled by varying the voltage	Not as easily controlled	Not as easily controlled
Consistency of brightness	Consistent	Dims/flickers with age	Consistent
Durability	Easily broken	Easily broken	Withstands bounces
Energy wasted as heat	90% wasted	30% wasted	Very little wasted
Contains toxic mercury	No	Yes (harms the environment)	No

First aid methods for treating accidents

Accidents **during electricity use** can result in injuries ranging from minor to severe. The following describe how **first aid treatment** can be provided for some accidents.

Electrical shock

- **Switch off** the electrical supply if the victim is still connected to it. If that is not possible, then separate the victim from the supply using a non-conducting object, for example a dry wooden stick. Never touch the victim directly.
- Call for emergency medical help.
- If the victim's heart has stopped beating, or he or she has stopped breathing, **cardio-pulmonary resuscitation (CPR)** should be performed (see below).

Burns

Minor burns are those affecting only the outer layers of skin and which are less than 5 cm in diameter. They may be treated as follows:

- Remove any clothing that is not stuck to the burn.
- Wash hands with antibacterial soap.
- Soak the affected area in cool running water for several minutes. Do not use ice since this may damage the tissue even more.
- Clean the affected area with a mild soap and soothe with aloe vera.
- Cover with a sterile, non-adhesive gauze.
- Take a pain reliever such as ibuprofen, aspirin or acetaminophen.

More severe burns that have damaged underlying layers of skin, especially burns on the face or large areas of the skin, should be seen by a doctor.

Cardiac arrest and/or not breathing

CPR should be administered to a victim whose heart has stopped beating or who has stopped breathing. This consists of two procedures, **chest compressions** and **mouth-to-mouth resuscitation (rescue breathing)**. Depending on the situation, these procedures may be used **individually** or **together**.

If the victim's heart has stopped beating, **chest compressions** should be performed:

- Lay the victim on his or her back.
- Kneel next to the victim's shoulders, place the heel of one hand over the centre of the victim's chest and place the other hand over the first.
- Push firmly down on the chest so that it is compressed by approximately **5 cm**.
- Repeat compressions at a rate of about **100 per minute** until the heartbeat resumes or until medical help arrives.

If the victim is not breathing, **mouth-to-mouth resuscitation** should be performed:

- Lay the victim on his or her back and gently tilt the head backwards to open the airways by lifting the chin.
- Open the victim's mouth and remove any debris.
- Pinch the victim's nostrils to close them.
- Inhale, seal your lips over the victim's mouth and breathe out into the mouth for **1 second**.
- If the victim's chest rises, breathe into the mouth a second time.
- Continue rescue breathing by giving **one breath** every **5 seconds** until normal breathing resumes or until medical help arrives.

Both procedures are usually administered together. In such instances, **30 chest compressions** are alternated with **two rescue breaths** until the victim is breathing again or medical help arrives. If the victim's breathing resumes, he or she should be placed in the recovery position shown in Figure 11.12:

- Tilt the victim's head back and pull his or her chin forward to allow air flow.
- Point the victim's mouth downward to allow fluids to drain.
- Bend the victim's legs and lock his or her arms to prevent rolling.

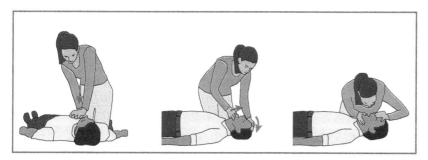

Figure 11.11 *Chest compressions and rescue breathing*

Figure 11.12 *Recovery position*

Methods used to extinguish fires

Fuel, oxygen and heat are all required to start and sustain a fire. They constitute the '**fire triangle**'. Removing **any one** or more of these will stop the fire.

Table 11.6 *Removing elements of the 'fire triangle'*

Element(s)	Method of removal
Heat	Adding a suitable material to absorb heat.
Oxygen	Covering with a fire blanket, sand or other inert substance to separate oxygen from the burning material.
Oxygen and heat	Spraying with cold carbon dioxide or other suitable chemical agents to separate the material from oxygen and remove heat.
Fuel	Turning off the flammable gas supply.

Figure 11.13 *Fire triangle*

A **fire extinguisher** is typically a **hand-held** vessel containing an **agent under pressure** which can be discharged to extinguish **small fires**. Table 11.7 indicates the various agents used depending on the type of fire. Larger fires, e.g. bush fires, can be extinguished by water hoses connected to a large reservoir; if these fires are difficult to reach, aircraft can drop water or chemical agents onto them.

Table 11.7 *Types of fires and methods used to extinguish them*

Type of fire	Method(s) of extinguishing	Additional information
Bush fires, paper, cloth, plastics	Drench with water, or cover with foam or dry powder.	• **Removes heat.** Water and foam are very effective. • Carbon dioxide is ineffective in pushing away the oxygen if there is **wind** or the fire is **large**.
Flammable liquids (oils, paints, spirits)	Cover with carbon dioxide, foam, sand or dry powder.	• **Removes oxygen and some heat.** • Water cannot be used since it will instantly **boil** and **splatter**, spreading the fire.
Flammable gases	Turn off gas supply.	• **Removes fuel.** • Gases are difficult to smother since they readily **diffuse**.
Electrical fires	Cover with carbon dioxide or dry powder.	• **Removes oxygen and some heat.** • Water cannot be used since this can result in **electrocution**.

Type of fire	Method(s) of extinguishing	Additional information
Burning metals	Cover with dry powder.	• **Removes oxygen and some heat.** • Other methods do not smother the metal effectively. • Water is not used since it may **react** with the metal.
Cooking oils, fats and greases	Cover with wet chemical agent or fire blanket.	• **Removes oxygen and some heat.** • A wet chemical agent is the **only type** that can **thoroughly** smother the oil, but a fire blanket may also be useful.

Hazards of careless handling of appliances and equipment

Appliances and equipment should always be handled with **care** in order to **avoid harm** to humans and other organisms, as well as to **protect** other aspects of the natural and built environment.

Table 11.8 *Hazards of careless handling of appliances and equipment*

Hazard	Reason for danger	Prevention
Faulty electrical equipment	Loose electrical contacts or damaged power cords having exposed conducting wire can produce short circuits resulting in **overheating, electrical fires** and **electrocution.**	Always maintain electrical equipment using **qualified technicians**.
Overloading electrical outlets by connecting too many appliances	Each appliance draws its own current. **Overheating** and **electrical fires** can occur if the total current is larger than that allowed for the wire.	Do not connect several appliances in the same outlet circuit.
Handling electrical equipment with wet hands or in wet areas	Wet environments provide an **easy conducting path** for high currents that can lead to **death by electrocution.**	Wear **dry, electrically insulated** boots and gloves.
Exposed high voltage power lines	These voltages will cause **death by electrocution** if they discharge current through a person.	**Stay away** from high voltage power lines.
Radiation from power lines and electrical equipment such as cell phones, radios, televisions, computers and microwave ovens	This may be **harmful to our body systems** including the nervous, cardiovascular, hormonal, immune and reproductive systems.	**Do not remain close** to such equipment for **extended periods**.
Radiation from radioactive materials and X-ray machines	Excessive exposure to this type of radiation can **damage body cells** and lead to the **development of cancer.**	Wear **lead-lined coats** to block the radiation.
Faulty gas supplies	Combustible gases are **harmful if inhaled** and can **cause fires** if they make contact with very hot surfaces or flames.	Always **maintain** gas hoses and associated equipment.
Careless handling of hot kitchen appliances and equipment	Contact with hot pots and pans can result in severe **burns**; contact with hot liquids or steam can produce severe **scalds**.	Carefully manoeuvre hot kitchenware by their handles, using insulated mittens.
Overheating of cooking oils	Excessive heating can ignite the oil, resulting in **violent flames.**	Never leave heated cooking oil unattended.

Table 11.9 *Applications of protective gear in work and in sport*

Gear	Protection	Examples of users
Gloves	• Thick, padded, heavy duty leather gloves protect the hands from being **cut** and **bruised**.	• Construction workers
	• Gloves made of **sterile** latex, nitrile rubber, PVC or neoprene protect from **germs** and **viruses**.	• doctors, nurses, chemists
	• Anti-corrosive gloves protect the hands from **harmful chemicals**.	• farmers, gardeners
	• Heat insulating gloves protect the hands from **hot objects**.	• cooks
Boots	• Heavy duty leather boots, usually with a steel cover over the front, protect the feet from being **cut** or **bruised**.	• Construction workers, farmers, gardeners
	• Waterproof and anticorrosive rubber boots protect against **dangerously reactive chemicals** and some **pathogens**.	• firemen
	• Light duty sports boots protect the feet from being **bruised**.	• cricketers, footballers
Goggles	• Protect the eyes from airborne **particles**, splashing **chemicals** or **water**.	• Swimmers, chemists, gardeners
	• Dark goggles or visors protect the eyes from **ultraviolet radiation**.	• welders
Earmuffs	• Protect the ears from **loud noises** and **low temperatures**.	• Construction workers, skiers, airport workers
Helmets	• Protect the head from **cuts**, **bruises**, and **skull and brain damage** by absorbing shock and preventing penetration.	• Construction workers, cyclists, climbers
	• Some have visors and cages to protect the face from **airborne objects**.	• cricketers
Coats/aprons	• Protect against **caustic chemicals** or **hot materials** in laboratories, industrial sites and kitchens.	• Chemists, factory workers, cooks
Respirators	• **Filter particles** such as dust and smoke from the air.	• Firemen
	• Some can also **remove harmful gases**.	• painters, fumigators
	• Some **provide clean air** for environments with poor or limited air.	• astronauts
Chest guards	• Protect against obtaining **broken bones** and **damaged organs**.	• Racing drivers
Back braces	• Support and protect the **spine** when lifting **heavy objects**.	• Construction workers, dock workers
Groin boxes	• Protect the groin from the impact of **fast-moving cricket balls**.	• Cricketers
Sports pads	• Protect the elbows, knees and shins from the impact of **collisions**.	• Cricketers, footballers

Revision questions

1. Distinguish between electrical conductors and electrical insulators.

2. Draw a circuit diagram containing a switch, a cell, a filament lamp, a variable resistor, an ammeter to measure the current through the lamp and a voltmeter to measure the voltage across the lamp. The lamp and variable resistor are to be connected in series.

3. A voltage of 6 V exists across a device of resistance 3 Ω. Determine:

   a the current   **b** the power (wattage) of the device

   c the energy converted in 2 minutes.

4. **a** State the colours used for the live, neutral and earth wires of a conventional wiring system.

   b **i** Describe what can happen when a circuit is overloaded.
   ii What change can be made to the wires of the circuit to prevent this problem?
   iii Why does the current increase and cause the fuse to blow during a short circuit?

5. A 10 kW electric stove is used for 30 minutes each day and four 60 W lamps are used for 5 hours each night. Calculate the total weekly energy used by these appliances in kW h.

6. On 30 March, an electricity meter reading was 15 237 kW h and on 30 April, it was 15 397 kW h. Electricity is charged at $0.50 per kW h, with a fixed charge of $10. Calculate the electricity bill for the period.

7. **a** State THREE ways of reducing energy consumption in the home.

   b Of the incandescent, fluorescent and LED types of lighting, state which:
   i has the longest life.
   ii is most efficient.
   iii contains toxic mercury.
   iv is most durable.
   v has the lowest operational cost.
   vi has an easily controlled brightness capability.

   c Contrast the shadows produced by a 'small (point)' light source and a 'long tube' light source.

8. State the first aid steps necessary in dealing with a victim who:

   a has a minor burn   **b** has stopped breathing

9. Suggest a suitable extinguisher to extinguish fires involving the following:

   a gasoline   **b** cooking oil

   c a wooden shed   **d** electricity

10. Suggest, with reasons, TWO types of protective gear for each of the following persons:

    a a welder   **b** a construction worker

    c a fumigator   **d** a cricketer

12 Machines and movement

*A **machine** is a device that makes doing work (converting energy) easier.*

Some examples of simple machines are levers, inclined planes and pulleys.

Some simple machines

In discussing machines, we generally use the terms **load** and **effort**.

* **Load** is the force to be overcome without the use of the machine (usually the weight of an object).
* **Effort** is the force required when using the machine.

Table 12.1 *Some simple machines*

Levers	Levers each consist of a rigid beam or rod that can rotate on a fixed pivot. An effort applied at one point along the beam or rod can move a load from some other point along it. Figures 12.1 through 12.5 show the various classes into which levers may be divided, with reference to practical levers commonly encountered and levers of the mammalian skeleton.	
Inclined planes	Inclined planes each have a flat, sloping surface along which an object can be pushed or pulled to a higher level, for example from the road into the back of a truck. The longer the slope, the more gradual it is, and the easier it becomes to force the object up the incline.	
Pulleys	Pulleys each consist of a wheel on an axle that carries a rope (chain or belt) wrapped around its circumference. An effort applied to one end of the rope (chain or belt) creates a tension that is transmitted throughout its length and moves an attached load. Pulleys are particularly useful in raising loads through large distances. Systems of several pulleys can be arranged to lift very heavy loads, as shown in Figure 12.7.	

Types of levers

Levers may be divided into three classes dependent on the relative positions of the pivot and the points of application of the effort and load.

In each case shown on the next page, an **effort** (*E*) is balancing a **load** (*L*) and the lever is **pivoted** at **P**.

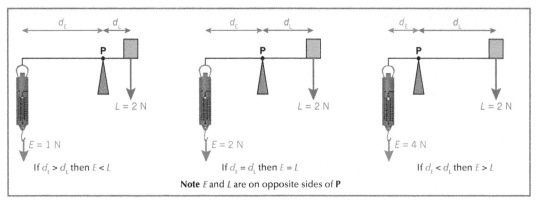

Figure 12.1 *Class 1 lever*

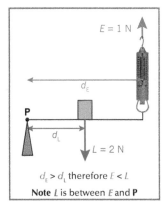

Figure 12.2 *Class 2 lever*

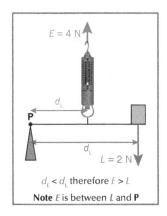

Figure 12.3 *Class 3 lever*

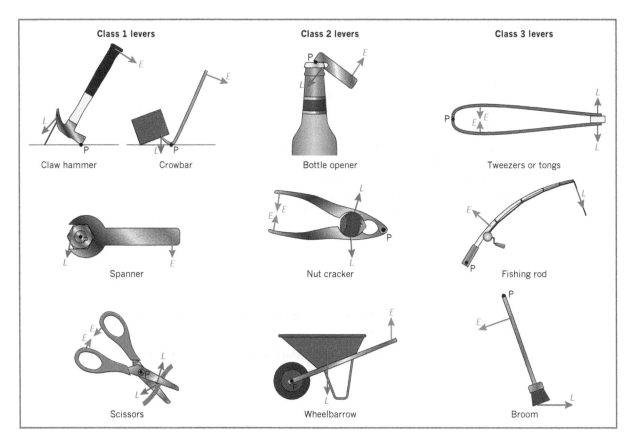

Figure 12.4 *Examples of practical levers*

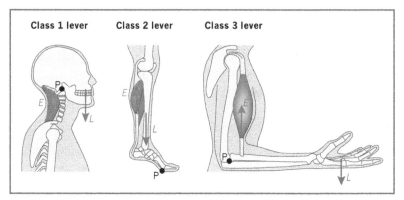

Figure 12.5 *Levers in the mammalian skeleton*

Mechanical advantage and energy conversion

mechanical advantage (MA) $= \frac{\text{load}}{\text{effort}}$

Work and energy were discussed in Chapter 10. A given amount of work or energy can be the result of different combinations of a force and the distance through which that force moves an object.

For example: 40 J = 20 N × 2 m or 40 J = 2 N × 20 m.

So, a **smaller force** can convert the same energy over a **larger distance**. Machines simply alter the force and distance necessary to do work or convert energy.

Efficiency

- **Useful energy output** is the energy converted in **moving the load without using the machine.**
- **Energy input** is the energy converted **by the effort using the machine.**

The useful energy output from a machine is always less than the energy input, since some energy is always wasted in overcoming forces other than the load. The efficiency, expressed as a percentage, is calculated as follows:

efficiency $= \frac{\text{useful energy output}}{\text{energy input}} \times 100\%$

Force and distance multipliers

- **A force multiplier** is a machine that alters the forces so that the **effort is smaller** than the load.
- **A distance multiplier** is a machine in which the **distance moved by the effort is smaller** than the distance moved by the load (the **effort is then greater** than the load).
  - **Class 2 levers** are always **force multipliers.**
  - **Class 3 levers** are always **distance multipliers.**

Example 1

Jide uses a bar as a lever in order to lift a stone of weight 500 N through a distance of 12 cm. He exerts an effort of 100 N through a distance of 80 cm. Determine the following:

a The useful energy converted in lifting the load.

b The energy converted by the effort using the machine.

c The mechanical advantage.

a Useful energy converted in lifting the load = load × distance moved by load

$$= 500 \text{ N} \times 0.12 \text{ m} = 60 \text{ J}$$

b Energy converted by the effort using the machine = effort × distance moved by effort

$$= 100 \text{ N} \times 0.80 \text{ m} = 80 \text{ J}$$

c Mechanical advantage $= \dfrac{\text{load}}{\text{effort}} = \dfrac{500 \text{ N}}{100 \text{ N}} = 5$

Example 2

Figure 12.6 shows a block of weight 20 N being raised to a height of 3 m using an inclined plane. The block is pushed by an effort of 12 N up the incline.

a Calculate the following:

  i The energy converted if the block was lifted vertically.

  ii The energy converted by the effort in using the machine.

b Which is less, the useful work output or the work input?

c How does the user benefit by using such a ramp?

d Is this machine a force or distance multiplier?

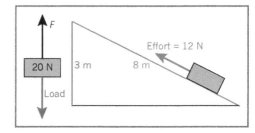

Figure 12.6

a **i** useful energy output = load × distance moved by load

$$= 20 \text{ N} \times 3 \text{ m} = 60 \text{ J} \text{ (Note that the force and distance are parallel.)}$$

  ii energy input = effort × distance moved by effort

$$= 12 \text{ N} \times 8 \text{ m} = 96 \text{ J} \text{ (Note that the force and distance are parallel.)}$$

b The useful work output is less. (You can never get out more than you put in!)

c The user benefits by using the ramp since, although the work input is greater than the work output (96 J > 60 J), the force of the **effort** needed is less than the force of the **load** (**weight**).

d This machine is a force multiplier since the effort of 12 N raises a larger load of 20 N.

A closer look at pulleys

- An **effort** applied to the string sets up an **equal tension** within it that **raises the load**.
- Figure 12.7 shows that the sum of the tensions **raising the load** is equal to the load; therefore the greater the number of strings raising the load, the smaller the required effort.
- A **system** of two or more pulleys enables a small effort moved through a long distance to raise a heavier load over a shorter distance.

The following pulleys are **assumed** to be completely efficient for ease of calculations, that is no work needs to be done against friction or any resistance. If they were not, the MA would be less. In a practical system, the effort required in each case will be more due to the inefficiencies discussed in Table 12.2.

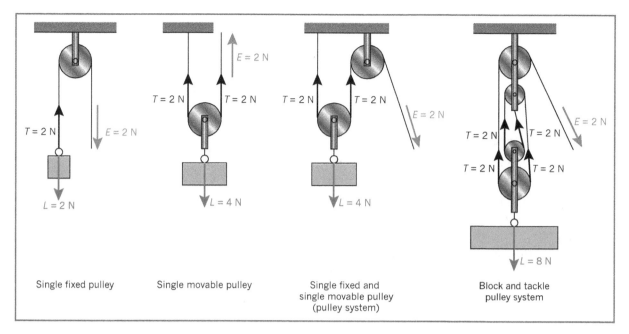

Figure 12.7 *Single pulleys and pulley systems*

Single fixed pulley

The load is equal to the effort and

$$MA = \frac{L}{E} = \frac{2\,N}{2\,N} = 1$$

There are two reasons why we would use this pulley although the effort is not less than the load.

1. The user may use his body weight to provide part of the effort since he is **pulling downwards.**

2. Loads may be raised to great heights without the user having to move through those heights.

Single movable pulley

The load is twice the effort and

$$MA = \frac{L}{E} = \frac{4\,N}{2\,N} = 2$$

Single movable and single fixed pulley system

This is like the single movable pulley except that the user can stand on the ground and pull downwards.

The load is twice the effort and

$$MA = \frac{L}{E} = \frac{4\,N}{2\,N} = 2$$

Fixed and movable pulleys – block and tackle pulley system

In the block and tackle of Figure 12.7, **the load is four times the effort** and

$$MA = \frac{L}{E} = \frac{8\,N}{2\,N} = 4$$

Hydraulic machines

A **small effort** (*E*) is applied at the narrow cylinder through a **large distance** (E_d). This forces the **large load** (*L*) to rise through a **small distance** (L_d) in the other cylinder. The **hydraulic press** in Figure 12.8 is assumed completely efficient and so the energy input is equal to the energy output. In a practical system, the effort needed will be more than 8 N due to the inefficiencies discussed in Table 12.2.

$E \times E_d = L \times L_d$ 8 N × 10 cm = 80 N × 1 cm

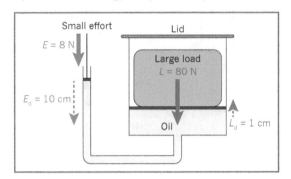

- Materials placed in the compartment above the larger piston can be compressed.

- By removing the lid, the machine becomes a **hydraulic jack** such as that used to lift vehicles.

- **Car brakes** work in a similar way. The brake pedal creates an effort at a narrow piston and this creates a greater force at a larger piston onto the wheel of the car.

Figure 12.8 *Hydraulic press or jack*

Gears and cogged wheels

Figure 12.9 shows connected cogged wheels having identically sized and spaced teeth. The wheel with the lesser number of teeth will spin faster than the other.

A **bicycle** regulates its gears in this way. The pedals produce a rotation in the larger cogged wheel, which causes rotation of the back wheel connected to the smaller cogged wheel. Some **lawnmowers** also use cogged wheels to drive their rotating blades.

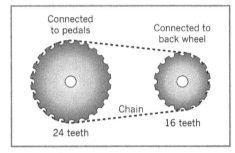

From the diagram, for every **1 revolution** of the pedals, the back wheel makes **1.5 rotations**.

Figure 12.9 *Gears and cogged wheels*

(gear ratio = $\frac{24}{16}$ = 1.5).

By switching between several cogged wheels, different gear ratios are produced.

Screws

An effort applied to the head of a screw can cause the screw to revolve about its axis and be driven forward into a material such as wood. The resistance of the wood acts as the load. Each revolution of the screw causes it to advance by its **pitch** (the distance between successive threads on its shaft). The smaller the pitch of the screw, the smaller is the effort required to advance it.

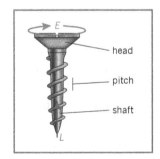

Figure 12.10 *Screw*

Inefficiencies of machines and ways to overcome them

Table 12.2 *Inefficiencies of machines and ways to overcome them*

Factors causing inefficiency of machines	Overcoming the inefficiency
Friction between moving parts wastes energy in bearings, joints, gear wheels, axles of pulleys, pistons and cylinders.	**Lubricating oil** reduces friction. A **fine powder** is often used to reduce friction on inclined planes.
Corrosion leads to instability and increased friction.	Rust-proofing of iron or steel parts using special paints and greases prevents corrosion.
The weight of the lower rising block of a pulley system and the **weight of the plate** supporting the load in a hydraulic press, result in additional energy being required to raise the load.	Pulleys and their harnesses, as well as any equipment being raised with the load, should be made of a **strong, light material** such as aluminium.

Revision questions

1 Name the class of each of the following levers:

  a a wheelbarrow   **b** tweezers   **c** scissors

2 What makes a machine:

  a a force multiplier?   **b** a distance multiplier?

3 **a** Curwin raises a load of 200 N using the pulley system shown in Figure 1. Determine:

    i The minimum effort *E* required and the forces *X* and *Y* at this time.

    ii The mechanical advantage relating to this minimum effort.

  b How will the mechanical advantage be affected if the machine becomes less efficient?

  c State TWO factors that can cause this pulley system to be inefficient.

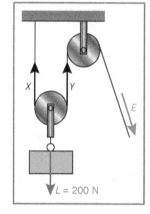

Figure 1

4 Figure 2 shows a machine where an effort of 20 N turns a handle to raise a load of 100 N. It is assumed that the machine is very well oiled and is completely efficient.

  a Through what height will the load be raised if the effort moves through 2 m?

  b How would using a longer handle affect the effort required?

5 Cogged wheels of a bicycle, A of 60 teeth and B of 15 teeth, are connected by means of a chain. How many times will B rotate if A makes 2 rotations?

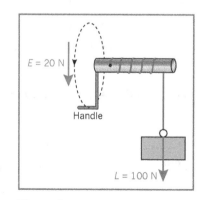

Figure 2

13 Metals and non-metals

Chemical elements can be classified as **metals** or **non-metals**, and **materials** used in everyday life can be classified as **metallic** or **non-metallic materials** based on their properties. Each class of materials has its own unique properties which make the materials suitable for different uses.

Properties and uses of metals

Most **metals** have the following common **physical properties**:

- They have **high melting points.**
- They are **good conductors** of electricity and heat.
- They are **malleable**, meaning that they can be hammered into different shapes, and **ductile**, meaning that they can be drawn out into wires.
- They have **high tensile strengths**, meaning that they are strong and do not break easily under tension.
- They are **shiny** in appearance or can be **polished** to make them shiny.
- They have **high densities.**
- They are **sonorous**, meaning that they make a ringing sound when hit.

Metals have a variety of **uses** because of their specific **properties**.

Table 13.1 *Properties and uses of some important metals*

Metals	Specific properties making the metal suitable for its uses	Uses
Aluminium	• Good conductor of electricity and heat • Relatively low density • Very malleable and ductile • Very shiny and reflective • Resistant to corrosion	To make overhead electrical cables, window frames, cooking utensils, cans to store drinks and foil for cooking (see pages 151–152). **Alloys** made mainly of aluminium are used to construct aircraft.
Copper	• Good conductor of electricity and heat • Very malleable and ductile • Very resistant to corrosion	To make electrical wires, bases of saucepans and water pipes.
Iron	• High tensile strength • Very malleable and ductile • Easily welded	To make ornamental iron work. **Steel**, an **alloy** made mainly of iron, is used to construct buildings, bridges, oil rigs, ships, trains and motor vehicles, and to make wire, nails, cutting tools, drill bits and many household items (see page 152).
Zinc and **tin**	• Resistant to corrosion	To coat iron and steel items to prevent rusting; for e.g. zinc is used to coat nails and roofing sheets, and tin is used to coat 'tin cans' (see page 153).
Silver and **gold**	• Very shiny • Very malleable and ductile • Very resistant to corrosion	To make jewellery and medals. Silver is also used to make cutlery and ornaments. Gold may also be used in dentistry to make crowns and fillings.

Properties and uses of non-metallic materials

Non-metallic materials include natural materials such as wood and rubber, and man-made materials such as plastics, glass, ceramics and carbon fibre. These materials have variable **physical properties**:

- They are all **poor conductors** of electricity and heat, i.e. they are **insulators**.
- Some are **flexible** whilst others are **brittle**.
- Some have **low tensile strengths** whilst others are **strong**.
- Most are **dull** in appearance.

Non-metallic materials have a great many **uses**.

Wood

Wood is a hard, fibrous material obtained from the trunks and branches of trees. It can be split fairly easily along its grain, but is hard to cut across its grain. Wood can be divided into two kinds: **hardwood**, e.g. mahogany and purple heart, and **softwood**, e.g. pine and cedar. Most hardwoods are hard, strong, tough and durable, whereas most softwoods are softer, easier to work with and not as durable.

Wood is **used** to build houses and boats, and to make furniture, flooring, cupboards, window frames, doors, musical instruments, toys, tool handles and handles for saucepans because it is an insulator.

Plastics

Plastics are made using chemicals obtained from petroleum (crude oil), and are composed of very large organic molecules known as **polymers**. They include polyethene (polyethylene), polystyrene, polyvinyl chloride (PVC), polyesters and nylon. Plastics have many uses because their properties make them **superior** to many other materials; however, they can have serious **harmful** effects on the environment.

Plastics are **used** to make bottles for drinks and cleaning products, food containers, shopping and garbage bags, toys, handles on saucepans, packaging materials, insulation for electrical wires, water pipes, guttering, window frames, clothing, boat sails, carpets, ropes, fishing lines and furniture.

Table 13.2 *Advantages and disadvantages of using plastics*

Advantages of plastics	Disadvantages of plastics
• They are **durable**, meaning they are resistant to damage, chemicals and decay.	• They are made from a **non-renewable resource**, petroleum. Their manufacture is contributing to the depletion of petroleum worldwide.
• They are easily **moulded** into many different shapes.	• Most plastics are **non-biodegradable**. When disposed of, they build up in the environment causing pollution of land and water.
• They are **light** in weight, but **strong**.	
• They can be made to be **rigid** or **flexible**.	• They are directly harmful to **aquatic organisms**, e.g. sea turtles, due to ingestion, entanglement and suffocation.
• They are good thermal and electrical **insulators**.	• Various **toxic chemicals** are released into the environment during their manufacture, and some continue to be released from plastic items during their use and when disposed of.
• They can easily be **welded** or **joined**.	
• They can easily be spun into **fibres** because their molecules are extremely long.	• Many plastics are **flammable**, therefore they pose fire hazards.
• They are easily **dyed** different colours.	• When burnt, plastics produce **dense smoke** and **poisonous gases**, which can lead to air pollution.

Figure 13.1 *Plastics in the environment*

Recycling plastic items should help to **reduce** the harmful effects on the environment of their extensive use (see page 100).

Materials used in sporting equipment

Materials used in making **sporting equipment** have evolved from natural raw materials such as wood, gut and rubber to high-technology materials such as **metals**, **plastics**, **ceramics** and **composites** which are made of two or more materials with different properties. Using these new materials enhances performance. These materials include:

- **Fibre-reinforced composites** which are made of fibres embedded in plastic, e.g. carbon fibre composite and fibreglass (glass-reinforced plastic). They are durable, lightweight, strong, stiff, have good shock absorption and allow freedom of design. **Carbon fibre composite** is used to make tennis rackets, bicycle frames, golf clubs, sailboat masts, hockey sticks and fishing rods. **Fibreglass** is used to make surf boards, kayaks, pole vaulting poles and the hulls of sailing dinghies.

- **Kevlar** which is a plastic of extremely **high tensile strength.** It is also lightweight, tough, durable, and abrasion and cut resistant. It is used to make racing boat sails, tennis racket strings, canoe hulls, skis and protective clothing used in motor sports, fencing and speed skating.

Reactivity of metals

Some metals react **vigorously**, even violently with other chemical substances such as **acids**, **oxygen** and **water**, whilst others are relatively **unreactive**. Potassium, sodium, calcium and magnesium are the most reactive whilst aluminium, zinc, iron and tin are less reactive, and copper and silver are relatively unreactive.

Reactions of metals with dilute acids

When a metal reacts with dilute hydrochloric or sulfuric acid, it forms a **salt** and **hydrogen**:

$$\text{metal} \; + \; \text{acid} \; \longrightarrow \; \text{salt} \; + \; \text{hydrogen}$$

e.g. aluminium + hydrochloric acid $\longrightarrow$ aluminium chloride + hydrogen

iron + sulfuric acid $\longrightarrow$ iron sulfate + hydrogen

Salts formed from hydrochloric acid are called **chlorides** and salts formed from sulfuric acid are called **sulfates**.

Reactions of metals with oxygen

When a metal reacts with oxygen, it forms a **metal oxide**:

$$\text{metal} \; + \; \text{oxygen} \; \longrightarrow \; \text{metal oxide}$$

e.g. zinc + oxygen $\longrightarrow$ zinc oxide

Reactions of metals with water as steam

When a metal reacts with **water** in the form of **steam**, it forms a **metal oxide** and **hydrogen**:

$$\text{metal} \; + \; \text{steam} \; \longrightarrow \; \text{metal oxide} \; + \; \text{hydrogen}$$

e.g. tin + steam $\longrightarrow$ tin oxide + hydrogen

Table 13.3 *Summary of reactions of some specific metals with dilute acids, oxygen in air and water*

Metal	Description of the reaction with dilute acids	Description of the reaction when the metal is heated in air	Description of the reaction with water
Aluminium (Al)	Reacts vigorously.	Burn when heated strongly, especially if powdered.	Do not react with cold or hot water.
Zinc (Zn)	Reacts fairly vigorously.		
Iron (Fe)	Reacts slowly.	Burn when powdered and heated strongly.	React with steam.
Tin (Sn)	Reacts very slowly.		
Copper (Cu)	Do not react with dilute acids.	Does not burn when heated but forms an oxide coating if heated very strongly.	Do not react with water or steam.
Silver (Ag)		Does not react, even when heated very strongly.	

Aluminium cooking and canning utensils

The surface of any item made of aluminium is coated in a thin layer of **aluminium oxide** which is relatively **unreactive**. This layer sticks to the metal surface and protects it from corrosion.

Using cooking and canning utensils made of aluminium has some **advantages** and some **disadvantages**.

Table 13.4 *Advantages and disadvantages of using cooking and canning utensils made of aluminium*

Advantages	Disadvantages
• The utensils are **resistant to corrosion** due to their aluminium oxide coating.	• The utensils can be **scratched** or **dented** easily, and they **warp** easily because aluminium is a soft metal.
• The utensils are **light in weight** because aluminium has a low density.	• The utensils can be **stained** easily, especially if cooking very acidic foods, such as tomatoes or citrus fruits.
• The utensils are very **good conductors** of heat.	• If the utensils are used to cook or store foods that are very acidic, the acid may **react** with the aluminium oxide coating, which reduces its effectiveness and causes aluminium ions to enter the food. Aluminium has been implicated in increasing a person's risk of developing **Alzheimer's disease**.
• The utensils can be polished to have a **shiny**, attractive appearance.	

The thickness of the aluminium oxide layer on items such as cooking and canning utensils can be increased by a process called **anodising**, which reduces or overcomes the disadvantages.

Alloys in the home and workplace

Alloys are mixtures of two or more metals, though a few also contain non-metals. They are produced to **improve** or **modify** the properties of metals. Alloys are usually **harder**, **stronger** and more **resistant to corrosion** than the pure metals.

Table 13.5 *Alloys commonly found in the home and workplace*

Alloy	Composition	Properties	Uses
Steel	**Iron** alloyed with up to 1.5% **carbon**.	Hard, strong, malleable and ductile.	To make tools, nails, door hinges, gates, fences and cookware.
Stainless steel	Usually about 70% **iron** alloyed with 20% **chromium** and 10% **nickel**.	Hard, strong, malleable, ductile and extremely resistant to corrosion. Has a very shiny, attractive appearance.	To make cutlery, kitchen equipment and appliances, sinks and surgical equipment.
Brass	**Copper** alloyed with up to about 45% **zinc**.	Malleable, ductile, strong and resistant to corrosion. Has an attractive golden yellow colour.	To make door and window fittings, taps, lamp fittings, nuts and bolts, ornaments and musical instruments.
Soft solder	About 60% **tin** alloyed with 40% **lead**.	Has a low melting point, so melts easily when joining metals.	To join metal items together, e.g. electrical wires and water pipes.

Electroplating

Electroplating is the process that uses an electric current to **coat** a metal object with a thin layer of another metal. It is used to **protect** the original metal object from corrosion, to make it look more **attractive** or to make an inexpensive object appear more **valuable**. **Silver**, **nickel** or **chromium** are often used to plate objects made of **steel**, which corrodes (rusts) easily but is relatively inexpensive.

Figure 13.2 *Chrome-plated wheel rims*

Tarnishing, corrosion and rusting

Tarnishing (dry corrosion)

A metal **tarnishes** when its freshly polished surface reacts with **oxygen** in the air. The oxygen **oxidises** the metal, forming a thin layer of the **metal oxide** on its surface, also known as **tarnish**. This layer causes the metal to become **dull** and sometimes **discoloured**, and it usually adheres (sticks) to the surface and **protects** the rest of the metal from reacting. Aluminium, zinc, iron, tin, copper and silver all tarnish; however, silver tarnishes by its surface reacting with any hydrogen sulfide or sulfur dioxide in the air, forming black **silver sulfide**.

Corrosion and rusting

Corrosion takes place when the surface of a metal is gradually worn away by reacting with **chemicals** in the environment, mainly **oxygen** and **water vapour (moisture)** from the air. The layer of tarnish on a metal helps to make most metals resistant to corrosion.

When **iron** and **steel** objects are exposed to **both** oxygen and water they immediately begin to corrode, forming **hydrated iron oxide**, commonly known as **rust**:

$$\text{iron} \ + \ \text{oxygen} \ + \ \text{water} \longrightarrow \text{hydrated iron oxide}$$

Rust does not stick to the metal as tarnish does, instead it **flakes off**. This exposes fresh iron to the environment, which in turn rusts and the rust flakes off. This process continues causing the iron to gradually wear away. The corrosion of iron and steel in this way is known as **rusting**.

Factors affecting the rate of rusting

The **rate** at which iron and steel rusts is affected by:

* **Temperature:** the higher the atmospheric temperature, the faster rusting occurs.
* **Humidity:** the more water vapour in the air, the faster rusting occurs.
* **Salts:** any salts such as sodium chloride dissolved in moisture in the air speed up rusting. Iron and steel fixtures in homes located near the **sea** rust at a faster rate than normal.
* **Pollutants:** certain pollutants in the atmosphere speed up rusting, e.g. sulfur dioxide and carbon dioxide speed it up because of their acidic nature. Iron and steel fixtures in homes near to **industrial plants**, especially those that burn fossil fuels, rust faster than normal.

Prevention of rusting

Iron and **steel** objects can be protected against rusting in various ways. Most of these methods aim to prevent **air** and **water** from coming into contact with the object.

* **Coating** the object with **paint, rubber, plastic, grease** or **oil**.
* **Coating** the object with a thin layer of **zinc**, a process known as **galvanising**. This is often used to protect nails and roofing sheets. An adherent layer of **zinc oxide** forms on the zinc, which protects it against corrosion. If damaged, the zinc is oxidised in preference to the iron because zinc is more reactive. Zinc is said to provide **sacrificial protection**.
* **Plating** (coating) the object with an unreactive metal or a less reactive metal. For example, **tin** can be used to plate 'tin cans' made of steel, or the objects can be **electroplated** with **silver, nickel** or **chromium**. However, if the coating is damaged, the iron and steel rust because iron is more reactive than any of these other metals.

Revision questions

1. Suggest TWO reasons for EACH of the following:
   a. Aluminium is used to make cans to store drinks.
   b. Copper is used to make electrical wires.
   c. Gold is used to make jewellery.

2. Give THREE reasons why plastics are used so extensively in today's world and THREE harmful effects that plastics can have on the environment

3. Discuss the use of non-metallic materials in sporting equipment.

4. Write a word equation to summarise EACH of the following reactions:
   a. Iron reacting with hydrochloric acid.
   b. The reaction between aluminium and steam.
   c. Tin reacting with oxygen.

5. Suggest TWO reasons why aluminium is used to make cooking utensils and TWO disadvantages associated with its use.

6. a. What is an alloy?
   b. Why are alloys often used in place of the pure metals?

7. Identify FOUR factors that can affect the rate at which an iron gate rusts and outline the effect of EACH.

8. Explain TWO different methods that can be used to prevent iron from rusting.

14 Acids, bases and mixtures

Acids and **bases** have opposite properties and they react with each other to form a **salt**. **Mixtures** are formed when two or more chemical substances are physically combined. Many of the chemicals found around our homes can be classified as acids, bases or salts, and most of them are mixtures.

Common household chemicals

Household chemicals are non-food chemicals that are commonly found and used in and around the home. They include **cleaning** products, **pest control** products and general **hygiene** products.

Table 14.1 *Some common household chemicals*

Household name	Chemical name of the main chemical component	Uses
Household bleach	Sodium hypochlorite	See page 161.
Oxygen bleach	Sodium percarbonate	See page 161.
Window cleaner	Ammonia and propanol	To clean glass windows and mirrors.
Oven cleaner	Sodium hydroxide	To clean the grease off the insides of ovens.
Limescale remover	Phosphoric or citric acid	See page 161.
Scouring powder	Powdered limestone, feldspar or silica	See page 163.
Toilet bowl cleaner	Hydrochloric or citric acid	To remove urine, mineral deposits and stains from toilet bowls.
Detergent	Sodium dodecyl sulfate	See page 162.
Caustic soda or lye	Sodium hydroxide	As a degreaser to remove grease, oils and fats. To unblock and clean drains.
Washing soda	Sodium carbonate	To soften hard water (see pages 163–164).
Bicarbonate of soda or baking soda	Sodium hydrogencarbonate	To absorb odours from the inside of refrigerators, whiten teeth and treat indigestion.
Vinegar	Ethanoic (acetic) acid	See page 161.
Epsom salt	Magnesium sulfate	As a laxative. Added to bath water to reduce inflammation and relieve stress.

A number of these chemicals are potentially harmful and they carry **safety symbols** to warn their users about their potential dangers.

corrosive   toxic   flammable   explosive

Figure 14.1 *Some important safety symbols*

Water

Water is the most **common chemical** used in the home because it **dissolves** a large number of substances. It is used to do laundry, wash dishes, clean floors, and for bathing, flushing toilets, watering gardens, cooking and drinking. Because water dissolves so many substances, most household chemicals in the liquid state contain water as a **solvent**.

Acids, bases and salts

Acids

Acids are substances that form positive **hydrogen ions (H^+ ions)** when they dissolve in water. Solutions of acids are described as being **acidic** and have the following properties:

- They have a **sour** taste.
- They are **corrosive**.
- They change blue litmus to **red**.
- They have a pH value of **less than 7**.

Hydrochloric acid, **sulfuric acid** and **nitric acid** are the common acids found in the laboratory, whilst **citric acid** and **ascorbic acid (vitamin C)** are found in fruits, and **ethanoic (acetic) acid** is found in vinegar.

Bases

Bases are chemically opposite to acids. Bases include **metal oxides**, e.g. calcium oxide, **metal hydroxides**, e.g. magnesium hydroxide, and **ammonia**. Bases react with acids to form a **salt** and **water**:

Some bases are **soluble** in water and these are known as **alkalis**. Alkalis include **sodium hydroxide**, **potassium hydroxide**, **calcium hydroxide** and **ammonium hydroxide,** formed when ammonia dissolves in water. Alkalis contain negative **hydroxide ions (OH^- ions)**. Solutions of alkalis are described as being **alkaline** and have the following properties:

- They have a **bitter** taste.
- They are **corrosive**.
- They feel **soapy**.
- They change red litmus to **blue**.
- They have a pH value **greater than 7**.

The concept of pH

The **strength** of an acid or alkali in solution can be measured on the **pH scale** by using **universal indicator paper** or **solution**. The paper or solution is placed in the test solution and its colour is compared to the pH colour chart shown in Figure 14.2.

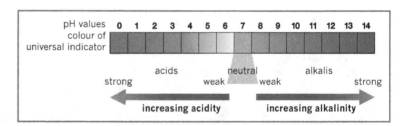

Figure 14.2 *The pH scale*

Salts

Salts are compounds formed when bases react with acids. Salts formed by hydrochloric acid are called **chlorides**, salts formed by sulfuric acid are called **sulfates** and salts formed by nitric acid are called **nitrates**. Other salts include **carbonates**, **hydrogencarbonates** and **phosphates**.

Classification of household chemicals

Household chemicals can be classified into **acids**, **bases** and **salts**. Most salts are **neutral**, but some can be acidic or basic.

Table 14.2 *Classification of some household chemicals as acids, bases or salts*

Classification	Household chemical	Main chemical component
Acid	• Limescale remover	• Phosphoric or citric acid
	• Toilet bowl cleaner	• Hydrochloric or citric acid
	• Battery acid	• Sulfuric acid
	• Vinegar	• Ethanoic acid
Base	• Drain cleaner	• Sodium or potassium hydroxide
	• Oven cleaner	• Sodium or potassium hydroxide
	• Chlorine bleach	• Sodium hypochlorite
	• Household ammonia	• Ammonia
	• Antacid	• Sodium hydrogencarbonate or magnesium hydroxide
Salt	• Washing soda (also basic)	• Sodium carbonate
	• Toothpaste (also basic)	• Sodium hydrogencarbonate
	• Epsom salt	• Magnesium sulfate
	• Baking soda (also basic)	• Sodium hydrogencarbonate
	• Table salt	• Sodium chloride

Neutralisation reactions

The reaction between a base and an acid is known as a **neutralisation reaction.** In a neutralisation reaction between an alkali and an acid, if just the right amount of each reactant is mixed, a **neutral** solution of the salt is formed that has a **pH of 7**. Neutralisation reactions can be used to **remove stains:**

- Alkaline **sodium hydrogencarbonate** can be used to remove acidic **fruit stains.**
- Alkaline **borax** can be used to remove acidic **fruit**, **wine** and **tea stains.**
- Acidic **lime juice** or **vinegar** can be used to remove basic **rust stains.**

In each of the above, the alkali and the acid react and make a **soluble salt** that can be washed away, removing the stain.

Solutions, suspensions and colloids

Solutions, **suspensions** and **colloids** are all **mixtures.** They consist of two or more substances that are **physically combined.** Each component in the mixture retains its own individual properties and has not undergone any chemical reaction with any other component. The components can be **separated** from each other by physical means (see pages 159–160).

Solutions

*A **solution** is a homogeneous (uniform) mixture of two or more substances; one substance is usually a liquid.*

A **solution** is made by **dissolving** one substance in another. The substance that does the **dissolving** is called the **solvent** and the substance that **dissolves** is called the **solute**. Examples of solutions include seawater, iced tea, carbonated drinks and rum.

Based on the **solvent**, solutions can be classified into **two** types:

- **Aqueous solutions** have **water** as the solvent. Water is known as the 'universal solvent' because it can dissolve a large number of substances.
- **Non-aqueous solutions** have substances other than water as the solvent. Common non-aqueous solvents include ethanol, kerosene, gasoline, acetone, turpentine and methylated spirits.

Suspensions

*A **suspension** is a heterogeneous (non-uniform) mixture in which minute, visible particles of one substance are dispersed in another substance, which is usually a liquid.*

Examples of suspensions include muddy water, chalk dust or flour stirred in water and oil shaken in water.

Colloids

*A **colloid** is a heterogeneous mixture in which minute particles of one substance are dispersed in another substance, which is usually a liquid. The dispersed particles are larger than those of a solution, but smaller than those of a suspension.*

Examples of colloids include fog, smoke, mayonnaise, milk, gelatin, whipped cream, emulsion paint and starch in water.

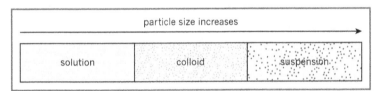

Figure 14.3 *Comparing the particle sizes in a solution, a colloid and a suspension*

Table 14.3 *Comparing solutions, colloids and suspensions*

Property	Solutions	Colloid	Suspension
Size and visibility of dispersed particles	Extremely small. Not visible, even with a microscope.	Between those in a solution and those in a suspension. Not visible, even with a microscope.	Larger than those in a colloid. Visible to the naked eye.
Sedimentation	Components do not separate if left undisturbed.	Dispersed particles do not settle if left undisturbed.	Suspended particles settle if left undisturbed.
Passage of light and appearance	Light usually passes through, making them appear **transparent**.	Most will scatter light, making them appear **translucent**. Some are **opaque**.	Light does not pass through, so they appear **opaque**.
Separation	Particles cannot be separated by filtration.	Particles cannot be separated by filtration.	Particles can be separated by filtration.

Classification of household chemicals

Household chemicals can be classified into **solutions**, **colloids** and **suspensions**.

Table 14.4 *Classification of some household chemicals as solutions, colloids or suspensions*

Solutions	Colloids	Suspensions
• Chlorine bleach	• Aerosol sprays, e.g. insecticides	• Liquid scouring (abrasive) cleaners
• Limescale remover	• Liquid detergents	• Metal polish
• Window cleaner	• Shaving cream	• Calamine lotion
• Household ammonia	• Hand cream	
• Vinegar		

Separation techniques

The **technique** used to separate the components of a mixture depends on the **physical properties** of the components.

Distillation

Simple distillation is used to separate and retain the **liquid solvent** and the solid solute in a **solution**, e.g. to obtain distilled water from tap water. The solute can also be retained by **evaporation** of the concentrated solution remaining after distillation if no impurities are present. The components are separated due to their different **boiling points**. The solvent must have a lower boiling point than the solute.

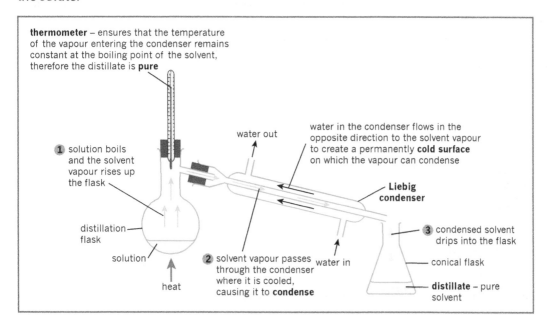

Figure 14.4 *Separating the components of a solution by simple distillation*

Distillation is used on an industrial scale in some parts of the world to remove salts from seawater to obtain fresh water for domestic and agricultural use. The process is known as **desalination** and it is carried out in a **desalination plant**.

Filtration

Filtration is used to separate a **suspended** or **settled solid** and a **liquid** when the solid does not dissolve in the liquid, e.g. to separate soil and water. The components are separated due to their different **particle sizes**.

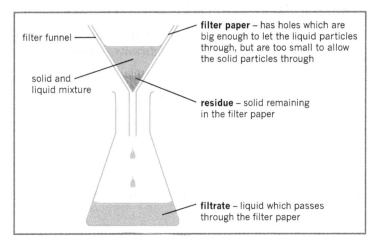

Figure 14.5 *Separating the components of a suspension by filtration*

Chromatography

Paper chromatography is used to separate **several solutes** that are present in a solution. The solutes are usually coloured and can travel through the absorbent paper used. Such solutes include the dyes in black ink or pigments in chlorophyll. The solutes are separated based on:

- How **soluble** each one is in the solvent used, which is usually water or ethanol.
- How strongly each one is **attracted** to the paper used.

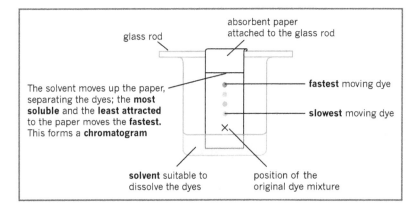

Figure 14.6 *Separating the coloured dyes in a mixture by paper chromatography*

Stain removal by solvent extraction

Some **stains** can be removed using the appropriate **solvent** to dissolve them:

- If the stain is soluble in **water**, it can be removed by soaking in water.
- If the stain is insoluble in water but soluble in a **non-aqueous solvent**, it can be removed by soaking in the appropriate solvent. For example, **acetone** dissolves nail polish, **turpentine** dissolves paint, **methylated spirits** dissolves greasy dirt on surfaces such as glass, and **tetrachloroethane** is used in dry cleaning to dissolve greasy dirt and stains from clothes.

The use of some common household chemicals

- **Disinfectants** are chemicals used to destroy or inhibit the growth of microorganisms in or on **non-living objects**, e.g. in water, and on counter tops and floors. Disinfectants include **alcohols, chlorine-releasing compounds** such as sodium hypochlorite (found in household bleaches) and **quaternary ammonium salts** (found in some disinfectants). Some disinfectants can **irritate** the skin and eyes, as well as the respiratory system if inhaled.

- **Antiseptics** are chemicals used to destroy or inhibit the growth of microorganisms on **living tissue**, e.g. in a cut or wound, or on unbroken skin before an injection. Antiseptics reduce the risk of infection; examples include **hydrogen peroxide, rubbing alcohol** and **iodine solution**. Antiseptics can dry out the skin and kill skin cells, and they may worsen a wound's condition if not used carefully.

- **Deodorisers** are chemicals used to remove unpleasant **odours**. They either **mask** the smell with a pleasant odour of their own, or they **absorb** the chemicals responsible for the unpleasant smell. Some deodorisers use chemicals which may be carcinogenic (cause cancer), aggravate asthma or cause an allergic reaction.

- **Household bleach (chlorine bleach)** is a solution of **sodium hypochlorite (sodium chlorate(I))** which is used to **remove stains, whiten clothes** and as a **disinfectant**. It must be used with care because:

  - Sodium hypochlorite is a powerful **oxidising agent** that can remove **colour** from fabrics.
  - Bleach is **alkaline** so it can weaken the fibres in fabrics, causing **holes** to appear.
  - Bleach has an unpleasant smell and can **irritate** the skin and eyes.
  - If bleach is used with certain other household chemicals, they may react and give off substantial quantities of poisonous **chlorine gas**.

- **Hydrogen peroxide** is used as a bleaching agent to **remove stains, lighten** hair and **whiten** clothes and teeth. It is also used as an **antiseptic**. Hydrogen peroxide is milder than chlorine bleaches, so is safer to use.

- **Rust removers** usually contain an acid such as **phosphoric** or **oxalic acid**. The acid reacts with the rust (iron oxide), which is basic, and forms a compound that can be washed away leaving the bare iron or steel. Rust removers can be harmful to the skin.

- **Limescale removers** contain an acid such as **phosphoric** or **citric acid**. The acid reacts with the **calcium carbonate** deposits, known as **limescale**, that build up inside kettles and shower heads, and around taps. The reaction forms a compound that can be washed away. Limescale removers can be harmful to the skin.

- **Vinegar** is a dilute solution of **ethanoic (acetic) acid** that is used in cooking, salad dressings and pickling. It can also be used to remove **limescale** from appliances, **stains** such as rust stains from fabrics and **tarnish** from silver and copper items.

The safe use of household chemicals

Guidelines for the **safe** use of **household chemicals** include:

- Read all labels carefully, follow the instructions given and use only as directed.
- Use only the amount of the chemical needed to do the job.
- Never mix household chemicals, especially chlorine bleach and products containing ammonia.
- Wear the appropriate protective clothing when using harmful chemicals and do not use chemicals near food.
- Wash hands immediately after using any household chemical.
- Store all chemicals in their original containers, and ensure the containers are tightly sealed and out of reach of children.

Detergents

Detergents are added to water to remove dirt from the skin, clothes, household surfaces and floors. They can be classified as **soapy** and **soapless**:

- **Soapy detergents** are made by boiling animal fats or vegetable oils with concentrated potassium or sodium hydroxide solution. They may be simply called **soaps**. An example is sodium octadecanoate.
- **Soapless detergents** are formed from **petroleum**. They are also known as synthetic detergents and may be simply called **detergents**. An example is sodium dodecyl sulfate.

Table 14.5 *Soapy and soapless detergents compared; (A) = advantage, (D) = disadvantage*

Soapy detergents	Soapless detergents
Manufactured from fats and oils, **renewable** resources which will not run out. (**A**)	Manufactured from petroleum, a **non-renewable** resource which will eventually run out. (**D**)
Do not lather easily in hard water. They form unpleasant **scum** (see page 163). (**D**)	Lather easily in hard water. They **do not** form scum. (**A**)
Are **biodegradable**, meaning they are broken down by microorganisms in the environment so they **do not** cause foam to form on lakes and rivers. (**A**)	Some are **non-biodegradable**. These can cause **foam** to form on rivers and lakes, which prevents oxygen dissolving in the water and leads to the death of aquatic organisms that depend on the dissolved oxygen. (**D**)
	Most modern soapless detergents are biodegradable.
Do not contain phosphates, so they **do not** cause pollution of aquatic environments. (**A**)	Some contain **phosphates** which pollute aquatic environments by causing **eutrophication** (see pages 203–204). (**D**)

Cleaning action of detergents

Detergent molecules, also known as **surfactants**, are long molecules composed of **two** parts: a **hydrophilic head** that is attracted to water but repelled by grease and oil, and a **hydrophobic tail** that is attracted to grease and oil but repelled by water. Detergents work by:

- **Lowering** the surface tension of the water, allowing it to **spread out** and **wet** surfaces more efficiently.
- **Breaking up** and **dispersing** grease and dirt.

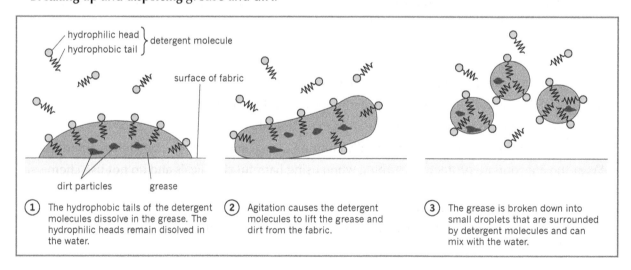

Figure 14.7 *How detergents remove grease and dirt from fabrics*

Detergents may also contain a variety of other active **components**.

Table 14.6 *Other components that may be found in detergents*

Component	Function
Oxidising agents	To oxidise stains, making them colourless, i.e. they act as **bleaches**.
Builders such as phosphates	To reduce water hardness and improve the cleaning ability of the detergent molecules.
Enzymes	To help remove biological stains such as blood and grass.
Optical brighteners	To make fabrics appear whiter and brighter.
Fabric softeners	To make clothes softer and reduce crinkling.
Fragrances	To give laundry a pleasant smell.

Scouring powders

Scouring powders are used to remove dirt and stains on hard surfaces. They contain **fine particles** of an insoluble mineral such as limestone, feldspar or silica mixed with other powders to help them clean. When mixed with water, they form a thick paste and the mineral particles act as an **abrasive** when rubbed on hard surfaces, **physically** removing solid dirt. They may also contain a **detergent (surfactant)**, a **bleaching agent** which can also act as a disinfectant, and a **rust remover**.

Cleaning household appliances made from metals

The correct cleaning agent must be used when cleaning **metal appliances** to avoid scratching, corroding or damaging the surface of the appliances.

- **Aluminium** scratches fairly easily. It can be cleaned using a **liquid detergent** such as dishwashing liquid, wiped with vinegar and polished with **glass cleaner**. Scouring powders can scratch aluminium, chlorine bleaches can discolour it and sodium hydroxide in oven cleaners can react with it, so must not be used.

- **Iron** and **steel** can be cleaned using scouring powders and oven cleaners, and rust can be removed using **rust removers**. The surface can then be sealed with oil to prevent further rusting.

- **Copper** and **silver** can be cleaned using the appropriate **metal polish** to remove the layer of tarnish, then polished to a shine with a soft, dry cloth.

Hard and soft water

Water can be classified as **hard** or **soft**:

- **Hard water** does not lather easily with soap because it contains dissolved **calcium** and **magnesium salts**. Soap is a compound called **sodium octadecanoate** and when it is added to hard water, insoluble calcium and magnesium octadecanoate form, which are also known as **scum**. Soap only lathers when all the calcium (Ca^{2+}) and magnesium (Mg^{2+}) ions have been converted to scum. Water in limestone-rich areas is hard.

$$\text{hard water} \quad + \quad \text{soap} \quad \longrightarrow \quad \text{scum}$$

- **Soft water** lathers easily with soap because it does not contain dissolved calcium or magnesium salts. Rainwater is soft.

Table 14.7 *Advantages and disadvantages of hard and soft water*

Type of water	Advantages	Disadvantages
Hard water	• When drunk, it is good for building strong bones and teeth due to the presence of calcium ions. • It does not dissolve lead from pipes so does not contribute to lead poisoning in homes with lead water pipes. • It tastes better than soft water.	• The **scum** that forms with soap discolours clothes and forms an unpleasant grey, greasy layer around sinks, baths and showers. • It **wastes** soap because all the calcium and magnesium ions have to be removed as scum before the soap lathers. • It causes **limescale (calcium carbonate)** to be deposited in kettles, boilers and hot water pipes. This wastes electricity and can block pipes.
Soft water	• It does not form unpleasant scum or discolour clothes. • It does not waste soap because it lathers immediately. • Limescale does not build up in kettles, boilers and hot water pipes.	• It does not help build strong bones and teeth because it lacks calcium ions. • It dissolves lead from water pipes so can cause lead poisoning. • If softened using an ion exchange process, it has a higher content of sodium ions than normal which may lead to hypertension (high blood pressure) when drunk.

There are two **types** of water hardness:

- **Temporary hardness** which is caused by dissolved **calcium** and **magnesium hydrogencarbonate**. It is found in limestone-rich areas and **can** be removed by **boiling** the water.

- **Permanent hardness** is caused by dissolved **calcium** and **magnesium sulfate**. Permanent hardness **cannot** be removed by boiling.

Softening hard water

Hard water can be converted into **soft water** by removing the dissolved calcium and magnesium ions.

- **Boiling** – This removes **temporary hardness** by causing dissolved calcium and magnesium hydrogencarbonate to decompose, forming **insoluble** calcium and magnesium carbonate. These insoluble carbonates, known as **limescale** or **kettle fur**, remove the dissolved calcium and magnesium ions from the water.

- **Adding washing soda (sodium carbonate)** – This causes dissolved calcium and magnesium ions to form **insoluble** calcium and magnesium carbonate, thereby removing the dissolved ions from the water.

- **Distillation** – Boiling the water and condensing the steam forms pure **distilled water**, and any dissolved salts are left behind.

Revision questions

1. Identify the most common chemical used in the home and state why it is used so extensively.

2. a State THREE properties of an acid and THREE properties of an alkali.

   b What is the pH scale used for?

3. a What is a neutralisation reaction?

   b How can neutralisation reactions be used to remove stains? Support your answer with specific examples.

4. a Using particle size, passage of light and sedimentation, distinguish between a solution, a colloid and a suspension.

   b Name TWO different household chemicals that are solutions, TWO that are colloids and TWO that are suspensions.

5. a Explain the principles involved in separating a mixture of sand and water.

   b What technique would you use to obtain pure water from tap water?

6. a Distinguish between a disinfectant and an antiseptic, and give a *named* example of EACH.

   b Suggest THREE guidelines to follow to ensure that household chemicals are used safely.

7. Explain how:

   a A detergent removes greasy dirt from a shirt.

   b A scouring powder removes solid dirt from a cooker top.

8. Give THREE differences between a soapy and a soapless detergent.

9. Distinguish between hard and soft water, and suggest TWO advantages and TWO disadvantages of hard water.

Exam-style questions – Chapters 9 to 14

Structured questions

1 **a)** With reference to heat, give TWO examples of each of the following:

    i) good conductors

    ii) good insulators. **(2 marks)**

  b) Distinguish between conduction and convection. **(2 marks)**

  c) Solar energy is incident on the panels of Desean's hot water heater system.

    i) By what method of heat transfer does energy from the Sun reach the heater? **(1 mark)**

    ii) Explain why the surface of each panel is painted a dull black. **(2 marks)**

    iii) Explain why the tubes carrying the water are narrow. **(2 marks)**

    iv) Suggest a suitable material for the tubes mentioned in iii) above. **(2 marks)**

  d) Samarah's father has installed a new roof on his house. He has made small vents in it, in such a way that rain water cannot enter through them. Comment on how this new roof feature will keep the house cooler and provide a healthier environment within their home.

(4 marks)

Total 15 marks

2 **a)** Define:

    i) energy

    ii) work. **(2 marks)**

  b) Show, by means of an arrow diagram, the energy conversions taking place when:

    i) Jacob recharges the battery of his cell phone using the power outlet in his room. **(1 mark)**

    ii) Photosynthesis takes place. **(1 mark)**

  c) Anita sits in a box and Jacob pulls her horizontally at constant speed across the room through a distance of 5 m. If the force he uses is 80 N, calculate the following:

    i) The energy converted by Jacob. **(2 marks)**

    ii) The work done by Jacob. **(1 mark)**

  d) Draw a diagram to show how Jacob can focus radio waves onto a receiver aerial by using a curved reflector. **(3 marks)**

  e) **i)** State the principle of conservation of linear momentum. **(1 mark)**

    Jacob and Anita each have cars of mass 2000 kg. Jacob's car travels at a speed of 4 m s^{-1} towards Anita's car, which is stationary.

    ii) Determine the momentum of Jacob's car as it moves towards Anita's. **(2 marks)**

    iii) After the collision, Jacob's car comes to rest. With what speed does Anita's car move off? **(2 marks)**

Total 15 marks

3 **a)** Complete Table 1, which relates to good and poor electrical conductors. The examples are to be chosen from the following: rubber, graphite, copper, plastic, aluminium.

Table 1

	Example 1	Example 2	One use
Good conductor			
Poor conductor			

(4 marks)

b) Akim finds a short, thin rod in the yard. Draw a diagram of the circuit he can use in order to determine if the rod is a good conductor of electricity, clearly showing where the rod will be connected. **(2 marks)**

c) Akim plugs a 480 W device into a 120 V electrical power socket. Calculate

   i)   the current **(2 marks)**

   ii) the resistance **(2 marks)**

   iii) the energy used in 10 minutes. **(2 marks)**

d) To protect the device, Akim's father chooses a 5 A fuse from fuses of ratings 3 A, 5 A and 13 A.

   i)   Comment on why each of the other fuses is unsuitable. **(2 marks)**

   ii) To which wire of the three-core flex should he connect the fuse? **(1 mark)**

Total 15 marks

4 **a)** State the function of a simple machine. **(1 mark)**

b) **i)** Distinguish among the THREE classes of levers. **(3 marks)**

   ii) Give TWO examples of a class 2 lever. **(1 mark)**

c) A block of weight 100 N is to be raised to a platform 2 m from the ground. Jai uses an inclined plane of length 6 m to do the job and pushes the block up the slope using an effort of 50 N.

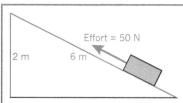

   i)   Determine the mechanical advantage of this machine. **(2 marks)**

   ii) Suggest whether the machine is a force multiplier or a distance multiplier. **(2 marks)**

   iii) Determine the energy converted as Jai pushes the block up the slope. **(2 marks)**

   iv) Calculate the energy wasted in using the machine. **(3 marks)**

   v)   Suggest how the effort is affected if the length of the slope is increased in order to reach the same height. **(1 mark)**

Total 15 marks

5 **a)** Questions **i)** to **iv)** below refer to the following metals:

zinc, copper, tin, aluminium, silver, iron

    i)   Arrange the metals in decreasing order of reactivity.   **(1 mark)**

    ii)   Which metal would be the best to use to make cans to store drinks?
        Suggest TWO reasons for your choice.   **(3 marks)**

    iii) Which two metals are alloyed to make brass? Give ONE reason for alloying
        these metals.   **(2 marks)**

    iv) Write a word equation for the reaction between zinc and sulfuric acid.   **(1 mark)**

b) Anya set up the experiment illustrated in Figure 2 to investigate the
conditions needed for an iron nail to rust.

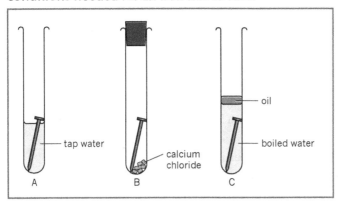

Figure 2 *Experiment to investigate the conditions needed for an iron nail to rust*

    i)   If boiling water removes dissolved oxygen and calcium chloride absorbs moisture,
        in which tube would Anya expect to see the nail rust?   **(1 mark)**

    ii)   Give an explanation for your answer to **i)** above.   **(2 marks)**

    iii) What was the purpose of the oil in tube C?   **(1 mark)**

    iv) Victor recently moved from his home in the countryside to live close to a
        factory that burns fossil fuel, and he notices that the rust spots on his car
        seem to be quickly increasing in size. Suggest a possible explanation for
        Victor's observation.   **(2 marks)**

    v)   Suggest the best way to prevent EACH of the following steel items from rusting:

        - the chain of a bicycle

        - a roofing sheet.   **(2 marks)**

                                Total 15 marks

Structured essay questions

6 **a)** Coastal regions have their temperatures moderated by cool sea breezes. Explain how these breezes are produced on a hot day and state what change occurs at night.

(7 marks)

b) Identify FOUR main problems associated with inadequate ventilation and suggest FOUR ways by which we can overcome these problems. **(8 marks)**

Total 15 marks

7 **a)** Describe THREE hazards which may be encountered due to the careless handling of electrical appliances and equipment and state how we can prevent each of these hazards. **(6 marks)**

b) **i)** Identify the THREE elements necessary to start and sustain a fire. **(1 mark)**

ii) An electrical fire is started in Angie's kitchen due to a toaster having a faulty plug. She is unsure whether she should use the water spout connected to her kitchen sink or the carbon dioxide cylinder hanging on the kitchen wall to extinguish the fire. State which of the extinguishers is suitable and discuss the reasons for your choice. **(4 marks)**

iii) Angie's father is a fire fighter who extinguished a large bush fire at work. Suggest TWO pieces of protective gear he would have worn and state, with reason, the type of extinguisher that would have been suitable for that job. **(4 marks)**

Total 15 marks

8 **a)** **i)** Outline the relationship between an acid, a base and a salt. **(3 marks)**

ii) Name ONE household chemical that is acidic and ONE that is basic. **(2 marks)**

iii) Explain how you would determine the pH of the two chemicals named in **ii)** above. **(2 marks)**

b) Explain how distillation can be used in the laboratory to obtain pure water from tap water and how paper chromatography can be used to separate the dyes in black ink. Your answers must include the principles involved in EACH separation process. **(8 marks)**

Total 15 marks

Section C – Earth's place in the universe

15 The universe and our solar system

The universe is vast. It takes light just 8 minutes to travel 152 000 000 km from the Sun (our nearest star) to Earth, but more than 4 years to reach us from the next nearest star! Scientists believe that there are more stars in the universe than there are grains of sand on the entire Earth.

Location of Earth in the universe

Table 15.1 *The universe and some important bodies within it*

Body	Definition
Earth	The celestial body that supports life and is home to humans.
Star	A luminous sphere composed of plasma and held together by gravitational forces.
Sun	An average star and the closest to **Earth**.
Our solar system	A system having the Sun as the focus and several bodies, including Earth, orbiting it.
Galaxy	A group of billions of stars.
Milky Way	The galaxy containing our solar system.
Universe	The entire cosmic system composed of all the matter and energy within and between billions of galaxies.

Earth

Our solar system

Small part of the observable universe

Milky Way

Figure 15.1 *Location of Earth in the Universe*

The Milky Way galaxy

- The Milky Way is a typical **spiral** galaxy made of **hot gases, dust** and over **200 billion stars.**
- It has a diameter of more than **100 000 light-years** (meaning that it takes light more than 100 000 years to travel across it).
- It is bulged at the centre and has **four spiral arms** where the stars are most concentrated.
- Our solar system is located near the centre of the galaxy.
- As the spirals spin, hot gases and dust forced through them lead to the birth of more stars.
- At its centre is a huge **black hole** with a mass that is billions of times greater than that of the Sun.

Characteristics of outer space

- Outer space is the expanse that lies between celestial bodies such as the stars and planets.
- A **plasma** of **hydrogen** and **helium**, as well as **cosmic dust,** exists in a **vacuum** between these bodies.
- Since there are no large bodies nearby, the **lack of gravity** causes objects to float around.
- Due to the vacuum, there is **no air to breathe** and **sound cannot be transmitted.**
- As an object travels away from the Sun (or any star), its temperature falls until it **becomes extremely cold.**
- **Radiation levels** in space are **extremely dangerous.**
- **Dark matter** (a concept not fully understood) is believed to represent 90% of the mass of outer space.

Satellites

*A **satellite** is a body that orbits another body of larger mass.*

Satellites may be **natural** or **artificial** (man-made). The Earth is a natural satellite of the Sun and the Moon is a natural satellite of the Earth. The force of **gravity** on a satellite keeps it in its orbit. The gravitational attraction of the Earth to the Sun is just sufficient to maintain its orbit around the Sun (see chapter 19, page 219, 'Satellites'). Some artificial satellites are described below.

Geostationary satellites

These orbit the Earth with a **period of 24 hours** in the same direction as the Earth revolves, and are always **directly above the same point on the equator.** They have the following uses:

- **Communication** – They relay TV, radio, and telephone signals. Since they are always above the same point on the Earth, their **signals can be easily located.**
- **Storm monitoring** – They can observe continuous data from a region within the hemisphere of the planet that faces them, and so are useful in monitoring large scale systems such as hurricanes.

Polar satellites

These orbit in planes that are almost **parallel to longitudinal lines** as the Earth spins on its axis. Since they can obtain data from the Earth in an east–west as well as a north–south direction, they are useful **as weather satellites.** Unlike geostationary satellites:

- They can monitor conditions anywhere around **the entire planet.**
- They **produce images of good resolution** since they orbit close to the Earth's surface.
- They have periods of about **90 minutes** and therefore orbit the Earth several times in 24 hours, gathering **important data within a short period.**

Global positioning system (GPS) satellites

This is a system of approximately **30 satellites** that orbit with **periods of about 12 hours** (two revolutions per day). They produce information of **location and time** at various points on or above the Earth's surface. See chapter 17, page 206, 'Navigational devices used at sea'.

Other artificial satellites include the **Hubble Space Telescope,** which researches the formation of the planets, stars and galaxies, and the **International Space Station (ISS)** (see page 176). The Hubble Telescope is scheduled to be replaced by the **James Webb Telescope** in 2021.

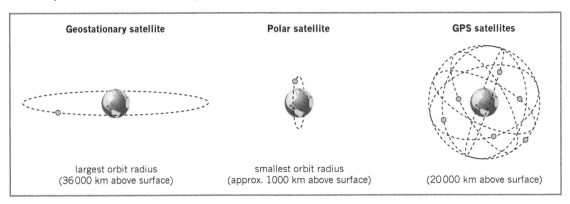

Figure 15.2 *Artificial satellites in orbit around Earth*

The solar system

Our solar system has the Sun at its centre and planets, dwarf planets, moons, asteroids, meteoroids and comets that orbit it in **elliptical paths.**

Planets are bodies that **rotate** on an axis as they **revolve** around (orbit) a star. Planets are large enough to have gravitational forces that have made them approximately **spherical** and that have **cleared their orbital paths** of most bodies.

* **Terrestrial planets** or **inner planets:** Mercury, Venus, Earth and Mars. These have **hard, rocky** surfaces.
* **Gas giants** or **outer planets:** Jupiter, Saturn, Uranus and Neptune. These are mainly made of gaseous **hydrogen** and **helium** and **liquid ammonia**; they have **no solid surface.** They are **larger and colder** than the terrestrial planets, and have dust, or ice and dust, orbiting them in **ring systems.**

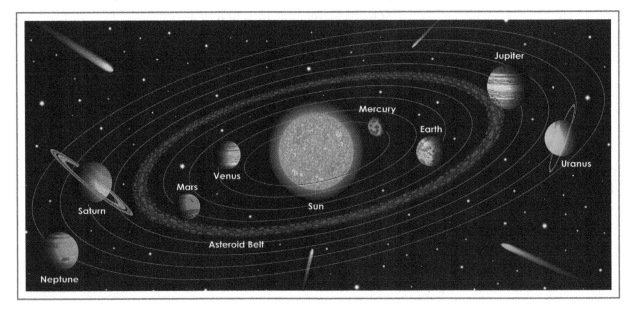

Figure 15.3 *Our solar system*

Table 15.2 *Characteristic features of the planets of our solar system*

Planet	Characteristic features
Mercury	• The **smallest** planet. • Rotates slowly about its axis, taking 59 Earth days to make 1 rotation, but orbits the Sun in only 88 days. Approximately 3 Mercury days occur during 2 Mercury years! • The only planet that has virtually **no atmosphere** to prevent heat from entering or leaving it. The side facing the Sun is very hot and the opposite side is very cold.
Venus	• A dense atmosphere of **carbon dioxide** traps heat by the greenhouse effect (see chapter 18 page 210, 'Global warming and the greenhouse effect'), making it the **hottest** planet even though it is not the closest to the Sun. • Rotates very slowly about its axis taking 243 Earth days to make 1 rotation. This is even longer than the year on Venus, which is 225 Earth days! • Spins about its axis in the **opposite direction** to the other planets. • Covered by an opaque cloud of **sulfuric acid.** • **Brightest** planet since sunlight is reflected from the thick cloud that surrounds it. • More than a thousand large **volcanoes** are scattered over its landscape.
Earth	• Largest of the terrestrial planets. • Completes one rotation in 24 hours and one revolution in $365\frac{1}{4}$ days. • **Supports life**, since its temperature allows water to exist in the liquid state. • Has a strong magnetic field that protects it from the **solar wind** (high speed electrical charges streaming out from the Sun).
Mars	• Known as the **red planet** due to the rusted iron in its surface of rock, ice and dust. • Has two moons, Phobos and Deimos. • Has the **largest dust storms** and the **tallest mountain** in our solar system. • There is evidence of the **presence of water** – which is necessary for life – on Mars. However, evidence of life has not yet been detected on Mars. • The second smallest planet; it is half the size of Earth but has the same land area as Earth's continents. • UV and cosmic radiation penetrate the **thin atmosphere** consisting mainly of carbon dioxide. This radiation **sterilises** the surface. • The thin atmosphere causes ice to change directly to vapour, **leaving the planet dry**.
Jupiter	• Has the **shortest day** of all the planets; rotates once every 9 h 55 min. • Has a **Great Red Spot**, which is a huge raging storm. • Has the **largest mass** and **volume**. • Has the **largest number of moons** (**67**). The largest moon (Ganymede), is bigger than all other moons and is even larger than Mercury. • Has a ring system of dust particles.
Saturn	• Known for its profound **ring system** which is made mainly of ice and dust (see Figure 15.3). • Has **62 moons,** all of which are frozen. Titan and Rhea are the largest.
Uranus	• Known as an **'ice giant'** and has a ring system of ice and dust. • Its axis of rotation is tilted at an angle of 98°, so that it appears to be on its side (see Figure 15.3).
Neptune	• Known as an **'ice giant'** and has a **ring system** of ice and dust.

Table 15.3 *Comparing and contrasting the planets*

Planet	Distance from Sun (km)	Diameter (km)	Number of moons	Mean temperature (°C)
Mercury	60 million	5 000	0	167
Venus	110 million	12 000	0	464
Earth	150 million	13 000	1	15
Mars	230 million	7 000	2	−65
Jupiter	780 million	143 000	67	−110
Saturn	1430 million	121 000	62	−140
Uranus	2870 million	51 000	27	−195
Neptune	4500 million	50 000	14	−200

- **Dwarf planets** are approximately spherical, but unlike planets, have orbital paths that are **intercepted by other bodies** such as asteroids. Three examples of dwarf planets are **Ceres**, **Pluto** and **Eris**.

- **Asteroids** are rocky masses that orbit the Sun but which are **too small to have an atmosphere** or to be called a planet. Unlike planets, they are not approximate spheres. The **asteroid belt** is located between Mars and Jupiter and contains millions of asteroids and one dwarf planet, **Ceres**. The asteroid belt separates the inner and outer planets.

- **Meteoroids** are smaller than asteroids but also orbit the Sun. They are usually the remnants of comets or broken pieces of asteroids.

- **Comets** are masses of frozen water and super-cold carbon dioxide, methane and ammonia 'ices' mixed with smaller quantities of rock and dust, which orbit the Sun in **elliptical paths**. When they are close to the Sun the ices vaporise, producing a **'tail'** of gas and dust that is always directed away from the Sun. If a planet's orbit passes through this material, it falls onto the planet as **meteor showers**.

- **Meteors (shooting stars)** are bright trails of light produced when meteoroids or other materials experience friction on passing through the atmosphere.

- **Meteorites** are the remains of meteoroids or other debris that have **fallen to the Earth**.

How Earth is affected by other bodies

Day and night

As the Earth spins on its **axis** (rotates), the surface that faces the Sun experiences **daylight**, and the surface on the side away from the Sun experiences **night**. The Earth rotates about its axis once every **24 hours** and so most places on the planet will undergo a period of daylight and darkness in this time.

Effect of tilted axis

The axis of rotation of the Earth is tilted at 23.5°. This results in the northern hemisphere receiving more hours of daylight than the southern hemisphere for six months, and then more hours of darkness than the southern hemisphere for the next six months.

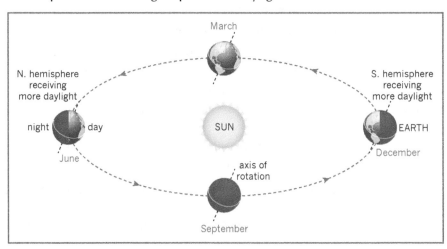

Figure 15.4 *Day and night through the year*

Eclipse of the Moon (lunar eclipse)

*A **lunar eclipse** occurs when the Earth passes between the Sun and the Moon and casts a shadow on the Moon.*

The Moon is a **non-luminous** body and is therefore seen from the Earth **by reflection** of light from the Sun. The orbit of the Moon normally passes outside of the Earth's **umbra** (cone of complete shadow). However, at times the Moon enters the umbra and is only dimly visible. It can take as much as $1\frac{1}{2}$ hours before it emerges from the other edge of the shadow.

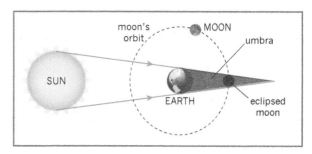

Figure 15.5 *Eclipse of the Moon*

Eclipse of the Sun (solar eclipse)

*A **solar eclipse** occurs when the Moon passes between the Sun and the Earth and blocks the visibility from Earth of all or a portion of the Sun.*

At times, the orbit of the Moon can pass through the rays directed from the Sun to the Earth. The Moon's **umbra** then reaches the Earth over a region from which **a total solar eclipse** is observed. People who find themselves in the partial shadow of the **penumbra** observe a **partial solar eclipse**.

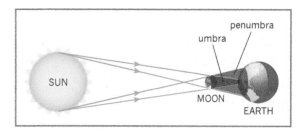

Figure 15.6 *Eclipse of the Sun*

Observing the Moon over a 30-day period

The Moon takes $29\frac{1}{2}$ days (approximately 30 days) to orbit the Earth and to return to the same position relative to the Sun as seen by an observer on Earth. As it does so, the side facing the Sun is always lit and the opposite side is always in darkness, as shown in Figure 15.7 (a).

Figure 15.7 (b) shows how the Moon appears from Earth during this time. When the Moon is between the Earth and Sun we view the side that is in darkness, a **new moon**. For the next few days an increasing amount of light from the Sun reflects from its surface until **half of the disc** appears lit and we observe the **first quarter moon**. As the Moon continues in its orbit, an increasing amount of its surface reflects light until a **full moon** is observed after approximately 15 days. The reflected light then becomes less, displaying next a **third quarter moon**, and finally a **new moon** again as the cycle completes.

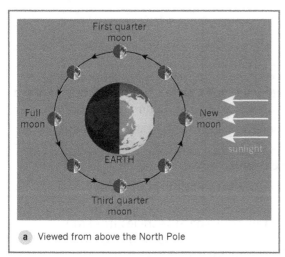

a   Viewed from above the North Pole

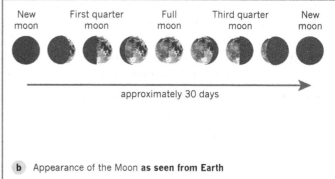

b   Appearance of the Moon **as seen from Earth**

Figure 15.7 *Observing the Moon over a 30-day period*

Exploration of the universe by humans

Humans have been interested in **space exploration** for a very long time. **Astronomers** have used **telescopes** to study celestial bodies for centuries, but humans lacked the technology to carry out the **physical exploration** of space until the latter half of the 20th century. During that time, powerful **rockets** and **space probes** were developed which allowed much more knowledge of the universe to be gained.

Table 15.4 *Reasons for space exploration by humans*

Reason	Details
Scientific research	• Certain scientific research is better done in the absence of gravity.
Asteroid collisions	• Approximately every 10 000 years, an asteroid crashes into Earth. By learning more of 'space', we may avoid being wiped out by such a collision.
Mining	• Important materials can be extracted from the planets, moons and asteroids.
Migration	• Population increase may reach levels that are unsustainable by Earth. • Climate change may force us to search for a less harmful environment.

Table 15.5 *Some problems of space exploration faced by humans*

Problem	Action required
Lack of atmosphere	• Oxygen, stored in liquid form, must be constantly added to the air within a space vehicle. • Carbon dioxide must be constantly removed from the air. • Temperature and pressure levels must be carefully maintained. • Sound cannot pass through a vacuum so communication outside the space vehicle is done by using radio waves.
Lack of gravity	• Astronauts need to learn to move around in the absence of gravity. • Food must be in liquid or semi-liquid form so that it may be sucked from its container and then forced down the oesophagus using the muscles. • Urine and body waste must be passed to sealed containers. • It is recommended that astronauts exercise $2\frac{1}{2}$ hours per day, six days per week to avoid **muscle atrophy** (shrinking of the muscles) and **reduced bone mass**.
Radiation	• Special clothing must be worn to protect against the high radiation levels in space. The outer layers of space vehicles contain similar protection.

The International Space Station (ISS)

Table 15.6 *The International Space Station*

Brief description	This is the largest **artificial satellite** put into space by humans. It has laboratories, living quarters, docking ports for space vehicles, solar panels to provide power and a crew of about six, whose responsibilities also include maintaining the station.
Orbit	It is a low orbit satellite with an average height of 400 km (see page 177, Figure 15.8) and it orbits the Earth every 90 minutes.
Functions	It is used as an **intermediate port** for space exploration. Within it, **scientific research** is performed under the conditions of a space environment.
Ownership	It was built in orbit at a cost of 100 billion dollars by space agencies from four countries (the USA, Russia, Canada and Japan) and one collection of countries (Europe). Each of these space agencies has a control centre on Earth.

Exploration of Mars

Mars exploration began in the 1960s and continues today, as humans try to find out more about one of Earth's closest neighbours. All the types of space probes listed in Table 15.7 relay their information to receivers on Earth.

Table 15.7 *Obtaining information about Mars*

Probe	Function	Important tasks and accomplishments
Flybys	Space probes that get close enough to gather information and then shoot off into space.	• **Mariners 4, 6 and 7** obtained photos, detected a thin atmosphere of carbon dioxide as well as a magnetic field, and measured temperatures.
Orbiters	Satellites placed around planets to obtain information from the surroundings or from data collected by **landers** and **rovers**.	• **Mariner 9** investigated the Martian moons and produced maps of the planet indicating past volcanoes and rivers. • **Mars Global Surveyor** investigated the ionosphere, the atmosphere and the surface.
Landers	Spacecraft designed to land and remain on a planet in order to gather information and relay it to **orbiters**. Landers are also used to deliver vehicles known as rovers to the planet.	• **Viking 1 and Viking 2** looked for signs of life on Mars and found the essential ingredients: carbon, nitrogen, hydrogen, oxygen and phosphorus. • **The Mars Pathfinder lander** delivered the **Sojourner rover**. • **The Phoenix lander** was designed to detect microbial life and the possibility of water on the planet.
Rovers	Vehicles that explore and take samples of a planet for analysis. They usually report their findings to a lander, which then communicates with Earth via an orbiter. Figure 15.9 shows three generations of Mars rovers.	• **The Sojourner rover** was only 60 cm long. It stayed within 12 metres of the **lander**, as it gathered, analysed and relayed information about the planet's surface. • **Spirit** and **Opportunity** were put on opposite sides of Mars to search for water. • **Curiosity** is the size of a small car. It investigates the geology and climate, as well as the possibility of Mars being able to support life.

Figure 15.8 The International space station

Figure 15.9 Three generations of Mars Rovers

Revision questions

1 Describe the location of Earth in the universe in terms of the Sun, other stars, our solar system, our galaxy and galaxies in general.

2 Give a brief description of the Milky Way galaxy.

3 a Distinguish between geostationary satellites and polar satellites, and cite ONE use of EACH.

b Briefly describe GPS satellites and state what they are used for.

4 a List FIVE types of bodies that orbit the Sun.

b Name the planets belonging to the following groups in order of increasing orbital radius:
i The gas giants.
ii The terrestrial planets.

c For each of the following items, identify the planet of our solar system that is:
i the smallest.
ii orbited by 67 moons.
iii known for its profound ring system.
iv the largest.
v spinning on its side with its axis of rotation tilted at 98°.
vi known as the 'red planet'.
vii the hottest.
viii known for having many volcanoes.
ix orbited by a moon larger than Mercury.
x the brightest when seen from Earth.
xi virtually without an atmosphere.
xii known for its 'Great Red Spot'.
xiii covered by dense carbon dioxide and a cloud of sulfuric acid.
xiv known for its dust storms.

5 a How long does the Earth's moon take to orbit the Earth and to return to the same position relative to the Sun as seen by an observer on Earth?

b Approximately what percentage of the Moon's disc reflects light to Earth during a:
i Full moon?
ii New moon?
iii First quarter moon?

16 The terrestrial environment

Terrestrial organisms live and grow predominantly or entirely on **land. Soil** forms an important part of the environment of these organisms, and the terrestrial environment as a whole is influenced by events occurring in the **atmosphere**, within the **Earth** itself and in the **oceans**.

Soil formation

Soil is the upper layer of the Earth, comprising inorganic and organic matter, air and water, in which plants grow.

Soil forms continuously, but slowly, from the gradual breakdown of rocks by **physical** and **chemical weathering** and **biological action**.

Physical (mechanical) weathering

During **physical weathering**, rocks are broken down by **physical processes** into smaller pieces without altering the chemical composition of the rocks. Several factors can bring it about.

- **Temperature changes** between day and night cause rocks to expand and contract, especially in desert regions. This causes the rock surfaces to crack and break up into smaller pieces which then peel off, a process known as **exfoliation**.
- **Water** in cracks in rocks **freezes** when the temperature drops below 0 °C, causing **ice** to form. Ice expands as it forms and exerts pressure within the cracks. When temperatures increase above 0 °C, the ice **melts**. This repeated **freeze-thaw** widens the cracks and causes pieces of rock to break away.
- **Wind** can blow small particles of rock against other rocks, which causes small pieces to break away.

Chemical weathering

During **chemical weathering**, rocks are broken down by **chemical processes** that alter the chemical composition of the rocks. Chemical weathering is common in locations with a lot of **rainfall** and occurs more rapidly in high temperatures or polluted air. Several processes can bring it about:

- **Carbonation** occurs when **carbon dioxide** in the air reacts with **rainwater** forming a weak acid, **carbonic acid**. This acid **reacts** with the softer parts of rocks, especially limestone rocks, forming soluble compounds that are washed away, leaving the harder parts that break away or crumble.
- **Hydrolysis** occurs when **water reacts** with certain minerals in rocks to form new compounds that are often softer than the original rock. This weakens the original rock, so it breaks apart more easily.
- **Oxidation** occurs when some minerals in rocks **react** with **oxygen** in the air to form compounds called **oxides** which wash away or crumble more easily.
- **Solution** occurs when some minerals in rocks **dissolve** in **rainwater** and wash away. This weakens the original rock so that it breaks apart more easily, and it is speeded up if the rainwater is slightly acidic, which occurs particularly in areas where **pollution** produces **acid rain** (see page 210).

Biological action

During **biological action** or **weathering**, rocks are broken down by **living organisms**:

- **Plant roots** grow into cracks and crevices and make them wider and deeper as the roots grow. This causes the surrounding rocks to break up.
- **Burrowing animals** burrow into cracks and crevices. This makes the cracks and crevices larger and causes rocks to break up.
- **Earthworms** eat soil with their food, grind it up in their guts and pass out the finely ground remains.

Functions and types of soil

Soil has **six** basic components (see Table 16.1).

Table 16.1 *The components of soil and their functions*

Component	Functions
Inorganic rock particles: formed from rocks by weathering.	• Provide support and anchorage for plant roots. • Provide shelter for soil animals.
Water: held in a thin film around rock particles.	• Provides plants with water for photosynthesis. • Dissolves mineral nutrients for plants. • Prevents animals without waterproof body coverings from drying out (desiccating), e.g. earthworm.
Air: present in the spaces between rock particles.	• Provides plant roots and animals with oxygen for respiration. • Provides microorganisms with oxygen to decompose dead organic matter.
Mineral nutrients (salts): dissolved in water in the soil.	• Provide elements which are essential for the healthy growth of plants.
Organic matter or **humus:** derived from dead and decaying plant and animal material.	• Adds mineral nutrients to the soil. • Binds rock particles together forming **soil crumbs** (see page 182).
Living organisms: plant roots, microorganisms, earthworms and other burrowing animals.	• Plant roots bind soil particles, preventing erosion. • Microorganisms (bacteria and fungi) decompose organic matter. • Earthworms and other burrowing animals increase soil aeration and fertility.

Types of soil

Soils can be classified into **sandy soil, clay soil** and **loam** based on the **size** of the rock particles they contain. This can be determined by the **sedimentation test**, in which soil and water are shaken in a jar and the mixture is left to settle.

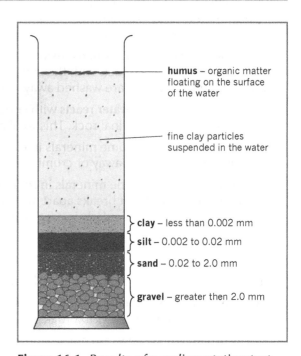

humus – organic matter floating on the surface of the water

fine clay particles suspended in the water

clay – less than 0.002 mm

silt – 0.002 to 0.02 mm

sand – 0.02 to 2.0 mm

gravel – greater then 2.0 mm

Figure 16.1 *Results of a sedimentation test*

Table 16.2 *Clay and sandy soils compared*

Property	Sandy soil	Clay soil
Particle size	**Large:** 0.02 to 2.0 mm	**Small:** less than 0.002 mm
Air content	**High:** large particles have large air spaces between.	**Low:** small particles have small air spaces between.
Water content	**Low:** large particles have a small total surface area to retain water.	**High:** small particles have a large total surface area to retain water.
Drainage	**Good:** water passes through large air spaces quickly. Does not become waterlogged.	**Poor:** water passes through small air spaces slowly. Easily waterlogged.
Mineral nutrient content	**Low:** rapid drainage causes minerals to be washed through the soil (leaching).	**High:** slow drainage prevents leaching of minerals.

Loam

Loam is the **ideal soil**. It contains a mixture of sand, clay and silt. The **advantages** of both sand and clay are combined in loam. Loam retains water well but does not become waterlogged, and it contains an adequate quantity of air and mineral nutrients.

Soil profiles

Soil is composed of layers known as **soil horizons**. A **soil profile** is a vertical section through the soil showing the horizons. The soils in the horizons differ in composition, structure, texture and colour. Most soils have **three** horizons, **A**, **B** and **C**. Some also have an **O** horizon, and the parent rock is known as the **R** horizon.

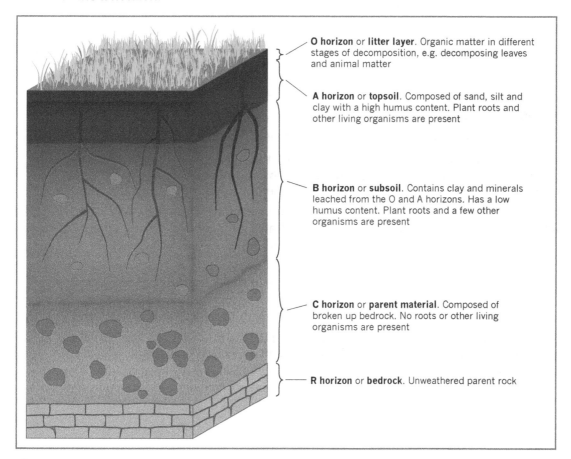

O horizon or **litter layer**. Organic matter in different stages of decomposition, e.g. decomposing leaves and animal matter

A horizon or **topsoil**. Composed of sand, silt and clay with a high humus content. Plant roots and other living organisms are present

B horizon or **subsoil**. Contains clay and minerals leached from the O and A horizons. Has a low humus content. Plant roots and a few other organisms are present

C horizon or **parent material**. Composed of broken up bedrock. No roots or other living organisms are present

R horizon or **bedrock**. Unweathered parent rock

Figure 16.2 *A typical soil profile*

Soil fertility

A **fertile soil** is able to support the healthy growth of a large number of plants. **Soil fertility** is affected by the **physical** and **chemical properties** of the soil.

- **Physical properties** depend on the soil's **texture**, i.e. the proportions of sand, silt and clay particles, and its **structure**, i.e. how the particles are clumped together into **soil crumbs**. A fertile soil must have a balanced mixture of small and large particles and a good crumb structure so that it:
  - Contains adequate quantities of **water** and **air**.
  - **Drains** well and does not become waterlogged, but still retains adequate quantities of water.
  - Is **loose** enough for plant roots to penetrate easily and soil animals to burrow.

- **Chemical properties** depend on the nature of the **parent rock** and the amount of **organic matter** the soil contains. These determine the soil's **mineral nutrient** content and **pH**. A fertile soil:
  - Contains all the essential **mineral nutrients** for healthy plant growth, including nitrate, sulfate, phosphate, potassium and magnesium ions.
  - Has a **pH** between about **6.0** and **7.5** which is suitable for most plants to grow, ensures that most minerals are available for plant roots to absorb and encourages earthworms to move into the soil.

Humus and soil fertility

Humus is formed by bacteria and fungi decomposing dead and waste **organic matter** in the soil, e.g. dead plant and animal remains, and faeces. It is a dark brown sticky material that coats soil particles and improves **soil fertility**. Humus:

- Improves the **mineral nutrient content** by adding minerals when the organic matter decomposes, and by absorbing and retaining minerals.
- Improves the **water content** by absorbing and retaining water.
- Improves the **air content** and **drainage** by binding finer soil particles together into larger **soil crumbs**.

Soil organisms and soil fertility

Soil organisms are important in increasing **soil fertility**:

- **Bacteria and fungi** decompose dead organic matter, releasing mineral nutrients back into the soil.
- **Earthworms** improve **aeration** and **drainage** by burrowing through the soil. They **fertilise** the soil by feeding on plant debris and soil particles, and egesting **worm casts** that are rich in minerals. They also add **humus** to the soil by pulling plant debris into their burrows, which then decomposes.
- **Nematodes** are microscopic roundworms. They consume bacteria and fungi in the soil and release **ammonium compounds** which can be converted into nitrates for plant use (see page 185). They also **spread** useful bacteria and fungi through the soil on their bodies.

Soil erosion

Soil erosion is the wearing away of the upper layers of soil due to the action of wind and water.

Soil is one of the world's most **important natural resources**. It is essential for the growth of **plants**, including agricultural crops. Plants are essential to supply all other living organisms directly or indirectly with **food** and with **oxygen**. Soil also provides a **habitat** for a wide range of organisms. If soil is removed, plants cannot grow, and if plants cannot grow, **food production** is substantially **reduced** which can lead to starvation.

Causes of soil erosion

Soil erosion occurs naturally and is speeded up if the soil has **no plants** growing in it to bind the particles together with their roots. The following can cause soil to erode:

- **Rainfall** on the soil surface breaks down soil crumbs and disperses soil particles, which can then be washed away by water **runoff**.
- **Wind** picks up loose soil particles and carries them with it.
- **Deforestation**, where trees are cut down and not replanted, removes leaves that break the force of the rain and roots that bind the soil together. This leaves the soil barren and exposed to rain and wind.
- **Bad agricultural practices** such as leaving the soil barren after harvesting, not rotating crops, using chemical instead of organic fertilisers, overgrazing animals and ploughing down hillsides.

Prevention of soil erosion

A variety of measures can be implemented to **reduce soil erosion** and **conserve soil**:

- Never leave soil barren:
  - Practise **reforestation**, i.e. plant new young trees in areas where trees have been removed by cutting, or destroyed by fire or disease.
  - Replant **crops** immediately after harvesting.
  - Plant other **vegetation** on barren soil, such as grass and shrubs.
- Practise **crop rotation** to ensure the soil remains fertile and does not lose its crumb structure.
- Grow crops using **contour ploughing, terracing** or **strip-planting** to prevent erosion caused by water running down slopes (see Table 3.1, page 33).
- Cover soil with **mulch**, i.e. plant material such as leaves, compost and crop residues.
- Prevent **overgrazing** of animals.
- Improve **drainage** of land.

Recycling in nature

The different **chemical elements** that make up the bodies of all living organisms, such as carbon, oxygen and nitrogen, are continually **cycled** through these living organisms and their physical environment to ensure that they never run out. **Decomposers** are essential for much of this recycling. These are **bacteria** and **fungi** that feed on dead and waste organic matter causing it to **decompose**. Decomposers are also known as **saprophytes**.

The oxygen cycle

The cycling of **oxygen (O) atoms** occurs between **oxygen (O_2) gas** in the air and **oxygen-containing compounds**, mainly carbon dioxide (CO_2) and water (H_2O).

- **Oxygen** is **removed** from the air and converted to carbon dioxide and water by:
  - **Respiration** occurring in all living organisms including animals, plants and decomposers.
  - **Combustion**, mainly of **fossil fuels** such as coal, oil and natural gas.
- **Oxygen** is **returned** to the air during the day by **photosynthesis** occurring in green plants.

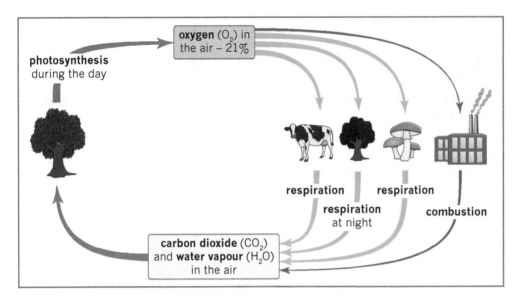

Figure 16.3 *The oxygen cycle*

The carbon cycle

The cycling of **carbon (C) atoms** occurs by them being converted into different **carbon-containing compounds** including carbon dioxide (CO_2) present in the **air** and organic compounds, mainly carbohydrates, proteins and lipids, present in **living organisms**.

- **Carbon dioxide** is **removed** from the air and converted into organic compounds by green plants during **photosynthesis**. These organic compounds are passed on to **animals** when the plants are eaten, and to **decomposers** when plants and animal die.

- **Carbon dioxide** is **returned** to the air by:

  - **Respiration** of organic compounds occurring in all living organisms.
  - **Combustion**, mainly of **fossil fuels**.

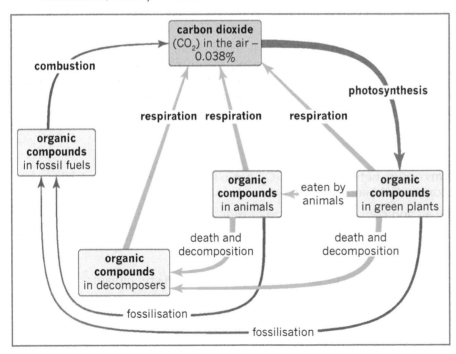

Figure 16.4 *The carbon cycle*

The nitrogen cycle

Most living organisms are unable to use nitrogen (N_2) gas directly. The cycling of **nitrogen (N)** atoms occurs mainly by them being converted into different **nitrogen-containing compounds** including proteins present in living organisms and ammonium (NH_4^+) compounds, nitrites (NO_2^-) and nitrates (NO_3^-) present in the soil.

- **Nitrogen** is **removed** from the air and converted into ammonium compounds by **nitrogen-fixing bacteria** in the soil and in the root nodules of legumes, such as peas and beans. The legumes use these compounds to make proteins.

- **Nitrogen** is **returned** to the air by **denitrifying bacteria**, which convert nitrates in the soil to nitrogen.

- **Nitrate ions** in the soil are **removed** from the soil by **plants** and used to make protein. This protein is passed on to **animals** when the plants are eaten.

- **Nitrate ions** are **returned** to the soil by the decomposition of dead plants and animals by **decomposers**. This forms ammonium compounds which **nitrifying bacteria** convert into nitrites and nitrates.

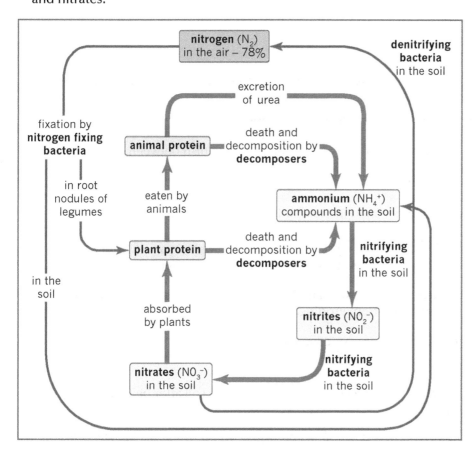

Figure 16.5 *The nitrogen cycle*

The water cycle

The cycling of **water** involves the following processes:

- **Evaporation** – Water **evaporates** from the soil and from bodies of water, including streams, rivers, ponds, lakes, seas and oceans. The water vapour that forms enters the atmosphere.

- **Transpiration** and **exhalation** – Plants lose water vapour to the atmosphere from their leaves when they **transpire** and animals lose water vapour when they **exhale**.

- **Condensation** – Water vapour in the atmosphere cools and **condenses** to become water droplets that form **clouds**.

- **Precipitation** – Water from clouds falls back into bodies of water or onto land as rain, hail, sleet and snow. Water falling onto land can run off the land into bodies of water as **surface runoff**, or it can enter groundwater by **infiltration** and **percolation**, and may eventually return to bodies of water.

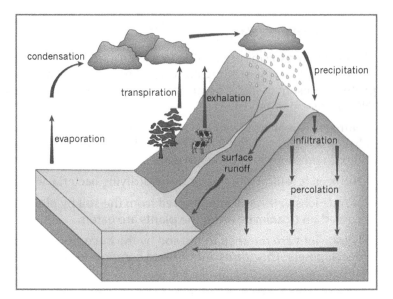

Figure 16.6 *The water cycle*

Revision questions

1 **a** What is soil?

   b Identify the THREE main factors that influence the formation of soil and distinguish among them.

2 Outline the importance of soil to living organisms.

3 **a** Using air content, water content and drainage, distinguish between a sandy soil and a clay soil.

   b What is loam?

4 Name the THREE horizons found in most soils and distinguish among them.

5 Explain how EACH of the following affects a soil's fertility:

   a its physical properties   **b** its chemical properties   **c** its humus content

6 Identify THREE causes of soil erosion and THREE methods farmer Giles can employ to prevent the soil on his farm from eroding.

7 Describe how the following are cycled in nature:

   a carbon   **b** water

8 **a** Explain how nitrates in the soil can be returned to the soil after being absorbed by grass growing in a field.

   b What are nitrogen-fixing bacteria and what is their role in the nitrogen cycle?

Air masses

Air masses are extensive bodies of air with approximately uniform characteristics of temperature and humidity at any given altitude.

The longer an air mass remains over a particular region, the more it will acquire the properties resulting from its contact with the surface. These air masses affect the **weather** and can **transport pollutants** over thousands of miles to other parts of the Earth.

Table 16.3 *The main types of air masses*

Type	Region of formation on surface of Earth	Features
Maritime tropical (mT)	Tropical and sub-tropical seas and oceans, such as the Caribbean Sea	warm/humid
Continental tropical (cT)	Tropical land areas, such as the Desert Southwest of the USA	hot/dry
Maritime polar (mP)	Polar oceans, such as the Atlantic Ocean east of Newfoundland	cool/humid
Continental polar (cP)	Large land areas near to the poles, such as Canada	cold/dry

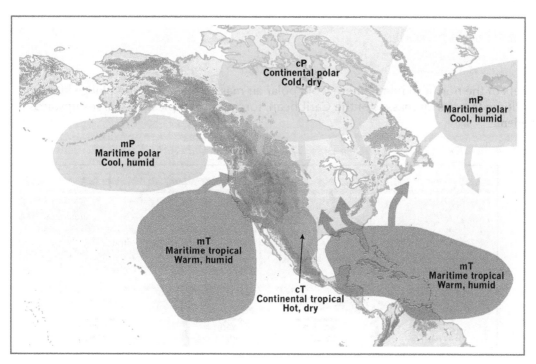

Figure 16.7 *Air masses affecting North America and the Caribbean*

Table 16.4 *Pollutants transported by air masses*

Pollutant	Associated problems
Industrial gases	Carbon dioxide, nitrogen dioxide and sulfur dioxide emitted by **industrial processes** dissolve in rain water and in oceans, producing acids that have a negative effect on plant and animal life. Nitrogen dioxide and sulfur dioxide also cause respiratory problems.
Landfill fumes	Landfill fumes contain the greenhouse gases carbon dioxide and methane, which contribute to global warming, as well as ammonia and hydrogen sulfide, which produce unpleasant odours and cause breathing difficulties.
Particulate matter	Smoke and dust can cover the leaves of plants reducing photosynthesis and can also lead to respiratory problems. They can originate from **industrial processes, volcanic eruptions** or even **desert regions. Sahara dust** presents problems in the Caribbean.
Radioactive fallout	Material from **nuclear explosions** can be shot high into the air and transported for hundreds of miles before it returns to the surface and threatens all forms of life.

Local fronts and their effects on weather

*A **front** is a boundary or transition zone formed where air masses of different temperatures meet.*

At a front, the warm, less dense air rises above the cooler air. If the rising air is humid, its water vapour may **condense** as it cools to produce **rain**.

Table 16.5 *Fronts and their weather map symbols*

Type of front	Cold front	Warm front	Stationary front	Occluded front
Map symbol	▲▲▲▲	⬤⬤⬤⬤	⬤⬤⬤	▲⬤▲⬤▲

Cold fronts and warm fronts

*A **cold front** is the boundary where a cold air mass advances into a warm air mass.*

During the winters of the northern hemisphere, cold polar air masses from the USA **plunge into** the warm, moist maritime tropical air masses of the Caribbean, forcing the tropical air masses upwards with a **steep gradient**.

*A **warm front** is the boundary where a warm air mass advances towards a cold air mass.*

As warm air masses advance towards cooler ones, they **glide over** them producing fronts of a **gentle gradient**.

Figure 16.8
Weather at a cold front and at a warm front

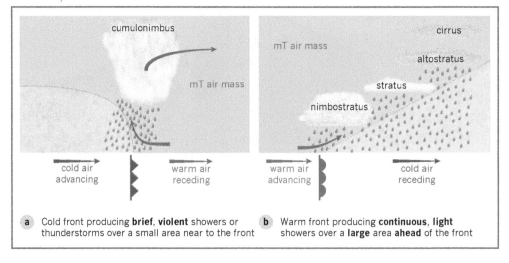

a Cold front producing **brief, violent** showers or thunderstorms over a small area near to the front

b Warm front producing **continuous, light** showers over a **large** area **ahead** of the front

Table 16.6 *Comparing the weather produced by cold fronts and warm fronts*

	Cold front	Warm front
Action	Cold polar air mass **plunges into** warm tropical air mass.	Warm tropical air mass **glides over** cold polar air mass.
Gradient at boundary	**Steep**	**Gentle**
Temperature	Becomes **cooler.**	Becomes **warmer.**
Clouds	**Vertical cumulonimbus** clouds form rapidly due to rapidly rising air.	**Horizontal stratus-type** clouds form slowly due to gently rising air.
Showers	**Brief, intense** showers with possible thunderstorms at the front.	**Continuous, light** to moderate showers ahead of the front – can last for a few days.
Region affected	Relatively **small** due to the steep gradient between the air masses.	Relatively **large** due to the slight gradient between the air masses.
Frontal speed	**Fast**, compared to warm fronts.	**Slow**, compared to cold fronts.

Stationary front

*A **stationary front** occurs at the boundary between two air masses of different temperatures when neither air mass is capable of displacing the other.*

Weather at the stationary front is normally **clear** to **partly cloudy**, but if there is moisture, there can be light or heavy rain which may fall for long periods until the front moves again.

Winds blowing parallel to the front help to keep it stationary, as shown in **Figure 16.9b**. If the wind direction changes, the front can begin to move again, becoming a cold front or a warm front depending on which air mass advances against the other.

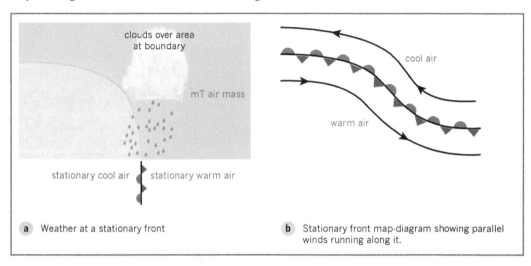

a Weather at a stationary front

b Stationary front map-diagram showing parallel winds running along it.

Figure 16.9 *Stationary front*

Occluded front

*An **occluded front** occurs where a fast-moving cold front catches up with a warm front travelling in approximately the same direction, raising the warm air between them upwards and off the ground.*

Cold fronts advance faster than warm fronts. Figure 16.10a shows the air masses just before the formation of an occluded front. The cold air mass plunges into the warm air, squashing it onto the cool air ahead of the warm front. The warm air rises steeply at the cold front and more gently at the warm front, producing **cumulonimbus** and **stratus** clouds respectively. The cold front catches up with the warm front, squeezing the hot air mass **off the ground** and producing **major precipitation** as shown in Figure 16.10b. This is the last stage of the storm since the hot air has now all been lifted.

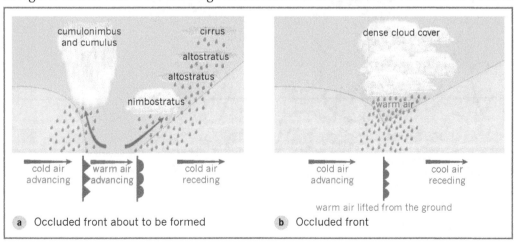

a Occluded front about to be formed

b Occluded front

Figure 16.10 *Weather at an occluded front*

Figure 16.11 shows a sequence of map diagrams during the formation of an occluded front. When the cold front catches up with the warm front, an occluded front is formed and they 'zip together'. Note that **winds in the northern hemisphere blow anticlockwise around a low pressure centre.**

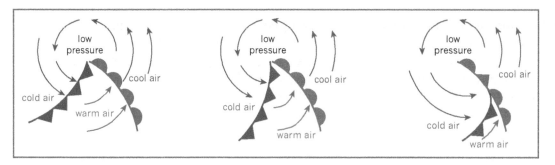

Figure 16.11 *Map diagram showing the formation of an occluded front*

Cyclonic storms

*A **cyclone** is a large-scale wind system that rotates around a low-pressure centre.*

Tropical cyclones

- Temperatures in excess of 27 °C can cause large areas of hot, moist air to expand and rise, producing regions of **low pressure**.
- Winds pulled by the low-pressure region are deflected by the Earth's rotation in an **anticlockwise direction in the northern hemisphere** and in a clockwise direction in the southern hemisphere.
- As water vapour condenses, latent heat of condensation further heats the air, sucking water vapour from over the ocean at an **increased rate** and producing **cumulonimbus** clouds and **torrential rains**.
- The centre of the storm, known as the **eye**, is a **calm low-pressure** region with **few clouds** and **little or no rain**.
- The eye is surrounded by the **eyewall.** This is the most destructive region of the storm, as this is where the **strongest winds** and **heaviest rainfall** occur.

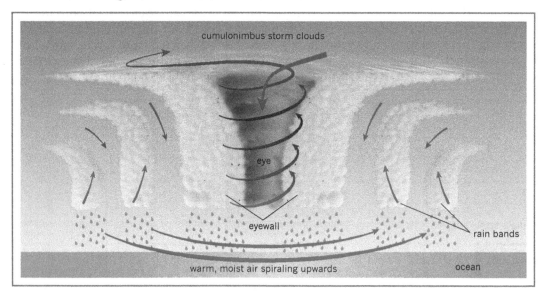

Figure 16.12 *Cross-section through a hurricane*

Table 16.7 *Classification of tropical cyclones*

Classification	Tropical depression	Tropical storm	Hurricane
Wind speed (km h⁻¹)	Less than 63	63 to 118	Greater than 118

The **Atlantic hurricane season** runs from June 1 to November 30. This is when the ocean is **warmest** and the air near the surface is very **humid**.

Weather during the passing of a hurricane

- Hurricanes in the Atlantic **progress westward** across the ocean, strengthening until they reach land.
- The approaching storm is signalled by a **drop in atmospheric pressure. Wind gusts** become **strong** and dark nimbus clouds (rain clouds) appear in bands, bringing **heavy rain.**
- As the eye approaches, the strong winds and heavy rainfall become severe, destroying buildings, uprooting trees and causing landslides.
- On arrival of the eye, the pressure drops significantly and **calm** sets in.
- As the eye passes, the **rains return** and the **wind speed increases** once more, this time in the **opposite** direction. The very low-pressure region of the storm pulls water upwards, producing high sea levels known as **storm surges** that result in coastal flooding.
- This bad weather persists for quite some time, gradually weakening as the storm leaves the region.
- Wind speed **decreases over the land:**
  - due to **friction** with the landscape.
  - since the storm is **no longer being fed with energy** from evaporation of the ocean.

Hurricane preparedness

- Have charged battery packs or generators available in case the electricity is cut off.
- Stay tuned to the news media via a battery-operated radio.
- Ensure that your flashlights and lamps are functioning.
- Ensure that vehicles have a full tank of fuel.
- Secure doors and windows with straps or shutters and place tape on glass to reduce splintering.
- Trim or remove damaged trees or limbs, and remove any trees that are close enough to fall onto buildings.
- Anchor or store indoors any objects that could become projectiles.
- Pack loose objects in cupboards and secure important documents in sealed plastic bags.
- Have a stock of canned and dried foods that do not require refrigeration.
- Keep pets indoors and ensure that they wear identification or are microchipped.
- Know the whereabouts of the nearest secure shelter in case you need to evacuate.

Tidal waves and tsunamis

A *tidal wave* is a **shallow-water** wave that is produced by gravitational interactions among the Sun, the Moon and the Earth.

Tidal waves are not tsunamis, although some people generally use the same term for both.

A *tsunami* is a large **deep-water** wave produced by a coastal landslide, an undersea volcano or earthquake, or a huge meteorite crashing into the ocean.

Normal **ocean waves** produced by the wind carry energy only **along the surface. Tsunamis**, however, are created by disturbances **on the ocean floor** and carry energy through a massive amount of water. Tsunamis can travel at speeds ranging from 40 km h^{-1} near land to **800 km h^{-1}** in deep water!

- **In open water** the tip of the swell is seen appearing only about 1 m above the surface, but as the wave approaches land, this can grow as tall as **30 m**!

- **Just before reaching the coast**, water is sucked outwards and upwards into the swell, which then approaches with a devastating force, flattening buildings as far as 1.5 km inland.

- **As the water retreats** into the ocean, it drags debris with it, causing even more destruction.

Volcanoes

A volcano is an opening in a planet's crust from which molten lava, rock fragments, ashes, dust and gases are ejected from far below its surface.

Formation of volcanoes

The Earth's core consists of very hot molten rock known as **magma** which is constantly trying to expand outwards. Large sections of rock, known as **tectonic plates**, slowly drift on the magma. When these plates slip or collide against each other, magma can make its way upwards through cracks and fissures.

The pressure in the **vent** can cause it to explode outwards, throwing **pyroclastic** materials (rocks, ashes and gases) as well as **molten lava** (magma that has reached the surface) high into the air and producing **thick clouds** of **pungent smoke**.

Table 16.8 outlines the factors that result in the types of volcanic eruptions shown in Figure 16.13.

Table 16.8 *Causes of the different types of volcanic eruptions*

Cause	Effect
Viscosity of magma	• **Viscous** lava is thick and contains much silica, solidifying quickly to produce **steep slopes**. It tends to block the vent, leading to **explosive** eruptions as the pressure increases.
	• **Non-viscous** lava contains little silica and quickly spreads, forming **gentle slopes**. This type of lava does not block the vent to cause explosions.
Water	• **High water content** in the vent results in intense steam pressure that can produce violent explosions and scatter solid rock fragments, ash and cinder.
	• **Low water content** results in steady lava flows that are not explosive.
Gases	• **High concentrations** of gases in the vent have the same effect as high water content.

Cinder cone

- **Very viscous** (very thick) magma results in a **steep** slope.
- Vents block easily in this **small** volcano, causing **explosions** which **eject rock, ash and cinder** forming a conical shape as the pyroclastic materials are thrown away from the vent as '**volcanic bombs**'.

Example – La Soufriere, St Vincent

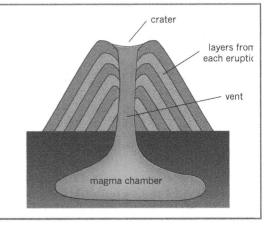

Composite cone (stratovolcano)

- **Viscous** magma leads to a **steep** slope.
- **Steam** in the vent causes **explosions** of rock, ash and cinder forming a conical shape as the pyroclastic materials are thrown away from the vent as 'volcanic bombs'.
- **Alternate layers** of lava and rock, ash and cinder occur with each eruption.
- **Parasitic cones** are produced at secondary vents.

Example – la Grande Soufriere, Guadeloupe;
          Soufriere Hills, Montserrat;
          Soufriere, St Vincent;
          Mount Pelee, Martinique

Lava dome

- **Viscous** magma produces a **steep slope** around the vent.
- Since there is **very little gas or steam** to cause explosions, the thick, slow-moving magma flows **steadily**, forming a **dome** instead of a cone.

Example – Soufriere Hills, Montserrat

Lava shield

- **Non-viscous** lava flows **steadily** since there is **little gas or steam to cause explosions.**
- Lava can spread for hundreds of kilometers giving an appearance of a **gently sloped** warrior's shield.

Example – Kilauea, Hawaii

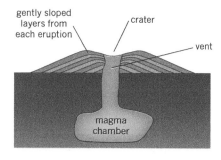

Fissure volcano

- **Non-viscous** lava flows **steadily**. Largest lava flows.
- **Very little gas and steam** together with a **long crack for magma to escape**, generally makes them **not explosive.**
- **Occurs along long fissures** where plates separate or on the flanks of some large volcanic vents. This makes them **different from all other volcanoes**, which only erupt at a **point** source.

Example – Holuhraun, Iceland

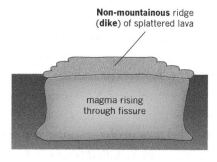

Figure 16.13 *Types of volcanoes*

Figure 16.14 *Lava dome volcano*

Figure 16.15 *Fissure volcano*

Kick 'em Jenny

- Kick 'em Jenny is an active **submarine volcano** located **8 km** north of Grenada. See Figure 16.16.

- It is **1300 m** above the sea floor and its highest point is **180 m** below the sea surface.

- It erupted in 1939 sending a cloud of steam and debris almost 300 m into the air and causing a small tsunami. Since then it has erupted at least 12 times.

- There is a **maritime exclusion zone** of radius **1.5 km** around the volcano.

- The volcanic islands of the Lesser Antilles were initially all submarine volcanoes.

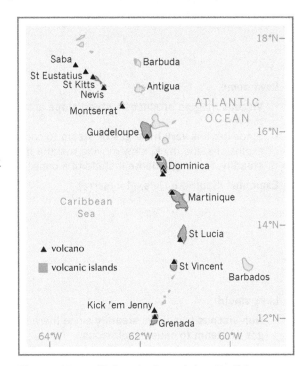

Figure 16.16 *Volcanic Arc of the Caribbean*

Ecological consequences of volcanoes

Table 16.9 *Ecological consequences of volcanoes*

Negative	Positive
• Rapidly moving flow of materials from the volcano destroys plants, animals, and anything in its path.	• Volcanic material can contain important minerals such as copper and gold.
• Ash can block sunlight, reducing photosynthesis and plant growth.	• Weathered lava becomes fertile soil after a period of time.
• Ash and volcanic gases can cause respiratory illnesses.	• Hot springs provide geothermal energy.
• Landslides produced can cause massive destruction.	• Hot springs can be used for therapy.
• Decaying animals, killed by the volcano, can pollute the environment, including its water supplies.	• Tourism can be boosted by extraordinary volcanic features such as 'calderas'. A **caldera** is created when a magma chamber is emptied by massive eruptions causing the crater to collapse into itself.
• Active volcanoes are unsafe and so can reduce tourism.	
• Beautiful landscapes are destroyed.	

The relationship between volcanoes and earthquakes

Earthquakes

Earthquakes are produced when the forces between tectonic plates result in sudden bursts of energy in the form of shock waves known as **seismic waves**.

The **hypocentre** or **focus** is the point below the surface where the earthquake originates.

The **epicentre** is the point on the surface directly above the focus where vibrations are usually strongest.

A **seismograph** is a device that measures movement of the ground by producing a graph (known as a **seismogram**) which indicates the amplitudes of the vibrations over time.

The **Richter scale** is a scale of 1 to 10 used to compare earthquakes.

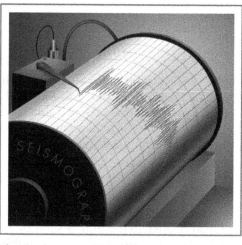

Figure 16.17 *Seismograph*

For each whole number increase on the Richter scale:

- the amplitude of the vibration increases by a factor of 10, and
- the energy released increases by a factor of about 30!

Table 16.10 *Interpreting the Richter scale*

Magnitude	Effect
< 5	Generally no damage, but indoor objects can vibrate and rattle.
5–6	Damages poorly constructed buildings.
6–8	Damages well-built structures; major damage may occur even 250 km from the epicentre.
8–9	Damages even 'earthquake-resistant' buildings.
>9	Almost total destruction producing permanent changes, even to the natural landscape.

Table 16.11 *The relationship between volcanoes and earthquakes*

Volcanoes	Earthquakes
Occur along the edges of tectonic plates.	Occur along the edges of tectonic plates.
Result from magma being forced upwards as plates collide, separate or slide past each other.	Result from vibrations produced as plates collide, separate or slide past each other.
Volcanoes can cause earthquakes as heat and pressure from the magma can crack rocks and so produce vibrations.	Earthquakes can cause volcanic eruptions by creating cracks for magma to rise through or by weakening the top of a magma chamber allowing the release of heat and pressure.

Tides

Tides are the changes in sea level on Earth caused by the gravitational attraction of the Moon and the Sun on the Earth, and by the Earth's rotation.

High tides and low tides

High tides occur on the sides of the Earth closest to the Moon and furthest from the Moon, as shown in Figure 16.18. Since the Earth takes 24 hours to rotate once on its axis, there are **two high tides** and **two low tides** at each point around the Earth on a **daily** basis.

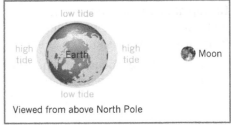

Figure 16.18 *High tides and low tides*

Spring tides and neap tides

The Moon takes $29\frac{1}{2}$ days (approximately one month) to orbit the Earth and to return to the same position relative to the Sun as seen by an observer on Earth (see chapter 15, Figure 15.7). Within each month there is a **spring tide** or a **neap tide** occurring each **week**.

Spring tides occur twice each month, at **new moon** and at **full moon**. This is when the gravitational attraction of the Earth by the Sun is in the same direction as the gravitational attraction of the Earth by the Moon, producing a maximum combined attraction of the Earth. These tides are therefore the **highest high tides** and the **lowest low tides.**

Neap tides occur twice each month, at the **1ˢᵗ quarter** and **3ʳᵈ quarter** phases of the Moon. This is when the gravitational attraction of the Earth by the Sun and the gravitational attraction of the Earth by the Moon produce a minimum combined attraction of the Earth. These tides are therefore the **lowest high tides** and the **highest low tides.**

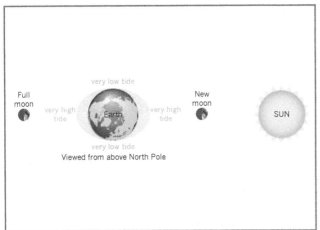

Figure 16.19 *Spring tides*

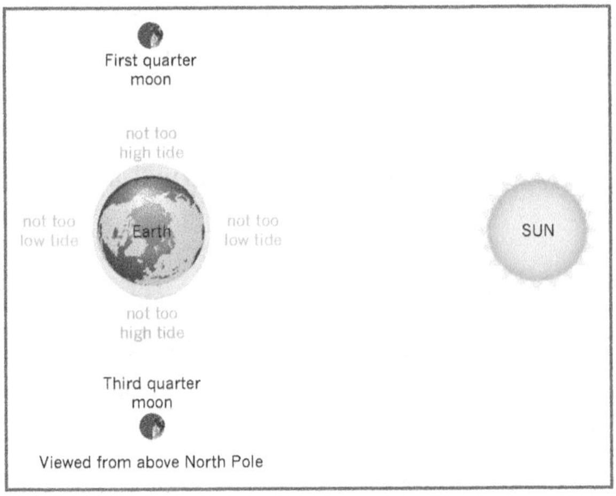

Figure 16.20 *Neap tides*

The effects of tides

- **A storm surge** occurs if the low-pressure eye of a hurricane sucks the ocean water into a swell and pulls it on to a coastal region. If this occurs during a spring tide, the sea level can rise significantly.
- **Tidal bores** occur at the mouths of rivers when the flow of water downstream meets a rising high tide and raises the water level even higher. If the river banks are steep and the width of the river upstream decreases significantly, the rise in water level can be very pronounced.

Coastal erosion due to tides

Coastal erosion of land and beaches can be caused by **changing tides** and **constant wave action**. The force of the water can continuously erode the soil and rock, or move sand from one place to another. This can cause trees to be uprooted, destroying habitats of plants and animals. Landscapes can be drastically changed, and the organisms that live there can be forced to **migrate** or **die**.

Effects of tides on organisms

Life along the shoreline is subjected to **harsh** physical conditions, dependent on the tides. Organisms must be capable of existing above and below the saline (salt) water. The areas of shoreline exposed to the Sun and air at low tide but covered by water at high tide can be divided into **intertidal zones**. These zones are subjected to variations in:

- moisture
- temperature
- salinity
- water turbulence

Table 16.12 *Coastal intertidal zones*

Intertidal zone	Conditions
Splash zone	This is splashed by sea spray but is mainly hot and dry.
High tide zone	Few animals live here since it is the **most stressful zone**. Organisms are exposed to high temperature and low moisture for long periods, and are pounded by the waves at high tide. Land animals living here usually have a tough exoskeleton and are mobile so that they can move to more comfortable places when necessary.
Mid-tide zone	This is exposed to the Sun and air, and then submerged in salt water for an equal period. Animals live here mainly in pools that remain when the tide recedes. The pools protect them from dehydration but make them easy targets for predators.
Low tide zone	This zone is usually submerged and so fluctuations in temperature, moisture and salinity are not drastic. A wide variety of aquatic plants and animals are found here.

9 Four important air masses are maritime tropical, maritime polar, continental tropical and continental polar. For EACH, state its TWO main characteristics and give an example of a region in which it is formed.

10 a What is meant by EACH of the following terms?
   i   Cold front
   ii Warm front
   iii Occluded front
   iv Stationary front

   b Use coloured pencils to draw map symbols of:
   i   a warm front
   ii an occluded front.

   c With the aid of a diagram, describe and explain the type of weather experienced at a cold front where a polar air mass meets a warm maritime tropical air mass.

11 a Distinguish among a tropical depression, a tropical storm and a hurricane in terms of wind speed.

   b Describe and explain how a tropical cyclone can develop into a hurricane and suggest TWO reasons why hurricanes weaken as they pass over land.

   c State FIVE ways you can prepare for a hurricane.

12 a Distinguish between a tsunami and a tidal wave in terms of how they are formed.

   b Describe a tsunami as it travels from its source, approaches land and causes destruction.

13 a Define the term 'volcano'.

   b i   How does thick lava affect the explosive nature of a volcano and the steepness of its slopes?
   ii How does lava with high water content affect the explosive nature of a volcano?
   iii What makes a fissure volcano different from all other types of volcanoes?
   iv Describe the type of lava produced by a 'lava shield' volcano.

   c Draw labelled diagrams of the following types of volcano.
   i   Composite cone
   ii Lava shield

   d State THREE advantages and THREE disadvantages of the ecological consequences of volcanoes.

14 What is meant by:

   a a seismograph?

   b the Richter scale?

15 Describe the physical conditions experienced by animals and plants living along the seashore.

17 Water and the aquatic environment

Water is **essential** for life on Earth. The bodies of living organisms contain between 60% and 70% water and water provides a **habitat** for aquatic organisms. Humans **use** water in many different ways.

Uses and conservation of water

Table 17.1 *Uses of water*

Where used	How used

Living organisms	• For **drinking**.
	• As a **solvent** to:
	    ♦ dissolve chemicals in cells so that they can **react**,
	    ♦ dissolve other useful substances such as food and minerals so that they can be **absorbed** into, and **transported** around, organisms' bodies,
	    ♦ dissolve waste and harmful substances so that they can be **excreted**.
	• As a **reactant**, e.g. in **photosynthesis**, which enables plants to make their own food.
	• As a **coolant** to remove heat from organisms when it **evaporates**, e.g. during sweating in humans or transpiration in plants.
	• As a **habitat** for aquatic organisms.

The home	• To do laundry, wash dishes, clean floors and wash cars. • For bathing, flushing toilets, watering gardens, cooking and drinking.
Agriculture	• To **irrigate** crops when there is insufficient rainfall. • To grow crops using **hydroponics** (see Table 3.1 page 33). • To provide **drinking water** for farm animals.
Fire fighting	• To create a barrier between the fuel and the air, and also to cool the fire.
Electricity generation	• In **thermo-electric** power plants, where water is boiled to produce steam for generating electricity. • In **hydro-electric** power plants, where the kinetic energy of flowing water is used to generate electricity.
Industry	• To **manufacture** a variety of products, e.g. soft drinks. • To **cool** and **clean** equipment and machinery.
Transportation	• To **transport goods** and **people** along rivers, and across seas and oceans.
Recreation	• For swimming, scuba diving, boating, fishing, surfing and water skiing.

Wastage and conservation of water

Less than 1% of the world's water is freshwater that is available for use. **Overusing** and **wasting** water can lead to food scarcity and starvation, loss of habitats for freshwater organisms, and a decrease in long-term, worldwide water security and availability.

The following measures can be implemented to **conserve** water in the home:

- **Meter** all domestic water supplies.
- Check regularly for **leaks.**
- Install **water saving devices** and **appliances** such as **low-flow** shower heads and taps, **low-flush** or **dual-flush** toilets, **aerators** on taps, and **water-efficient** washing machines and dishwashers.
- **Do not** leave taps running when brushing teeth, shaving, washing dishes and defrosting food.
- Use **greywater**, i.e. water used for washing dishes or fresh produce, to water gardens and wash cars.
- Collect **rainwater** and use it to flush toilets, wash cars and water gardens.

Methods of purifying water for domestic use

Water piped to homes usually comes from surface water sources such as **rivers**, **lakes** and **reservoirs**, or from groundwater sources such as **aquifers**. To make the water **potable**, i.e. safe to drink and use in food preparation, it must be **treated** to remove harmful contaminants such as bacteria, viruses, dissolved chemicals and suspended solid particles.

Large-scale treatment of water

The following steps are used to treat water before it is piped to homes.

- **Screening** – Water from water sources passes through grid screens that remove floating and suspended material.
- **Flocculation and sedimentation** – Chemicals such as **alum** are added to cause fine, solid particles suspended in the water to clump together to form larger particles called **floc**. The floc is then allowed to settle so it can be removed from the water.
- **Filtration** – The clear water above the floc is passed through **filter beds**, usually composed of sand, gravel and charcoal. This removes any remaining particles, and also removes some microorganisms (bacteria and viruses).
- **Chlorination** – **Chlorine gas** or **monochloroamine** are added to kill any remaining microorganisms. The water is then pumped to storage tanks for distribution.

Small-scale water treatment in the home

Table 17.2 *Methods used to treat water in the home*

Method	Explanation
Boiling	**Boiling** water for 15 minutes kills harmful microorganisms.
Filtration	**Fibre filters** can be used to remove suspended particles.
	Carbon filters containing **activated charcoal** can be used to remove dissolved organic compounds, odours and unpleasant tastes.
Chlorination	Adding **chlorine tablets** as directed or 2 drops of **chlorine bleach** per litre of water kills harmful microorganisms.
Distillation	Boiling the water to produce steam and condensing the steam to form pure **distilled water** leaves any dissolved salts and microorganisms behind.
Using additives	Adding **powdered alum** causes suspended fine particles to clump together and settle.

Desalination of seawater for domestic use

Oceans and seas contain 97% of the Earth's water, but this seawater contains **dissolved salts**. Before it can be used it must be **desalinated**, i.e. have the salts removed. Most desalination methods use large amounts of **energy**. The methods include:

- **Distillation** – See page 159 and Table 17.2.
- **Reverse osmosis** – Water is forced through a **semi-permeable membrane** under pressure and dissolved substances remain behind on the pressurised side. This removes any contaminants and microorganisms as well as the dissolved salts.

Properties of water

Water is the only natural substance that exists in **all three** physical states, solid, liquid and gas, at the temperatures found on Earth. **Pure water** has several unique **physical** and **chemical properties**:

- It is a colourless, tasteless, odourless **liquid** at room temperature.
- It has a **melting point** of **0 °C** and a **boiling point** of **100 °C**.
- It has a **maximum density at 4 °C**, therefore ice is less dense than liquid water and floats on water.
- It has a **high heat of vaporisation** and **a high specific heat capacity**, therefore it can resist temperature change and can moderate temperatures of living organisms and the Earth.
- It has a **high surface tension** because of the fairly strong attractive forces between water molecules.
- It **dissolves** a large number of substances, therefore is known as the **universal solvent**.
- It has a **pH of 7**, therefore is neutral.
- It **reacts** with reactive metals such as potassium and sodium.

Seawater, freshwater and aquatic life

Seawater has similar characteristics to freshwater, but some **differences** exist due to its salt content:

- Seawater has a **higher density** than freshwater.
- Seawater has a **lower melting point** than freshwater.
- Seawater has a **higher boiling point** than freshwater.

Most **aquatic organisms** are **adapted** to live in **either** seawater **or** freshwater and cannot survive if the salinity (salt content) of their environment changes very much. A few fish, such as salmon, can **migrate** between seawater and freshwater, but this takes time as their bodies adjust to the different salinities.

Archimedes' principle and flotation

Some bodies float in a fluid while others sink. The **density** of a body is an important factor in determining whether it will float or sink.

*The **density** of a body is its mass per unit volume.*

$$\text{density} = \frac{\text{mass}}{\text{volume}} \qquad \rho = \frac{m}{V}$$

The units of density are g cm^{-3} or kg m^{-3}.

Example

Figure 17.1 shows an object of mass 60 g placed into a displacement can filled with water to the level of the spout. The overflow is collected in a measuring cylinder. Determine the density of the object.

$$\rho = \frac{m}{V} = \frac{60 \text{ g}}{20 \text{ cm}^3} = 3 \text{ g cm}^{-3}$$

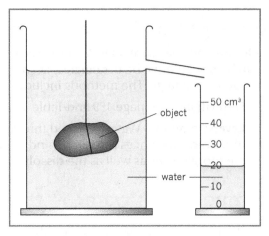

Figure 17.1 *Example 1*

*Archimedes' principle states that when a body is wholly or partially submerged in a fluid, it experiences an **upthrust** (buoyancy or upward force) equal to the weight of the fluid displaced (pushed away).*

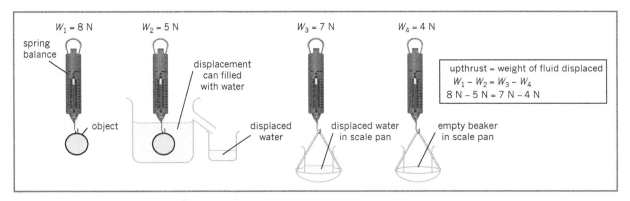

Figure 17.2 *Demonstrating Archimedes' principle*

Since the weight of the fluid displaced is proportional to its density, denser fluids provide greater upthrust.

- **Sinking** – An object will sink in a fluid if its density is greater than that of the fluid. The weight of the object is then greater than the upthrust (weight of fluid displaced).

- **Floating** – A heavy ship made of steel will float! This is so since its rooms contain air and therefore the overall density of the ship and its contents is much less than that of steel alone. The ship displaces just enough water to provide an upthrust equal to its weight.

  A ship travelling from the sea into the mouth of a river sinks deeper into the freshwater than it does into seawater, thereby displacing more of the **less dense freshwater** and so maintaining the upthrust at a value equal to its weight. A similar occurrence results when a ship travels from high latitude waters to **less dense, warmer, tropical waters**. The pilot of the ship must therefore be cautious when travelling to waters of lesser density.

- **Rising** – Hot air is less dense than cool air. A hot air balloon rises since the weight of its rubber casing plus the hot air inside of it is less than the upthrust on it (weight of cool air it pushes away).

Table 17.3 *Sinking, floating and rising*

Object sinks	density of object > density of fluid	weight of object > upthrust
Object floats at surface	density of object ≤ density of fluid	weight of object = upthrust
Object rises	density of object < density of fluid	weight of object < upthrust

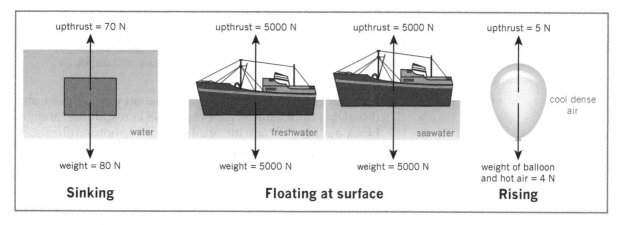

Figure 17.3 *Sinking, floating and rising*

The Plimsoll line

*A **Plimsoll line** is a line marked on a ship that indicates the maximum depth to which it should sink in the water in which it is loaded.*

Several '**load lines**' are used, corresponding to the density of the water where the ship is loaded. This makes it safe to travel between waters of different densities.

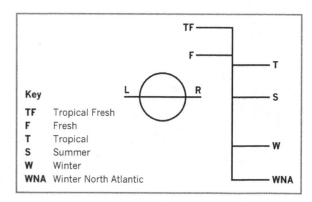

Figure 17.4 *The Plimsoll line*

Water pollution

Pollution is the contamination of the natural environment by the release of unpleasant or harmful substances into the environment.

Water can become **polluted** by harmful substances being released **directly** into lakes, rivers, seas and oceans, or by being **washed off** the land into these bodies of water.

Table 17.4 *Water pollutants and their effects on aquatic life*

Pollutant	Origin	Harmful effects
Nitrates and phosphates	• Fertilisers used in agriculture. • Synthetic detergents. • Improperly treated sewage.	• Cause **eutrophication**, in which these added mineral nutrients enrich the aquatic environment and cause the rapid growth of green plants and algae. This growth causes the water in lakes, ponds and rivers to turn green. The plants and algae die and are decomposed by **aerobic bacteria** that multiply and use up the **dissolved oxygen**. This causes other aquatic organisms such as fish to die.
Pesticides	• Used in agriculture to control pests, disease and weeds.	• Can be directly **toxic** to aquatic organisms. • Become **higher in concentration** up food chains and can harm the top consumers such as fish-eating birds.

Pollutant	Origin	Harmful effects
Oil spills	• From oil tankers and offshore oil rigs.	• Chemical constituents of oil can be **toxic** to aquatic organisms. • Form slicks on the surface of water that prevent **oxygen** from dissolving for aquatic organisms to use in respiration and block out light for aquatic plants to use in photosynthesis. • **Coat** sea birds and mammals with oil, causing birds to be unable to fly and keep warm, and causing mammals to be unable to keep warm. • **Smother** and **kill** plants and animals living in intertidal zones.
Heavy metals, such as mercury and lead	• Industrial waste. • Mining activities.	• May be directly **toxic** to organisms or become **higher in concentration** up food chains, harming top consumers such as large fish and birds of prey.

Figure 17.5 *Eutrophication*

Figure 17.6 *A seabird covered in oil*

Fishing methods

Fishing is an important industry in the Caribbean because it provides both **employment** and **food**. A variety of methods are used to catch fish.

Table 17.5 *Fishing methods*

Method	Description
By hand	Shellfish including lobsters, crabs, oysters and sea eggs (sea urchins) are **handpicked** from intertidal zones, or from the seabed by free divers or scuba divers.
Spearfishing and harpoon fishing	**Spears** and **harpoons** are held by hand or are shot from special guns. Free divers and scuba divers use spears to catch smaller fish such as snapper. Harpoons are used on boats to catch larger fish such as tuna.
Netting	Fish are caught within the mesh of **nets**. Mesh size determines the size of fish caught. Methods of net fishing include: • **Cast net** – A **circular net** with weights around its edge is thrown in shallow water close to shore. As the net sinks, it covers any fish below and traps them as the net edges are drawn together. • **Purse seining** – A **wall of netting** with weights at the bottom and supported by floats at the top is launched from a boat in a **circle** around a shoal of fish. A drawstring is pulled to close the bottom of the net and the fish are hauled aboard the boat. • **Trawling** – One or two boats tow a large **trawl net** through the water. Mid-water trawling catches fish in the open ocean. Bottom trawling catches fish close to or on the seabed and can damage the seabed. • **Dredging** – A net attached to a **frame** is dragged along the seabed to catch fish on the seabed and shellfish such as scallops and oysters. Dredging damages the seabed.
Lining	Fish are caught using **lines**: • **Hand line** or **rod and line** – A baited hook on a line is thrown into the water. As a fish bites the bait, the hook catches in its mouth and the fish is pulled or reeled in. • **Long-lining** – A long **main line** is held floating horizontally near the surface. Shorter, vertical, **branch lines** with baited hooks are attached to it at intervals to catch fish swimming below. Long-lining can kill seabirds and turtles.
Fish pots and traps	**Baited cages** made of chicken wire attached to a wooden frame are placed on the seabed with a surface buoy attached. Fish and shellfish enter through a cone-shaped funnel or trap door and cannot get back out. Lost traps can turn into 'death traps' for fish.
Fish farming	Freshwater and seawater fish and shellfish are raised commercially in **tanks**, **enclosures** such as ponds or **mesh cages** submerged in natural bodies of water. Species farmed include salmon, trout, tilapia, shrimp and oysters.

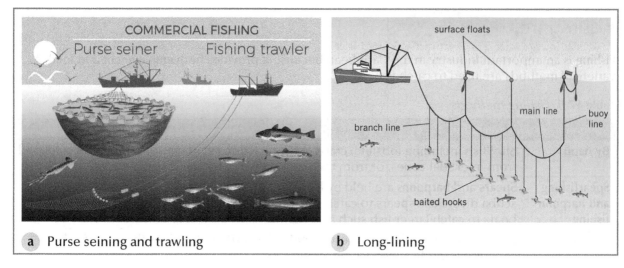

a Purse seining and trawling   **b** Long-lining

Figure 17.7 *Purse seining, trawling and long-lining*

Navigational devices used at sea

Sea-going vessels, such as ships, use a variety of **devices** to determine their **position** at sea, and to plan and steer a **course**. These devices are essential to ensure a vessel's **safety** and **prevent collisions**. The **International Maritime Organisation (IMO)** of the United Nations is responsible for setting **navigation rules** and **safety standards** for vessels at sea. **Regional boards** are responsible for implementing and enforcing these regulations, and can make modifications once they are consistent with the regulations.

The magnetic compass

A **magnetic compass** consists of a **magnetised needle** mounted on a pivot so that it spins freely and always points to **magnetic north**, and a **compass card** that shows the **cardinal points**, north (N), south (S), east (E) and west (W), and is divided into **360 degrees**.

A compass on a marine vessel is used to help **steer a course**. It has a fixed **lubber line** on its body that indicates the **direction** in which the vessel is pointing, and its compass card rotates freely so that **N** always points to **magnetic north**. A boat's course is shown by referring to the angle on the compass card indicated by the lubber line. If the card reads 0° the boat is heading due north, 90° due east, 180° due south and 270° due west. A compass does not need power or satellites to work.

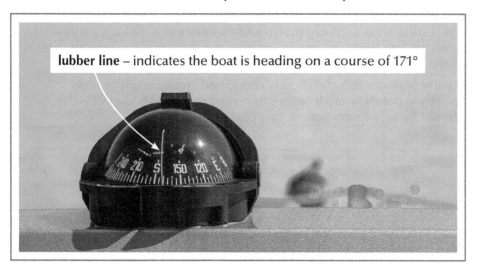

lubber line – indicates the boat is heading on a course of 171°

Figure 17.8 *A magnetic compass used at sea*

Sonar (Sound Navigation and Ranging)

Sonar is used to determine the **depth** of the seabed and to detect underwater **objects**. A sonar transducer emits **sound waves** into the water, which reflect off the seabed or an object and return an echo to the transducer. The **time** taken for the sound waves to return to the transducer is used to calculate the depth of the seabed, or the distance of the object.

Radar

Radar is used to detect **other vessels** and **coastlines**. It helps avoid collisions at sea by providing bearings of other vessels, their speed of movement and distances away. A **rotating antenna** on the vessel sweeps a narrow beam of **electromagnetic waves** around the surface of the water between the vessel and the horizon. The waves are reflected back to the vessel from any objects in their path and the objects show up as 'blips' on a **display screen**. Radar is especially useful in poor visibility conditions, e.g. during bad weather or at night.

GPS (Global Positioning System)

GPS is used to pinpoint the **exact location** of a vessel at sea by giving the vessel's latitude and longitude. The system consists of about **30 satellites** orbiting the Earth at an altitude of 20 000 km (see page 172). A GPS device receives **radio signals** from the satellites. Once a GPS receiver has information on how far away at least **three** satellites are, the exact location of the receiver can be pinpointed by a process called **trilateration**.

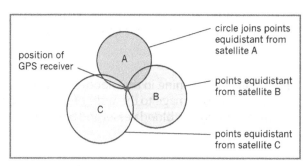

Figure 17.9 *Trilateration*

Water safety devices

Water safety devices are used to help keep people **afloat**, mainly in an emergency.

- **Life jackets** keep a person afloat even when unconscious and are always carried on sea-going vessels. Life jackets contain either **foam**, which is naturally buoyant, or are **inflated** when needed by a cartridge containing carbon dioxide. The person is kept afloat because the jacket weighs less than the water displaced by the person.
- **Buoyancy aids** help a person to float and swim, and are worn by people involved in water sports such as sailing, skiing and canoeing. Buoyancy aids usually contain foam. The person is kept afloat because the buoyancy aid weighs less than the water displaced by the person.
- **Life rafts** are small, rubber, inflatable boats carried on sea-going vessels. They have a **compressed air** or **carbon dioxide cylinder** attached that rapidly inflates the raft when its cord is pulled. Persons in need of rescue can then climb on board.
- **Inflatable tubes** or **rings** are worn around a person's waist and can be used to keep the person afloat when learning to swim.

Hazards associated with scuba diving

Scuba divers carry tanks of **compressed air** on their backs so they can breathe underwater. Divers experience **increasing pressure** from the water surrounding them as they descend and this can lead to a number of potential **hazards**:

Burst ear drum

As a diver descends, the pressure pushes his or her ear drums **inwards** causing **pain** which can be relieved by pinching the nose and forcing air from the throat up each eustachian tube into the middle ear (see page 87). If this is not done, an ear drum can **burst**.

'The bends' or decompression sickness

Increasing pressure increases the **solubility** of gases in liquids; therefore, as a diver descends and inhales air from the tank, more gases, mainly nitrogen, dissolve from the air into his or her blood and tissue fluids. If a diver dives too deeply for too long and does not ascend slowly enough, nitrogen forms **bubbles** in the bloodstream and body tissues during or soon after the ascent. These bubbles can cause joint pain, pressure bruising of the skin, paralysis and even death. 'The bends' is treated by immediate **recompression** and slow **decompression** in a **decompression chamber**.

Nitrogen narcosis

At depths greater than about **30 m** the nitrogen dissolved in a diver's blood and tissue fluids has a **narcotic effect** similar to that of drinking alcohol. This narcotic effect impairs the diver's judgement and sense of perception, and it increases as the diver goes deeper, increasing the risk of accidents. Narcosis can be reversed by ascending to a **shallower depth**.

Burst lung

If a diver holds his or her breath whilst ascending, the air inside the lungs expands as the surrounding water pressure decreases and can cause damage to the walls of the alveoli resulting in a **burst lung**.

Air or gas embolism

Nitrogen bubbles forming in the bloodstream during or after ascent, or **air bubbles** forming in the lung capillaries due to damage to the walls of the alveoli, can lead to an **air** or **gas embolism**. This is a **bubble** that becomes trapped in a blood vessel and **blocks** it, and can lead to a stroke or heart attack, and even death.

Revision questions

1. Outline how water is used:

   a by a hibiscus plant   b in the home   c in agriculture

2. Identify FOUR things Samara can do to conserve water in her home.

3. Explain THREE ways in which water can be treated in the home to make it safer to drink and identify TWO ways in which seawater can be treated for domestic use.

4. State FOUR properties of pure water and give TWO differences in the properties of seawater and freshwater.

5. a State Archimedes' principle and identify the conditions necessary for an object to float.

   b Define the term 'Plimsoll line' and suggest why a boat displaces more water as it travels from the ocean into the mouth of a river.

6. Outline the harmful effects of EACH of the following pollutants on aquatic life:

   a nitrates and phosphates b an oil spill   c pesticides

7. Describe how EACH of the following methods is used to catch fish:

   a purse seining   b long-lining   c trawling

8. a Name FOUR navigational devices that Akeem could use to help him safely navigate his cargo ship through the waters of the Caribbean.

   b What water safety devices should Akeem carry on his ship?

9. Outline what happens when a scuba diver suffers from EACH of the following:

   a 'the bends'   b a gas embolism   c nitrogen narcosis

18 Fossil fuels and alternative sources of energy

Earth receives energy from the **Sun** in the form of solar radiation. Plants absorb this energy during **photosynthesis** and convert it to chemical energy, which is then passed on to animals as they eat the plants. Solar energy can be used directly, but also provides us with other sources of energy.

Fossil fuels

*Fossil fuels are buried combustible deposits of decayed plant and animal matter that have been converted to **crude oil**, **natural gas** and **coal** by subjection to heat and pressure in the Earth's crust for hundreds of millions of years.*

Fossil fuels contain **chemical energy**. This is a type of **stored energy** that is released (converted to other forms of energy) when the fuel is **burnt**.

Table 18.1 *Types of fossil fuels*

Fossil fuel	Description	Formation
Coal	A black or dark brown rock consisting mainly of **carbon**.	Produced as the remains of **plants** of **swampy, forested areas** were covered by dirt and rock and subjected to intense **heat** and **pressure**. After millions of years these fossilised organisms converted to coal.
Crude oil	A yellow-to-black mixture comprised mainly of **hydrocarbon liquids**. Hydrocarbons are compounds consisting entirely of carbon and hydrogen.	Produced as the remains of microscopic **marine animals** and **plants** fell to the **ocean floor** where they were covered by layers of mud and subjected to intense **heat** and **pressure**. After millions of years these fossilised organisms converted to crude oil (petroleum). Crude oil is generally found **within layers of sandstone**.
Natural gas	A mixture including mainly **hydrocarbon gases**, the dominant constituent being **methane**.	Natural gas is formed together with coal and crude oil as described above. It is usually found trapped **under impermeable rock**.

Problems associated with the use of fossil fuels

Table 18.2 *General problems associated with the use of fossil fuels*

Problem	Details
Limited reserves	Supplies are diminishing.
Pollution (see Tables 18.3 and 18.4)	Burnt fossil fuels contaminate the environment with pollutants, including greenhouse gases. Unburnt fossil fuels also pollute the surroundings.
Rising cost of oil	The price of oil increases as it becomes less abundant.
Healthcare costs	Government funding of healthcare facilities to deal with illnesses associated with pollutants from the use of fossil fuels is a burden to economies.

Acid rain

The burning of fossil fuels produces **oxides of carbon, sulfur and nitrogen** which dissolve in rain water, lakes and oceans to form acids. These acids can:

- corrode metallic objects, buildings and landscapes
- negatively affect coral reefs
- damage soils and forests
- dissolve metals such as aluminium, which then flow to rivers and lakes and poison fish.

Global warming and the greenhouse effect

Energetic radiation from the Sun is mainly of a high frequency. It easily **penetrates** our atmosphere and warms the Earth. The Earth's surface then **emits** lower frequency **infrared** (IR) radiation which is **absorbed** by certain gases in the atmosphere known as **greenhouse gases**, mainly **carbon dioxide, water vapour** and **methane**. As the gases become warm, they **emit** their own radiation, much of it returning to Earth and preventing our seas and lakes from freezing.

However, with the increased burning of trees as forests are cleared and the extensive use of fossil fuels, the levels of greenhouse gases have risen to the extent that the planet is experiencing **global warming**. It is predicted that this will cause our weather to become more severe, the polar ice caps to melt and the ecology of the planet to be negatively affected.

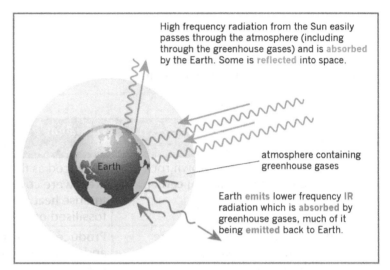

High frequency radiation from the Sun easily passes through the atmosphere (including through the greenhouse gases) and is absorbed by the Earth. Some is reflected into space.

Earth

atmosphere containing greenhouse gases

Earth emits lower frequency IR radiation which is absorbed by greenhouse gases, much of it being emitted back to Earth.

Figure 18.1 *The greenhouse effect*

Table 18.3 *Pollution due to burnt fossil fuels*

Pollutant	Associated problems
Particulate matter	• Dust and smoke diminish the amount of light reaching the Earth through our atmosphere and cover the leaves of plants, reducing photosynthesis. • Causes asthma, bronchitis and lung disease.
Carbon monoxide	• Reduces the blood's ability to transport oxygen. This can lead to nausea, headaches, blurred vision and even death through suffocation.
Carbon dioxide, sulfur dioxide and nitrogen oxides	• Produce **acid rain** – discussed above. • Carbon dioxide also contributes to global warming; sulfur dioxide combines with smoke particles and water vapour to produce **smog** (which causes respiratory problems); nitrogen oxides are irritants to the throat and lungs.
Heavy metal ions	• Lead, mercury, cadmium and other heavy metals are harmful to our bodies.

Table 18.4 *Pollution due to unburnt fossil fuels*

Pollutant	Associated problems
Oil from oil spills	• Poisons organisms if ingested or inhaled and can negatively affect the ecology of mangroves and coral reefs. • Irritates the skin and eyes of animals. • Smothers some species of small fish and invertebrates and covers the feathers and fur of many other animals, preventing them from flying or maintaining correct body temperatures. • Can travel across the sea, affecting regions far from the original spill.
Natural gas	• Wasted natural gas emissions contribute to **explosions** and **global warming**.

Using alternative sources of energy

Non-renewable energy sources are those that are not readily replenished and which become less with use.

Examples are **fossil fuels** and **nuclear fuel**.

Renewable energy sources are those which are readily replenished by natural processes.

Examples are **solar**, **hydroelectric**, **geothermal**, **tidal** and **wind** energy. Organic matter such as **wood** and **biomass** are considered renewable if the trees and crops from which they were obtained are **replanted**.

Due to the problems associated with fossil fuels, it is necessary to use alternative sources of energy.

An alternative source of energy is one which is not a fossil fuel.

Most alternative sources of energy:

• are renewable,

• produce zero or minimum net environmental pollution,

• require minimum operational costs, although initial plant costs may be high.

Table 18.5 *Various alternative sources of energy*

Energy source	Uses
Solar energy	**Water heaters** heat water directly and are relatively cheap to install. See chapter 9, page 111, 'Applications of heat transfer', Figure 9.8. **Photovoltaic (PV) panels** convert solar radiation into electrical energy. In the northern hemisphere they should be placed on a south-facing roof to more effectively receive the rays. **Advantages** • Low maintenance and operating costs. • Clean source of energy. • Energy can be stored in batteries. • Limitless supply of free sunshine. **Disadvantages** • High start-up cost. • Poor performance on cloudy days. • Large production requires much space. • Low efficiency of conversion to electricity. **Solar cookers** use mirrors to reflect solar radiation to a furnace or pot. See chapter 10, page 123, 'Reflection and focusing of waves'.

Energy source	Uses
	Solar driers absorb radiation through a glass cover. Air below the cover is heated and rises through the drying chamber, drawing cool unsaturated air from below. warm, moist air leaving tray of fish, meats, fruits or crops mesh grill door hot, dry air glass cover traps the heat inside dry air sucked in *A solar drier*
Biofuels or biomass	These provide energy from **plant** or **animal matter**. Although they produce carbon dioxide when burnt, the plants from which they are formed removed it when they were alive, producing a cancelling effect on environmental pollution. **Wood** can be burnt directly to be used as a fuel for cooking. **Biogas** is obtained from the decay of **plant** and **animal wastes** in the **absence of oxygen**. It is used for cooking or to drive generators on farms. Disadvantages of using biogas are that it is mainly methane, a greenhouse gas, and forested areas as well as agricultural lands and crops are used in producing it. **Biodiesel** is produced from **vegetable oils, animal oils/fats,** or **waste cooking oils** by a process known as **transesterification**. It produces less pollution than petroleum diesel and recycling waste cooking oil is a notable advantage. **Gasohol** is made from **gasoline mixed with ethanol** produced from the fermentation of crops such as **sugar cane**. It is cheaper than regular gasoline, emits less harmful gases when burnt, gives better engine performance and its production provides jobs. 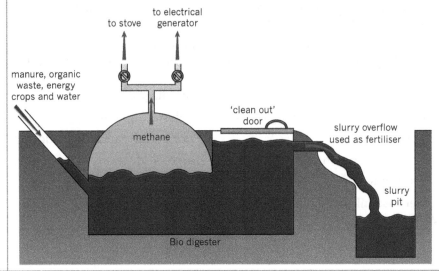 to stove to electrical generator manure, organic waste, energy crops and water methane 'clean out' door slurry overflow used as fertiliser slurry pit Bio digester *A biogas system*

Energy source	Uses
Wind energy	**Kinetic energy** from the wind can be used to turn the turbines of electrical generators. Offshore wind farms obtain stronger, more consistent winds than onshore wind farms. They also have less visual impact but are more expensive to construct and maintain. **Advantages** • Caribbean islands generally experience strong winds. • Clean source of energy. • Can be stored in batteries. **Disadvantages** • High costs in constructing the plant. • Causes noise pollution and unpleasant scenery. • Wind is variable between seasons. • Vulnerable to stormy weather.
Hydro-electric energy	Water collected behind a dam can be released to turn the turbines of electrical generators. **Advantages** • The ability to release the water as needed is a clear advantage of these systems over the less controllable solar and wind systems. • Clean source of energy **Disadvantages** • High cost in constructing the plant. • Disturbs the ecology of water bodies. • Danger of possible flooding.
Tidal energy	Water from the ocean can be collected at high tide and then released at low tide to produce powerful pressures that turn the turbines of electrical generators. High costs in constructing the plant, together with the negative impact on tourism due to the disturbance of the natural beauty of the coast, are the main disadvantages.
Wave energy	Energy of wave motion and ocean currents can be harnessed to turn the turbines of electrical generators near shorelines or floating far offshore. Low operational cost and consistent wave power are offset by disadvantages of the high costs in constructing the plant and the negative effect on the marine ecology.
Geo-thermal energy	It is common in volcanic islands for **hot water** and **steam** from within the Earth to be released in hot springs. The heat can be used directly for industrial processes or to heat buildings. **Geothermal energy plants** drill and install pipes so that hot water and steam can rise through them and be used to turn the turbines of electrical generators. The water is then cooled and returned to the geothermal reservoir in the Earth where it is reheated. *A geothermal energy plant*
Nuclear energy	This is an **alternative source** of energy that is **non-renewable**. Energy released by the nuclear disintegration of **uranium** and **plutonium** is used to produce steam to turn the turbines of electrical generators. A small amount of nuclear fuel produces an enormous amount of energy and greenhouse gases are not produced in the process. However, nuclear fuel, before and after use, is extremely dangerous, and spent nuclear fuel is difficult to dispose of.

Variables affecting solar and wind energy

Solar

- **Latitude** – Figure 18.2 shows that the intensity of received solar energy decreases at higher latitudes due to the increased region of the atmosphere and planet to be warmed by solar beams of given cross-sectional area.

- **Altitude** – High elevations receive more solar energy because there is less air above to absorb it.

- **Season** – The daily solar radiation received depends on the season (see chapter 15, Figure 15.4).

- **Time of day** – The intensity of solar radiation is greatest when the Sun appears highest in the sky.

- **Shadows** – Tall buildings, mountains and hills can block the direct rays from the Sun.

- **Cloud cover** – Clouds reduce the received solar radiation by absorbing and scattering it.

- **Small particles in the atmosphere** – General atmospheric pollution from factories, or dust and sand from quarries or sand storms, reduce the intensity of solar radiation reaching the planet.

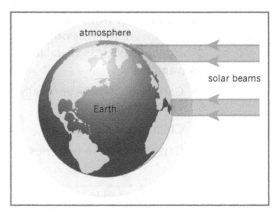

Figure 18.2 *Effect of latitude on solar radiation*

Wind

- **Wind speed** – Strong winds have more kinetic energy to turn wind turbines.

- **Wind consistency** – This is necessary for the continuous production of electricity.

- **Surface** – Wind speed and consistency is generally higher over the sea than over the land.

- **Altitude** – Wind speed over land is greater at higher altitudes as there is less obstruction from obstacles.

- **Hurricane-prone regions** – These deter the erection of wind turbines due to fear of destruction.

Appraisal of the use of alternative energy in the Caribbean

Reasons for switching from the use of fossil fuels

- Over 90% of the energy used in the Caribbean is obtained from fossil fuels at a huge annual cost.

- Fossil fuels harm humans and the environment, as previously discussed in this chapter.

- Caribbean islands are vulnerable to flooding due to climate change as a result of excessive use of fossil fuels.

Reasons for switching to alternative sources of energy

- Operational costs are low and the natural resource is free.

- Intense and consistent solar radiation is available.

- Locations with consistent and strong winds exist.

- The Caribbean is ideally located to use geothermal energy since it is near to tectonic plate boundaries.

- Hilly landscapes provide hydro-electric potential – Jamaica, St. Vincent and the Grenadines, Dominica and Suriname have hydro-electric plants. Guyana also has great potential.

- Tidal and wave energy is readily available around the islands.

Problems of implementing the switch

- Opposition due to the possible negative impact on the landscape and ecology of the surroundings.
- Lack of adequate education in technologies and technological skills.
- Large capital cost required to construct the energy plants.
- Local banks are hesitant to offer loans since they lack understanding of the technologies.
- Foreign banks are hesitant to offer loans to governments due to lack of transparency and accountability, and to local installers who have no firm credit history.
- Lack of economic incentives to stimulate the business and consumer sectors.

With improved technologies and an increasing awareness of climate change, the Caribbean is destined to be a significant producer of alternative energy as soon as it can obtain financial backing.

Revision questions

1 Describe the formation of EACH of the following:

    a crude oil

    b coal

2 Explain how 'acid rain' is formed and outline THREE problems that arise from it.

3 Explain the greenhouse effect and comment on how it is predicted to negatively impact on the planet.

4 Name THREE pollutants produced by the burning of fossil fuels and identify their negative effects.

5 Explain how natural gas leaks and oil spills can be harmful to the environment.

6   **a** How are each of the following produced?

      i biogas

      ii biodiesel

      iii gasohol

  b Explain, with the aid of a clearly labelled diagram, how a solar drier can be used to dry crops.

  c Distinguish between the methods of extracting tidal energy and wave energy.

7   **a** List THREE variables affecting EACH of the following.

      i solar energy

      ii wind energy

  b Write an appraisal on the use of alternative sources of energy in the Caribbean.

19 Forces

*A **force** is a push, pull or twist in a particular direction that can change the speed, direction, size or shape of a body.*

Principles of forces

If several forces act on an object, their directions must be taken into consideration when determining their **resultant force, F_R** (total or net force). Along a straight line, we take one direction as positive and the other as negative. The SI unit of force is the **newton, N.**

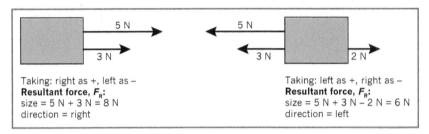

Taking: right as +, left as −
Resultant force, F_R:
size = 5 N + 3 N = 8 N
direction = right

Taking: left as +, right as −
Resultant force, F_R:
size = 5 N + 3 N − 2 N = 6 N
direction = left

Figure 19.1 *Summing forces*

Sir Isaac Newton, a famous English scientist, developed three **laws of motion.**

Table 19.1 *Newton's laws of motion*

1st Law	If the **resultant force (F_R)** on a body is **zero**, it continues in its state of **rest** or **constant velocity**. ($F_R = 0$ implies constant velocity (zero acceleration)).
2nd Law	A resultant force on a **mass (m)** produces an **acceleration (a)**. $F_R = m \times a$
3rd Law	If body A exerts a force on body B, then body B exerts an **equal but oppositely directed** force on body A. (For every action there is in an equal but oppositely directed reaction).

Friction

Friction is the force that acts along the surface of contact of a body to oppose its motion.

Some benefits of friction

- Friction provided by the brakes of vehicles **reduces speed.**
- Friction between tyres and road surfaces allows cars to go **round corners** and to **accelerate.** Tyres with worn treads can cause accidents since their smooth surfaces do not provide sufficient friction.
- Friction enables us to **walk** and **run**, as explained on page 217, by Newton's 3rd law of motion.
- Friction helps us to **grip** objects, preventing them from slipping away.

Problems caused by friction

- Friction **makes us do more work** when we try to slide objects across surfaces.
- Work done against friction **produces heat**, which can affect the proper functioning of machinery.
- Friction **erodes** and can destroy the surfaces of bodies.

Eliminating friction

- **Lubricating** with oil or grease can provide a layer between surfaces to reduce friction.
- **Sanding or polishing** reduces friction by making the surfaces smooth.
- **Streamlined shapes** reduce the **frictional drag** forces on bodies moving through fluids.
- **Rollers placed under objects** reduce friction by preventing their surfaces from **sliding** over other surfaces. Vehicles have wheels for the same reason.

Aerodynamic lift force on the wings of planes and birds

As the wing of a plane moves forward, air moves smoothly along its gently sloped, **streamlined** surface. Air over the wing moves faster than air under the wing since it travels a longer path. Since air above the wing is then more spread out, it exerts less pressure and the excess pressure from below produces an upward force known as the **lift force**. Birds are able to glide through the air for a similar reason.

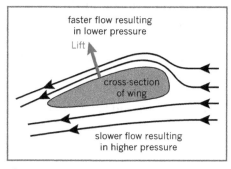

Figure 19.2 *Lift on wings of planes and birds*

Applications of Newton's laws of motion

- As our foot presses backwards on the ground, an equal force of the ground presses forwards on our foot, enabling us to walk or run. (3rd law: action = reaction)
- As the jet engine of an aircraft forces backwards on the air, an equal force (**thrust**) of the air pushes forwards on the engine propelling the aircraft forward. (3rd law: action = reaction)
- If an aircraft moves at constant horizontal velocity, there is **no horizontal acceleration**. The engine thrust and the drag force cancel each other so the horizontal resultant force is zero. Similarly, since there is **no vertical acceleration**, the weight and lift force cancel each other so the vertical resultant force is zero. (1st law: $F_R = 0$ ... no acceleration)
- If the aircraft **accelerates horizontally**, the resultant force is **not zero**; the forward thrust of the engine is then greater than the backward frictional drag. (2nd law: $F_R = ma$ ... acceleration)

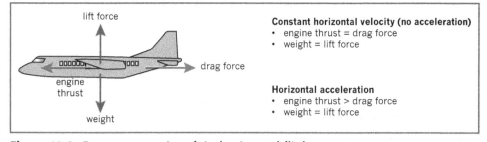

Figure 19.3 *Forces on an aircraft in horizontal flight*

Effect of winds on motion of aircraft

- A **tailwind** blows in the direction of travel of the aircraft and tends to increase its speed.
- A **headwind** blows in the opposite direction to the aircraft and tends to reduce its speed.
- A **crosswind** tends to cause the aircraft to shift off course. Figure 19.4 shows how the pilot must steer the plane through a crosswind blowing due north in order to continue its motion due east.

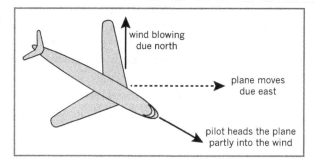

Figure 19.4 *Flying through a crosswind*

Gravitational force

Mass is the quantity of matter in a body.

Gravity is the force of attraction between bodies due to their masses.

*Weight is the **gravitational force** that a planet or other body of very large mass exerts on an object.*

- Planets of **larger mass** exert **greater gravitational forces**. The weight of a body on Earth is about six times its weight on the Moon, since the mass of the Earth is about six times the mass of the Moon.

- The **further apart** the objects are, the **smaller is the gravitational force**. As a rocket rises above the Earth, the gravitational force on it (its weight) decreases until it becomes zero in outer space. However, in outer space the rocket still has mass since it is still made of matter.

The gravitational force on a body of mass 1 kg pulls it to the Earth with an acceleration of 10 m s^{-2}.

From Newton's 2nd law $F_R = m \times a$ $\quad \therefore$ weight on the Earth $= 1 \text{ kg} \times 10 \text{ m s}^{-2} = 10 \text{ N}$

Example

On the Moon, the acceleration due to gravity is only 1.6 m s^{-2} and in space, it is zero. Determine the weight of a body of mass 2 kg:

   a on Earth   **b** on the Moon   **c** in space.

a weight $= 2 \text{ kg} \times 10 \text{ m s}^{-2} = 20 \text{ N}$

b weight $= 2 \text{ kg} \times 1.6 \text{ m s}^{-2} = 3.2 \text{ N}$

c weight $= 2 \text{ kg} \times 0 \text{ m s}^{-2} = 0 \text{ N}$

Escaping the pull of gravity

The speed and kinetic energy of an object shot vertically into the air diminish as it rises. The more kinetic energy it starts with, the higher it will rise before being pulled back to the planet. However, at increased height above the Earth, the force of gravity weakens until it becomes zero in outer space. A body given sufficient kinetic energy to reach outer space can therefore escape the pull of gravity.

Centripetal force and circular motion

*A **centripetal force** is the force on an object that is necessary to keep it moving in a curved path.*

A centripetal force always **acts towards the centre** of curvature of the path.

It increases if: **1** the mass of the object increases.

                     2 the speed of the object increases.

                     3 the radius of the curved path decreases.

Consider a ball at the end of a string being whirled in a horizontal circle. The string pulls outwards **on the hand**, but also exerts an inwards **centripetal force on the ball** to the centre of the circle. Releasing the string reduces the force in it to zero. The ball will shoot off at a tangent to the circle and take a curved path to the ground due to the Earth's gravitational force.

Similarly, a car moving around a curb requires a centripetal force to do so. This force is provided by friction between the tyres and the road surface. If oil is placed on the road, the reduced friction would not be sufficient and the vehicle will slide off at a tangent to the curve.

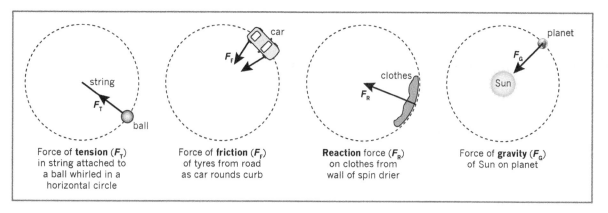

Figure 19.5 *Various types of forces acting as centripetal forces*

Satellites

Satellites depend on the **force of gravity** to provide the necessary centripetal force to keep them in orbit.

- **To remain in orbit**, the force of gravity must be **equal** to the required centripetal force.
- If the gravitational force is too large, the satellite will spiral inwards until it crashes to the planet. If it is too small, the satellite will move outwards into space.

Centre of gravity

*The **centre of gravity** of a body is that point through which its weight appears to act.*

Each particle making up a body has its own weight, as shown by the small arrows of Figure 19.6. The centre of gravity is that point where the resultant of all these forces **appears to act**. The centre of gravity (C of G) of a **regular shape**, such as a circle or a square, and a **regular solid**, such as a sphere or a cube, is at its **geometric centre**.

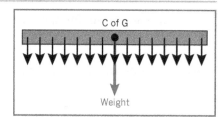

Figure 19.6 *Centre of gravity*

Finding the centre of gravity of an irregularly shaped lamina

A lamina is suspended so that it can swing freely from a pin through a small hole near its edge. A plumb line is hung from the pin and its position marked by small crosses. A line is drawn through the crosses. The process is repeated by suspending the lamina from another point near its edge. The point of intersection of the drawn lines is the centre of gravity.

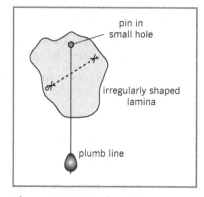

Figure 19.7 *Finding the centre of gravity of a lamina*

Finding the centre of gravity of solids

- **Uniform thin rod** – The mid-point of its length.
- **Non-uniform thin rod** – The point where a fine edge placed under the rod keeps it in balance.
- **Uniform cube or cuboid** – The point of intersection of its diagonals from **opposite** vertices.
- **Uniform sphere** – The mid-point of its diameter.

Moments, equilibrium and stability

When we open a door, we use a force that has a **turning effect** or **moment** about a **pivot**.

*The **moment of a force** about a point is the product of the force and the perpendicular distance of its line of action from the point.*

moment = force × perpendicular distance of line of action of force from point

The unit of moment is the newton metre, **N m.** We may also use the newton centimetre, **N cm.**

Example

Figure 19.8 shows a uniform trapdoor being opened by a minimum force of 4 N.

a If the trapdoor has a mass of 800 g, determine its weight.

b Calculate the **anticlockwise** moment about the hinge exerted by the force of 4 N.

c Calculate the **clockwise moment** about the hinge created by the weight of the door.

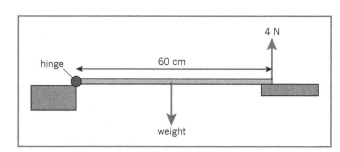

Figure 19.8

a First, express the mass in kg. 800 g = 0.8 kg

Then weight = mass × acceleration due to gravity = 0.8 kg × 10 m s^{-2} = 8 N

b anticlockwise moment about hinge = 4 N × 60 cm = 240 N cm

c Since the door is **uniform**, its centre of gravity is at its centre, 30 cm from the hinge.

∴ clockwise moment about hinge = 8 N × 30 cm = 240 N cm

Since moments are taken about the **hinge**, we must measure each distance **from the hinge** to the force.

Conditions for equilibrium under the action of parallel forces

1. The sum of the **forces** in any direction is equal to the sum of the **forces** in the opposite direction.

2. The sum of the clockwise **moments** about any point is equal to the sum of the anticlockwise **moments** about that same point.

Figure 19.9 shows a system in equilibrium. Objects hang from a uniform metre rule of weight 2 N suspended by a spring balance from its mid-point.

Sum of upward **forces** = sum of downward **forces**

$$9 N = 4 N + 2 N + 3 N$$
$$9 N = 9 N$$

Taking moments **about the 50 cm mark**

anticlockwise **moments** = clockwise **moments**

$$4 N × (50 - 20) cm = 3 N × (90 - 50) cm$$
$$4 N × 30 cm = 3 N × 40 cm$$
$$120 N cm = 120 N cm$$

The forces of 9 N and 2 N **have no moment** about the 50 cm mark since they have no distance to it.

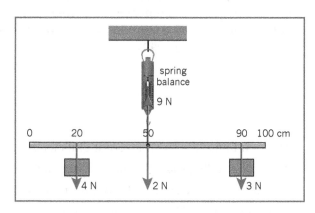

Figure 19.9 *Parallel forces in equilibrium*

Stable, unstable and neutral equilibrium

- A body is in **stable equilibrium** if when slightly displaced, its centre of gravity rises and a restoring moment is created that returns the body to its original equilibrium position.

- A body is in **unstable equilibrium** if when slightly displaced, its centre of gravity falls and a toppling moment is created that accelerates the body away from its original equilibrium position.

- A body is in **neutral equilibrium** if when slightly displaced, its centre of gravity remains at the same level and no moment is created, leaving the body in the displaced position.

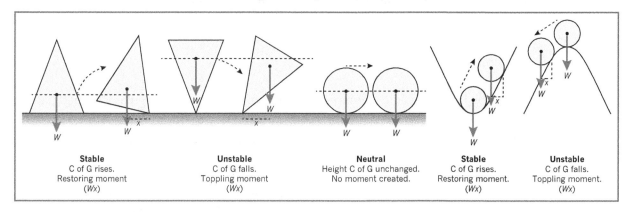

Figure 19.10 *Stable, unstable and neutral equilibrium*

Factors affecting the stability of an object

Figure 19.11 shows how the **height of the centre of gravity** and the **width of its base** affect the stability of an object. Go-karts have wide wheel bases and low centres of gravity in order to be more stable. When tilted, restoring moments are created which return them to their original position. Large cargo buses have their baggage compartments **below** the floor for a similar reason. The load is then closer to the ground, **lowering the centre of gravity** of the vehicle, and enhancing its stability.

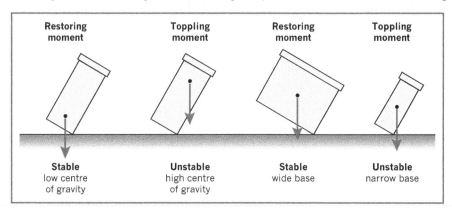

Figure 19.11 *Factors affecting stability*

Maximum loading capacity and tare – Loading the top of a vehicle such as a van or pick-up **raises its centre of gravity** making it less stable. Commercial vehicles therefore cannot exceed a maximum loading capacity. Their tare weight (unloaded weight) and their maximum loaded weight are usually marked on their sides to remind users.

Revision questions

1. State Newton's 3rd law of motion and cite an example that demonstrates it.

2. Explain, with the aid of a diagram, how the wing of an aircraft can produce a 'lift force'.

3. A toy aeroplane of weight 5 N travels due east at a constant speed and altitude. The thrust of its engine is 15 N. Draw a diagram labeling the FOUR forces acting on the plane including their values.

4. **a** Define:
    i centre of gravity
    ii weight

   b Describe how you can determine the centre of gravity of an irregularly shaped flat piece of metal.

5. **a** State the conditions necessary for a body to be in equilibrium under the action of parallel forces.

   b The diagram shows a uniform metre rule of weight 1 N pivoted on a fulcrum. Blocks of weight X and 4 N are suspended from the rule, keeping the system in balance. Determine the values of the weight X and the normal reaction R.

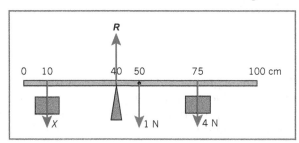

6. State TWO design features you can apply to a table lamp in order to increase its stability.

Exam-style questions – Chapters 15 to 19

Structured questions

1 **a) i)** List the planets of the solar system in order of increasing orbit radius. **(2 marks)**

   ii) Which planet:

   – has the shortest day?

   – takes more time to rotate once on its axis than to orbit the Sun?

   – has the most moons? **(3 marks)**

b) Illustrate each of the following occurrences with the aid of a diagram.

   i) A new moon and a full moon. **(3 marks)**

   ii) An eclipse of the Moon. **(3 marks)**

c) Suggest why:

   i) geostationary satellites are useful in transmitting radio and TV signals. **(2 marks)**

   ii) polar satellites are useful in obtaining weather information from around the planet. **(2 marks)**

   Total 15 marks

2 **a)** Table 1 below shows the results of Marianna's investigation to compare the water retention capabilities and drainage rate of a clay soil and a sandy soil. Both soil samples had the same mass and did not contain any water at the start of the investigation.

Table 1 *Water retention capabilities and drainage rate of two soil samples*

Type of soil	Volume of water poured into the soil/cm^3	Volume of water draining through/cm^3	Rate of drainage/ cm^3 min^{-1}
Clay soil	50	26	0.6
Sandy soil	50	32	3.4

   i) Calculate the volume of water retained by EACH soil. **(2 marks)**

   ii) Explain why the soils retained different volumes of water. **(2 marks)**

   iii) Explain why the sandy soil drained faster than the clay soil. **(2 marks)**

b) i) What is soil erosion? **(1 mark)**

   ii) At harvest time, farmer John and his neighbour, farmer Nick, harvest the yams from their fields. Farmer John decides not to replant anything whilst farmer Nick immediately replants his field with sweet potato seedlings. Whose soil is likely to erode faster? Explain your answer. **(3 marks)**

c) Figure 1 below shows part of the nitrogen cycle.

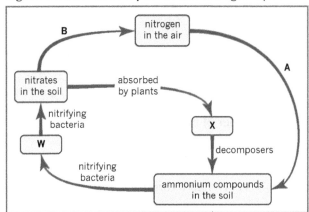

Figure 1 *Part of the nitrogen cycle*

i)   Identify the bacteria responsible for the processes occurring at A and B.   **(2 marks)**

ii) Name substances W and X.   **(2 marks)**

iii) Name ONE other important element that is recycled in nature.   **(1 mark)**

Total 15 marks

3 **a)** Complete Table 2 by placing a tick (✓) in the column indicating whether the weather feature is due to the approach of a warm front or of a cold front.

Table 2 *Weather features at warm fronts and cold fronts*

Weather feature	Warm front	Cold front
Temperature increases		
Tall cumulonimbus clouds		
Continuous light showers that can last several days		
Polar air mass plunges into maritime tropical air mass		
Gentle gradient between air masses		

(5 marks)

b) **i)** What TWO factors are responsible for the changing tides?   **(2 marks)**

ii) Draw a diagram illustrating how high tide and low tide are produced on Earth.   **(3 marks)**

c) Jared says that tomorrow we will experience a spring tide.

i)   Suggest the effect that a spring tide will have on the high tide.   **(1 mark)**

ii) Draw a diagram showing the relative positions of the Sun, the Moon and the Earth, and sea levels on the Earth during the spring tide. Clearly label the type of high tides and low tides.   **(3 marks)**

iii) Approximately how many days after the spring tide, will a neap tide occur?   **(1 mark)**

Total 15 marks

4 **a)** Define the following terms, giving an example of EACH, other than oil, solar or wind energy.

i)   Fossil fuels   **(2 marks)**

ii) Renewable energy sources   **(2 marks)**

   b) i) Comment on THREE ways in which solar energy can be used.   **(3 marks)**

      ii) Discuss TWO advantages and TWO disadvantages of using wind energy as an alternative source of energy in the Caribbean.   **(4 marks)**

   c) i) Define alternative energy.   **(1 mark)**

      ii) Kamal lives on the volcanic island of Dominica. State the type of alternative energy that volcanic islands are particularly capable of providing. Explain how this energy can be obtained by an energy plant and converted to electricity.   **(3 marks)**

                                                     Total 15 marks

5 **a)** Define each of the following:

      i)   frictional force   **(1 mark)**

      ii) gravitational force   **(1 mark)**

      iii) centripetal force.   **(1 mark)**

   b) Comment on:

      i)   TWO benefits of friction.   **(2 marks)**

      ii) TWO ways of reducing friction.   **(2 marks)**

   c) i) Sketch a diagram showing the centripetal force on the Earth as it orbits the Sun.   **(1 mark)**

      ii) Suggest the type of force that provides this centripetal force.   **(1 mark)**

   d) i) Distinguish between a body in stable equilibrium and one in unstable equilibrium.   **(2 marks)**

      ii) Comment on TWO ways of increasing the stability of an object.   **(2 marks)**

      iii) Comment on why there is a maximum allowable loading capacity for vehicles and state how we can attempt to ensure that it is not exceeded.   **(2 marks)**

                                                     Total 15 marks

Structured essay questions

6 **a)** Suggest THREE reasons for humans having the desire to explore space.   **(3 marks)**

   b) List THREE properties of space that present problems for its exploration and suggest THREE actions that may be taken to deal with these obstacles.   **(6 marks)**

   c) State TWO main functions of the International Space Station.   **(2 marks)**

   d) Name TWO types of space probes used to investigate Mars and outline the function of EACH.   **(4 marks)**

                                                     Total 15 marks

7 **a) i)** What is meant by the term 'pollution'?   **(2 marks)**

      ii) Explain how eutrophication is caused and how it affects aquatic life.   **(5 marks)**

   b) Naymar has a deep-sea fishing boat that he also uses for scuba diving. To ensure that he can safely navigate his boat when fishing and can locate the reef when he wishes to dive, he has a GPS unit, a magnetic compass and sonar on board.

      i)   Explain how Naymar uses his GPS unit and magnetic compass for navigation, and his sonar when he wishes to dive.   **(6 marks)**

      ii) Identify TWO health problems Naymar could experience whilst he is diving.   **(2 marks)**

                                                      Total 15 marks

Index

Note: figures and tables are indicated by 'f' and 't' after the page number. For example, 93t indicates a table on page 93.